a novel

CHRIS HEIMERDINGER

Covenant Communications, Inc.

AUTHOR'S NOTE

Although much of this book is based on Book of Mormon characters and events, it is primarily imagination and speculation. I'm most gratified when a reader tells me they went to the scriptures to see how much I got right. Better yet if they linger there.

C.H.

Cover illustration by Joe Flores

Published by Covenant Communications, Inc.
American Fork, Utah

Printed in the United States of America
First Printing: March 1995

06 05 04 03 02 01 00 99   10 9 8 7 6 5 4 3 2 1

ISBN 1-57734-487-1

For Larry McDonald,
A man in blue and a true-blue friend.

PROLOGUE

I'm entranced by the clouds. I especially love to watch them after a storm, when the billowing mass begins to break up, coil in on itself, and release the spiked rays of the sun.

As a little child, clouds would frighten me. Mostly because I had an older brother who attached macabre images to the evolving shapes over Rattlesnake Mountain. "Look, Jim, that one's an elk. It's been shot. See its tongue hanging out? There's a gargoyle. It's missing an eye and half its arm. That one's the ghost of the bogey man. If it rains on us, the rain will make our skin dissolve." Once he frightened me so badly that I scurried home in a panic as soon as the first droplet hit my arm, losing one shoe in the street. Fortunately, Judd grew out of that stage, and today serves in a bishopric in Billings, Montana. Still, I can't much resent him for frightening me. I later did the same thing to my little sister, Jennifer.

Few things take my breath away more than clouds. Not a canyon or a mountain or even an ocean can fill human vision with such immensity and power. I've seen distant billows so magnificent it looked like the neighboring county had erupted in a massive volcano or exploded under a nuclear bomb. To me, nothing in nature is more majestic. And it seems only appropriate, considering whom the clouds will one day bring.

So I watch them, anxiously, breathlessly, the wind causing my eyes to tear when I forget to blink, afraid that I might miss even a fraction of a second of this glorious event. I know now what I await. I know it with such conviction that I sometimes find it difficult to carry on with the day's tasks. I focus, I concentrate, and still my mind drifts back to the clouds. But I know it's only if I carry on that I can possibly abbreviate the wait. A short time ago I viewed this event as something that would inevitably occur, not as an event that I had the power to bring about; an event that all of us must bring about together.

So I carry on, and fervently. Because I will be there. Nothing fills me with greater anticipation. When those clouds finally part, if I am absent, I might as well shrivel into nothing. The thought of missing it makes me shudder.

A short time ago, these were unfamiliar emotions. It's not as if I had never known them. But sometimes our intimacy with the Spirit of God cools. It cools so gradually we don't know its gone. In college I had a Gospel Doctrine teacher who trumpeted the theme, "If you don't feel as close to God today as you did yesterday, who moved?"

So be it. I had moved. But I don't remember when exactly. All I remember is the pain. My heart was saturated with it. My bearings were lost. The future promised only blackness, thick and indispersable. Not even the simple things—a favorite food, a joyous song, or the laughter of my three children—could dispel it. Especially not the word of God. For I thought I'd been abandoned by Him. Punished for some unknown and unknowable sin.

Three years ago, my world shattered so decisively that I considered shutting the bedroom blinds and languishing in the dark until death took me home. I was prepared to quit my job, forget my family, and suspend my life as I had known it. Three years ago, on a stark October day, our family's vigil of futility came to an end.

Three years ago, she died.

Part One:

RETURN OF THE ENEMY

CHAPTER 1

I've been contemplating how I might start this.

Why don't you start at the beginning?

Yes. The beginning. How profound.

I should inform everyone, the sarcastic voice that you will hear from time to time belongs to my tempestuous daughter, Melody. She's sixteen. An age that parents have dreaded throughout the ages.

You make it sound like I'm just butting in. The fact is, there are major parts of the story that wouldn't make any sense if I didn't tell it from my own perspective.

All right. I confess. I *asked* Melody to help me. It's been a pleasant surprise to discover that my daughter can actually be quite insightful . . . on occasion.

Why don't you start by introducing yourself?

All right. My name is James Hawkins. The James part, or Jim if you prefer (and I do), is more of a nickname that I gave myself as a boy. The name on my birth certificate is Jamie. I never liked that name, though. Only one person in my life ever used it consistently; a girl I knew when I was thirteen years old. But a Cupid-smitten youngster will allow himself to be called just about anything. My wife, Renae, used the name a few times, but it never stuck. I've been Jim all my life, and I might as well keep it that—

Okay, okay, Dad. They get the point.

Melody, in case I need to remind you, I've told two stories prior to this one, and I did perfectly fine without your coaching.

Sorry. Please, go on. Most of us are still awake.

Anyway, this past April I turned the big "four-O." I guess that would be as good a place to start as any.

You mean your birthday? That's excellent!

Why is it "excellent"?

No reason in particular. It's just a funny story.

Funny?

And sorta pathetic . . . in a cute sorta way, of course. But never mind me. You just go ahead. I'll jump in if I don't think you're telling it right.

How comforting.

So it was my birthday. I was forty years old. I remember waking up before the sun. For a very self-indulgent purpose, the alarm clock had been set for 5:30 a.m. You see, when I was a teenager I happened to notice on my birth certificate that I was born at precisely 5:50 a.m. For some morbid reason, I felt compelled to count down those final minutes while I could still call myself thirty-nine. Those final minutes of youth. Someone decades back—parents or companions or society in general—convinced me that age forty marked the apex of life, the beginning of the end. Never again could I refer to myself as "young." I could only defer to the cliché "I'm as young as I feel," which, of course, never fooled anybody. Whenever I'd heard anyone declare it, I shook my head and said to myself, "That person is *old.* They're just living in denial."

For the last several years, knowing that my fortieth birthday was just around the corner, I worked hard to change such psychology, but my efforts floundered. As the digital clock on my nightstand changed to 5:31, I was hit by a wave of depression. Only nineteen minutes left before I was *old.*

As the display changed to 5:32, I realized it wasn't only because I was turning forty. It was because I was turning forty without her.

I wandered over by the bay window in my bedroom and sat in the window seat, cushioned by a thick, warm shag. It wasn't the first morning that my thoughts had turned to my wife. Since her death two and a half years before, I could only recall two mornings when my thoughts did not turn to her. Once when I was awakened by the screams of my youngest daughter, Steffanie, down in the kitchen, having just burned herself with a pan of hot butter, and exactly one year earlier when I was awakened by all three of my children singing "Happy birthday" at the top of their lungs and holding a tray with Jimmy Dean sausage, cranberry juice cocktail, and a three-stack of pecan pancakes—the very breakfast that my nineyearold son, Harrison (now ten), had prodded me to name the night before as my favorite. The pancakes supported no less than thirty-nine candles. Needless to say, I did not eat the top pancake, now buried under a layer of multicolored wax.

This year, I would have no such luck. The face of my beloved Renae floated in from its familiar corner of my mind and hovered there. The children were still fast asleep. Oh, they'd be in around seven, singing at the top of their lungs and carrying a tray that was one candle closer to presenting a serious fire hazard. But for the moment, as the sky behind the silhouetted Wasatch Range above Salt Lake glowed an increasingly brighter hue of red, it was just me and Renae.

The cancer was diagnosed fourteen months before she died. For a year prior to that time, Renae had complained of feeling a lack of energy. "All day long I feel like I'm walking through sand," she said. We took her to our family doctor. Probably stress or the mid-winter slumps, he concluded. So Renae took it easy for a few weeks, and when spring came around she thought she felt better. Before summer ended, she needed a four-hour nap every afternoon just to get through the day.

One evening, while dining with Renae's uncle in Provo, their cock-apoo, Misty, jumped up on her lap. The dog's landing hurt a little more than it should have. She examined her abdomen and found a tender knot of muscle.

After the test results came back, the doctor at the University of Utah Medical Center approached us with a solemn expression. Undifferentiated clear-cell carcinoma. Renae had ovarian cancer.

The hysterectomy took place four days later. Chemotherapy started within the month. Six months after that, we thought we had licked it. We thought the prayers, the blessings, the fasts, and the wisdom of modern medical science had prevailed. Within two months, her CA-125 count started rising. The cancer returned with more fury than ever before. It spread beyond the uterus and attacked her lungs and liver.

Her last words to me in the hospital were, "Don't be long." She said it as I got up to leave for the bathroom.

I took her hand. "Don't worry, honey. I'll just be a minute."

When I returned to the room, she'd fallen asleep. She never reawakened. Most of us were there when she died: our three children, her mother and father, one of her uncles, my kid sister, Jennifer, and her husband, Garth.

As friends and relatives embraced me in tearful consolation, they whispered things like, "She's in a better place," or "She's home now, Jim," or "We should feel grateful that she's been released from her pain-racked body." They spoke as if this had all been for the *better!* As if they'd forgotten the original injustice: Why had she gotten sick in the first place? And then the cruel joke of leading us to believe the chemotherapy had saved her. How could anything have been for the better? She was leaving behind an eight-year-old son who'd just made her a ceramic flower vase for a Christmas Day she would never see. She was abandoning a twelve- and fourteen-year-old daughter who needed her desperately to help cross the bridge from girlhood to womanhood, and a husband who had become so addicted to life with her that he had no idea how to go on without her.

For months, Renae's last words to me resounded. When she had said, "Don't be long," she hadn't been referring to my brief absence from the room. She'd meant a more eternal reunion. I wish so much that I might have responded correctly and cried, "I won't be long, my love. I'll finish whatever the Lord intends for me in this world as fast as humanly possible. And then I'll come to you. I promise, I'll come."

That's what I *wish* I had said, but it doesn't really matter now. I hadn't done much toward fulfilling my promise. Mostly I was just existing. Taking it one day at a time.

When I got around to looking at the clock again, it was 5:49. My final minute of youth was upon me. Like a person awaiting the descending ball in Times Square on New Year's Eve, I stiffened in anticipation. The digit flipped.

That's it, I thought. It's over. I am now officially, certifiably and unalterably . . . old.

Without further ado, I went back to bed.

* * *

I can tell Dad's just a bundle of joy right now, so why don't I tell you about the birthday dinner—

No, no, no. *I'll* tell about the birthday dinner. I'm perfectly capable of telling about the birthday dinner. But there are still one or two things I wanted to cover first. A few other crucial events took place on my birthday. Among them, I was demoted at work. Maybe "demoted" is too strong. Let's just say my job description changed markedly. I'm sure if they'd known it was my birthday, they'd have gone ahead and done it anyway.

For nine years I'd been working for a company called Entrepreneurial Marketing, Inc. The company served as a middleman for nationallyfamous financial gurus—those guys who materialize on television about 2:00 a.m. to pitch a book and tape package on saving tax money or buying real estate for nothing down. We sold those customers an upgrade package featuring a consultant or "expert" who would personally walk them through the process (over the telephone, of course) of reaching financial independence, or improving self-esteem, or losing weight. Sometimes an upgrade package cost upwards of ten thousand dollars, and the sales commissions were high.

Sound like a romantic line of work? Well, after getting married at the end of my second year at BYU, then dropping out at the end of my third year thinking I'd found a great career opportunity in multi-level marketing, and then nearly starving my wife and newborn daughter while working several more years in various dead-end jobs pushing everything from used cars to Israeli oil rights, I thought it was the most romantic job on earth. For the first time in our lives, bills were getting paid on the day we received them instead of three days before cutoff. We bought a second car, a house in West Valley with a view of the mountains, and a second honeymoon to the Caribbean.

The only shame I felt was dredged up at family reunions in Cody, Wyoming, as my mother introduced her sons to various acquaintances. "This is Mitch; he's an attorney. This is Steven; he's a pharmacologist. This is Judd; he owns three restaurants. And this is Jim; he's a salesman."

I'd try to correct her. "Mom, I'm a marketing consultant." But neither she nor anyone else was ever fooled. I was a salesman.

Someone might have expected more from a guy who had participated in so many extraordinary events in his youth. Events that might have thrust me into the spotlight as a worldwide celebrity if fate had made them known. Someone might have thought the Lord would allow such a guy to retire and live under a palm tree in the South Pacific, sipping coconut milk.

No such luck. I didn't find myself exempt from a single challenge of adulthood and marriage. At times I even wondered if I got more than my fair share of trials. But I never complained much, and I never felt resentment. That is, until I lost Renae.

Life is a funny thing. I've given up all hope of understanding it while living it. But as soon as it's over, I have a truckload of questions. Sometimes I think life isn't so much a journey to collect answers as a journey to gather questions. In the next life, those who have the most, or who ask the right ones, win.

I arrived at work a half hour late on the morning of my birthday. It took that long to blow out all of those candles and eat my pecan pancakes. My daughter, Melody, now sixteen, reminded me before she drove the kids to school that I should not make plans that evening. She had something special in mind, but she wouldn't tell me what it was. I nodded my consent, although I was very suspicious.

You were not. You didn't suspect a thing.

As soon as I arrived at work, the president of the company, Doug Bowman, called me into his office.

"Jim," he began, "how long have you been with us now?"

"A little over nine years."

"Nine years? That's incredible."

The compliment sounded hollow, especially since Doug had only been with the company eighteen months. I knew right away it was bad news.

"Jim, you're aware that Randy Carlson has been expanding his markets like crazy. His show broadcasts all over the country now."

Randy Carlson was one of the financial gurus that our company represented. He made his first couple hundred thousand buying and selling real estate, and the next twenty million teaching others how he did it.

Doug continued, "We're gonna have to expand our Carlson sales force by at least a hundred marketers just to keep up with the demand. We want you to head up the Carlson team."

My mouth dropped open. This meant that I'd have to return to the sales floor as a team leader. I hadn't worked the general sales floor for over two years. For the last twenty-six months my job had been grooming new clients. In fact, it was *me* who landed Randy Carlson in the first place.

"Doug," I pleaded, "you can't cut me off now. I'm *this close* to nailing Vincent Del Greco. If I can bring on Del Greco, we'll need a hundred new marketers just to—"

"Del Greco is in the bag, Jim."

"What?"

"Vincent and I had dinner last night in San Diego."

My heart skipped a beat. "You *what?*"

"Richard was there, too. We talked almost two hours. We're drafting the contract today."

Richard Elms was the sole owner of Entrepreneurial Marketing, Inc. Eighteen months earlier he'd gone into semi-retirement, despite the fact that he was only two years older than me. He spent most of his time now sailing the world in a 150-foot yacht. Just before he set sail, he hired Doug Bowman, a Wall Street hotshot who had worked with Richard on some other successful ventures.

"Why wasn't I told about this?" I asked.

I'd been corresponding with people at Del Greco's headquarters for over a month. Vincent Del Greco had recently published a book on financial strategy. It was a runaway bestseller. His seminar tapes were selling like hotcakes. For Bowman to go over my head and set up a meeting with Del Greco and Richard Elms without my knowledge was the most ruthless thing I'd seen in the nine years I'd worked for the company.

"Well," Doug Bowman replied, "we felt things had to move a little faster than you were able to do in your position."

My position. Not a Harvard business school graduate. Not a self-made millionaire. Just a salesman who had worked his way up through the ranks.

"What about my commission?" I demanded. "I made all the introductions. I designed the packages—"

"We're reviewing your packages," said Bowman. "If we use them, you'll get your commission on each sale as promised. The packages look good. I don't see any other way we could do it. There's nothing to worry about."

"I was grooming future clients, too," I said. "Barry Stapleton, Sunny Sampson, Zoomer Arakaki. What happens to all of them?"

"If all the deals we have in the works come through, the company might be forced to consolidate—focus on existing accounts for a year or so. We might have to let a few fish off the line."

Let go of potential clients? For nine years, the company's lifeblood had been the development of future clients. During the days when Richard ran the company personally, this had been his guiding philosophy.

Doug Bowman never ceased to infuriate me. In the beginning I really liked the guy. But after a few months, it became starkly evident that he didn't much like *me.* Maybe because I talked to him like an equal instead of a god. Who knows? But there wasn't much he could do about me. Richard had placed me in my position six months before hiring Doug. He told Doug that I was the company's most valuable asset. After all, I was the one who had landed the Carlson account, which was fast becoming our mainstay of income.

At that moment, I stuck my foot in my mouth. "Does Richard know about all this?"

Doug bristled. He leaned forward, one eye half shut. This was the expression he used to intimidate his subordinates. "Richard hired me to run this company, Jim. He doesn't care how I do it as long as it keeps paying the bills on that 150-foot yacht of his. You understand what I'm telling you?"

I nodded. "I understand."

Doug leaned back. "All right then. You've got your work cut out for you. I expect you to develop the sharpest sales team this company has ever seen. We started running the ad for new marketers this morning. Angie has already started taking applications. You'll probably be interviewing most of the day. You can use your old office today, but by Monday, you'll have to move your stuff out to one of the cubicles on the sales floor."

Richard had considered it a sin to use the word "cubicle." The telemarketers' particleboard booths were referred to as "suites." Flaky, but I think it boosted morale. After all, some of the seasoned salesmen who worked out of those cubicles brought in seventy-five thousand dollars a year. I had a couple years close to that myself. Then after Renae got sick, it dropped down to around thirty-five. The year after she died, I barely broke twenty.

On the day Richard made me the Executive of New Accounts, it was a new position. I think he astutely determined that I needed a change of scenery. The change was successful. I made the company a lot of money and saved our house from foreclosure. It would be hard to move back out onto the sales floor, but I tried to think positive. I'd made the big bucks once. I could do it again. For the rest of the morning I made apologetic phone calls to many of the "fish" I was letting off the line. About 11:45 I got a call from the receptionist, Angie.

"Do you have time to do one interview before lunch?" she asked.

"I told you," I said curtly, "that I didn't want to start interviewing until 1:00."

"Well, this young man's been waiting here since a little after 10:00," she explained. "At first I didn't think he even wanted a job. Now he's been sitting here for over an hour and a half. Says he wants to be the first one interviewed. I think he intends to sit here all the way 'til one o'clock."

I sighed. "All right, Angie. Send him up."

Some cocky little fireball who thought he could sell ice to a snowman. Might as well get it over with. There was no doubt that I would hire him. In fact, I'd probably hire just about everybody who filled out an application. Let them weed themselves out, more or less. The job tended to do that all by itself.

When the young man came into my office, it immediately struck me that I'd seen him somewhere before, but I couldn't figure out where. He was about five-eight, dark complexioned. Hispanic or Italian, I assumed. Yet he had no hint of an accent. What struck me most was the whiteness of his eyes, as if he carried around a bottle of Visine in his pocket. The kid looked fresh out of high school. We didn't hire them much younger. I figured his face was familiar because I had seen him in one of my daughters' classes or in some checkout line at Albertson's or Wal-Mart. And yet as he approached me, his hand boldly outstretched, my first impression was that he knew *me.*

"Jim Hawkins!" he exclaimed. "So pleased to finally meet you."

I shook his hand. "Have I seen you somewhere before?"

"People ask me that all the time," he said. "I think it's because I did a television commercial once for a Chevy dealership. They had me holding up a sign and eating a hotdog." He made a cheesy grin and displayed an imaginary hotdog, like Lady Liberty holding the torch.

"Ah," I said. "That must be it."

"The name's Alberto Sanchez, and I could sell ice to a snowman."

"I'll bet you could," I groaned inwardly.

"I hear today is your birthday. Congratulations."

"Well, thank you."

"So which one is this? No, don't tell me. I'm real good at this sort of thing. I'll bet today you'rrre . . . forty?"

I laughed clumsily. "That's right. How did you know that?"

"Like I said, I'm good. I'll wager in a month I'm your top salesman."

"Well, Alberto—"

"Just Al," he corrected.

"Al, you're hired."

"Just like that?"

"Just like that. We'll start training Monday morning. By Monday afternoon you'll be on the phone. If you can't cut it, you'll probably know it by week's end. We expect a minimum of eight hours a day, but during training, you'd be wise to put in ten or twelve."

"No problem. So that's it? No questions about my previous experience?"

"Nope. I can generally tell if a person can sell. That's something *I'm* good at."

"Well, all right then. Outstanding! I'll see you Monday morning."

"No later than nine."

"I'm looking forward to working with you, Jim. Really looking forward to working with you. In fact, I think I can change your life forever."

The way he said it had an oddly disconcerting edge.

I laughed it off. "It had better be a change for the better."

"Oh, absolutely," he grinned. "Absolutely."

Al Sanchez left my office. I made a couple more phone calls and then headed out for lunch. On the way out, I passed Angie.

"Sorry, Jim," she said. "I was starting to feel uncomfortable with him sitting there for so long. Did you hire him?"

"Sure," I said. "We'll give anyone a chance."

"I hope you like your new job," she added, mildly sympathetic.

"I hope so, too. Say listen, when you first called up to me you said something kind of strange. You said at first you didn't think this guy even wanted a job?"

"No. At first I thought he was just looking for you. I guess he heard you did all the hiring."

"How could he know that? I didn't even know it myself until this morning."

"News travels fast around here. As you well know."

"Yeah. No doubt about that." I turned to go. Remembering, I turned back. "Oh, and I'd appreciate it if you didn't tell the applicants that today is my birthday."

"Today is your birthday? Oh, I wish I'd known. I'd have baked a cake or sent up a sympathy card or something."

"You didn't tell Alberto Sanchez that today was my birthday?"

She shook her head. "I didn't even know it myself. I guess I should know those kinds of things. It's right here on my computer. I'll have to look up all that stuff and make a list one of these days."

I hesitated another moment. "Thanks, Angie." I turned and walked out the door.

CHAPTER 2

Okay. Now we come to the birthday dinner—

Not quite yet. There's one other matter I thought should be covered first.

You're deliberately avoiding this.

Not at all. I felt I better discuss your Aunt Jenny and Uncle Garth. It seems relevant because of my interview with Alberto Sanchez. The incident kicked loose some peculiar feelings. Sensations I hadn't felt for eighteen years. But such feelings connected with Alberto were ridiculous. Eighteen years ago he would have been an infant, if in fact he had been born at all. For much of the afternoon I pondered his face. I felt certain I'd seen it before, but at the same time, I felt an urge to use my hands and reshape it slightly. The chin seemed wrong, the nose a little too Roman. I suppose everyone meets people they think look like somebody else. But why did this particular person arouse in me such feelings of trepidation?

When I got back from lunch, I seriously considered calling Al Sanchez to say I'd made a mistake. All our positions were filled. It would be such an obvious lie. Then I realized he'd written the words "no phone" on his application. Even the address read only "temporarily living with friends."

I kicked myself. Why didn't I ever look at these things beforehand? Why even have people fill them out if I had no intention of reading them? I shoved the application back into my drawer. On Monday, I would insist on some sort of phone number.

Another event that day aroused similar feelings of discomfort. I might have forgotten this incident entirely if it hadn't occurred so soon after my meeting with Al Sanchez.

As I exited the building that evening after work, I glanced to my left and noticed a woman on the sidewalk. She just stood there, glaring at me. She was very short—five feet, if that. Definitely Hispanic. Dark hair. Dark eyes. Late forties. The stub of a cigarette smoldered in the fingers of her right hand. Her muscles were rigid, as if my appearance had startled her.

She mumbled in Spanish, "*¡Ay madre mia!*"

I nodded stiffly, politely, and headed toward my car. There must have been a logical explanation for the woman's expression. Undoubtedly, it had nothing to do with me, nor was it any of my business.

Before I climbed into my car, I looked back at the woman again. She was still gaping at me, fear projecting from her eyes. Her hand reached up to snatch at an insect before her face, but her eyes remained locked into mine. Maybe there's an emergency, I thought. Could she be stranded or lost? I shut my car door and started to approach her.

I called out, "Can I help—?"

After I'd taken a single step, the woman tossed away the cigarette and scrambled around the corner of the building. She was gone. Just like that. She'd looked as though she wanted to say something. Had she lost her nerve at the last second? Perhaps she didn't speak any English.

On the way out of the parking lot, I drove around the building to see if I could spot her. She'd disappeared. Lunatics. The world was full of lunatics.

During the trip home I felt a powerful urge to speak with my old friend, Garth Plimpton. I'd known Garth since grade school. He married my sister, Jennifer, the same year I married Renae. Garth had a unique gift. If something was wrong, he would know. He had a "sense" about these things. In fact, he'd probably have called me first.

But I couldn't expect a call from Garth. Nor could *I* call *him.* He and Jenny were far away, in a place without phones.

During those first few years after our college adventure in Mexico, the four of us, Garth, Jenny, Renae and myself, would frequently get together and discuss the notion of returning to the land of the Nephites. Renae would debate with us as to whether it was "moral" to go back. What right did we have to meddle in the affairs of an ancient culture? Besides, the world of the Nephites and Lamanites had proven considerably dangerous. Our chase in Mexico with Gadiantons and the sword of Coriantumr was about as much adventure as Renae desired in life.

But Renae had never been to the cave. She had never visited the past. The beauty of that place, the glory of its people and culture, had never been etched upon her mind. Not so for Garth, Jenny, and myself. We had been children, full of wonder and dreams, when that underground river in Frost Cave had swept us into another world.

Underground river. Another world. It all sounds so mythical now. So illusory. Yet it was real. As tangible as anything I've ever experienced. But for nine years, Jenny and I had lost the memories of what had occurred. These images were not returned until we were students in college, when Muleki, the son of Teancum, and the assassins of Gadianton had breached the portal of time and entered the twentieth century. Garth had retained his memories because he kept them a secret. This was the pact we had made with the Prophet Helaman—a pact that Jenny and I, as adolescent blabbermouths, had hastily broken.

Now that all three of us could remember and reminisce with every ounce of the clarity such events deserved, the place had come to represent a kind of paradise. A wonderland where the pains and trials of life could be left behind; where a simpler, nobler existence awaited. Such are the hazards of selective memory. Maybe we procrastinated our return because we feared this illusion would be shattered.

But truthfully, it just wasn't *practical* to go back. Over time, the idea faded into a pleasant fantasy. Renae and I decided that the life we were building here in *this* century took definite priority. We had a family now. Responsibilities. Obligations. A mortgage payment.

But for Garth and Jenny, the situation was different.

Garth and Jenny had numerous trials of their own, as well as tragedies. Soon after they were married, Jenny learned she could not become pregnant easily. There were many tests, experiments, drugs, priesthood blessings, and even an operation, but to no avail. They talked of adopting, but their financial situation, strained by all the doctors and fertility drugs, made it difficult.

Jennifer had begun to lose all hope of having children. For a long time it was hard for her to visit our home and see all the toddlers. Then one evening she and Garth came to dinner with wonderful news. The one-in-a-million miracle had occurred. Jenny was pregnant. But the pregnancy was very tenuous. At three months she confined herself to her bed. At seven months the situation became critical. The child was delivered prematurely. It was a boy. And he lived only fourteen hours.

My sister was devastated. All of this occurred shortly after the death of our mother in Wyoming. It was also the time when Renae underwent chemotherapy. Tragedy raged in our family that year. Because of my own pain, I almost failed to comprehend what my sister was going through. Renae was her closest friend, and when she died, I knew that something had to give. I did not, however, expect quite the solution that Garth proposed. Just after Renae's funeral, he pulled me aside to make an announcement.

"We're going back," he said.

"Back?" I asked naively. "Back where?"

"Back into the cave," he replied. "Back into the past."

I was speechless. My head was already so drunk with grief I could hardly think straight. I stood there with a baffled look on my face.

"I know it won't be easy for anyone to understand," said Garth. "And it will be impossible to explain for reasons that you and I both know. But this is a dream that Jenny and I have had for over fifteen years."

"What about your career?" I asked. Garth was currently on the faculty at BYU's Anthropology Department.

"My dean was kind enough to grant me leave for a couple of semesters. After all, I've worked nonstop for eight years."

"How long do you expect to be gone?"

"A year. About a year."

My eyes widened. "A *year!?* But what if something happens? How are we supposed to—?"

"We don't intend to put ourselves in any danger," Garth explained. "In fact, we don't intend to leave the borders of the land of Melek, where the Ammonites dwell. I've never seen a more peaceful place on earth. Jenny needs that peace, Jim. We both need it."

I remembered the land of Melek. It was the region where the Lamanites who had been converted to Christ finally settled; the city where we had met Ammon, the frail and aged missionary. Melek was also the land of the volcano. The subterranean passages of this volcano connected with the time portal. Well, at least *one* such route connected with Melek. Other routes would expel the time traveler in the heart of the hostile east wilderness.

"It's been twenty-seven years," I said to Garth. "How do you know that Melek is still a peaceful land?"

"I can't be sure," said Garth. "The Book of Mormon is sort of vague on that point, but I suspect that Melek remained peaceful until several hundred years after Christ. If I'm wrong, you can expect that we'll be back a lot sooner."

"There's something else to consider," I said. "Remember what we learned from Teancum's son? People we had known among the Nephites aged a decade faster than we had aged. The time barrier between our two worlds isn't very stable. How will you know for certain when a year is up?"

"We realize it might be longer," said Garth. "We've accepted that. There's really nothing to keep us here, Jim."

"Nothing? What about *us?*"

"That's it," said Garth. "Just you and your brothers. Jenny's parents are gone; so are mine. I don't think I have to tell you, Jim, that your sister is at the breaking point. I'm praying that by reliving this dream—this fantasy from our childhood—she'll be revitalized somehow, strengthened. We'll stay as long as it takes."

"What am I supposed to tell my family?"

"Tell them we've decided to travel for a year, like a couple of gypsies."

I knew that explanation wouldn't wash for long. Over time, Jenny had become my children's favorite relative. Some years it seemed they spent more weekends and summers in Provo with Jenny and Garth than they did with us. She became particularly close to my oldest daughter, Melody. The two of them developed their own secret codes and protocols. A third party in the room might not even follow the conversation.

Only you couldn't follow it, Dad.

I knew if they left for a year it wouldn't be easy on Melody, especially after the loss of her mother. But it didn't turn out to be a year. It turned out to be much longer.

Just before they drove off for Wyoming, their old Ford Escort packed to the hilt with camping equipment, Garth said to me, "We expect to show up on your doorstep on Christmas Eve, just about the time you start singing carols."

The following Christmas Eve came . . . and went. Garth and Jenny never appeared. They had been gone now for over two years.

But that's not the worst part. The worst part is that Dad never told us what happened to them! In fact, Dad never told us kids anything *about the passageway in Frost Cave or his adventures among the Nephites. Sometimes he would tell us these wild stories before we went to bed. But that's all we thought they were—wild stories from my dad's warped imagination.*

Just before they left, I asked Aunt Jen to write me often and send us pictures of their travels. She turned to Dad and gave him the queerest look I've ever seen.

I remember that look. Basically she was telling me to cover for her. It was the most unfair request she'd ever made of me. Every week, every month after they left, the situation grew increasingly awkward. After a year, the dean of BYU's Anthropology Department started calling. The police showed up to ask questions a month later. All I could say was that the last time I saw them they were headed north on I-15 in a Ford Escort full of camping supplies. And all this pressure as I struggled desperately with the loss of my wife.

The only thing I could think was that they had been murdered by hitchhikers or terrorists. It was horrible not knowing. We were comforted a little by Dad's confidence. He told us that Uncle Garth had said they might be gone longer than a year. He told us that everything would be all right.

That confidence was an act. For all I knew, Garth and Jen had been attacked by Lamanites or Gadianton robbers the minute they emerged from that tunnel. Several times I seriously considered driving to Wyoming, penetrating those caverns again and searching for them. But my life wasn't like Garth's. I couldn't just pick up and walk away. What if I were lost or killed? What would happen to my family?

As time went on we spoke of them less and less, but I'm certain they were never far from our thoughts.

Okay. That's it. I'm tired of talking about stressful things. I want to tell about the birthday dinner.

All right, fine. You can tell about the birthday dinner. But I'm not sure it'll mean we've stopped discussing stressful things.

Of course it won't. But to me the story is just so darling. First I better talk a little about myself—

My daughter's favorite subject.

Please, Dad. It's my turn.

My name is Melody Constance Hawkins. I'm sixteen years old and reasonably confident that I was blessed with most of the brains in this family. This becomes particularly apparent when one takes a minute to observe my tomboy sister, Steffanie, and my Neanderthal brother, Harrison. After all, only someone with brains like mine could have concocted, and then pulled off, such a brilliant plan for my father's birthday. Something like this would never even have occurred to Steffanie. She wouldn't have looked up from her basketball, soccerball, tennis racket or bowling ball long enough to think of it. And as for Harrison—well, let's just say that someone who would borrow my feather boa and silk bra to decorate a snowman isn't intelligent enough to think of anything.

So what did I arrange? A double date.

That's right. For the first time in two and a half years, my father was going out on a date. Of course my father had no idea. I knew if I told him beforehand that I'd set up a blind date with Sabrina Sorenson, he would have called her up that minute and told her it had all been a big misunderstanding.

I certainly would have. That is, after I had wrung your scrawny little neck.

But it wasn't exactly a blind *date. I mean, Dad knew who she was. Sabrina was this really pretty lady who had recently moved into our ward from Molalla, Oregon. She had one daughter about Harrison's age from a bad marriage that had ended in divorce about five years before. Her husband was this total jerk who up and left the roost one day.*

Anyway, I'd seen her try to flirt with Dad a couple of times at Church activities. Dad, of course, was totally oblivious.

She was *not* flirting. Can't people just be polite to each other? You think anytime a single woman says two words to me, she's flirting. It could be "Hey, you just ran over my schnauzer," and you'd still think she was flirting.

Like I said, Dad was totally oblivious. But I caught the hints. So I called Sabrina about a week before his birthday.

At first she was really reluctant about the whole thing. She hadn't dated much since her divorce, and when she did *date it was with the kind of guys that split the tab or never vacuum their car. I had never heard of anyone having worse luck with men. I convinced her that Dad thought she was nice and that he had told me he really wanted to ask her out. But I explained that he was so shy it might be a long time before he got up the nerve.*

In other words, you lied to her.

A white lie maybe. I know that you liked her.

I nev—! I don't think I like the way you're telling this story.

Stop interrupting.

I knew that the only way I could get Sabrina to agree was to promise that I'd tell Dad all about it before our date on Friday. She threatened to call him during the week to see if I'd carried through, but I had my doubts that she would actually do that. Thank goodness I was right, because I never told him. On Thursday I called Sabrina in the afternoon, when I knew she'd be at work, and left a message on the machine to remind her.

Before Dad got home on Friday, I shuffled off Harry and Steff to various sleepovers and got ready for my own date. Now I have to tell you about my boyfriend.

Melody's *second* favorite subject.

Oh, Dad, you are so wrong. Boys are unquestionably number one.

His name was Quinn. We'd been dating for about three weeks, which for me was kind of a record. He had dark hair. He was about six-one, with eyes that one day looked green and the next day looked brown. Quinn was about as arrogant as they come. He sincerely believed he was God's gift to women and frankly, he was, although I did my best to convince him otherwise and keep him on his toes. He was also a senior and inactive in the Church—two facts that my father didn't much appreciate.

I liked him mostly because he was smart. Intelligent conversation with a guy can be pretty rare. Some of his ideas were rather bizarre, but they were all interesting to listen to. I told him when I arranged this little excursion that he might do well to keep his philosophies to himself around my father. Unfortunately, I think he took it as a challenge. That day at school I reminded him that if he happened to make any remark that ruined my father's fortieth birthday dinner or his first date with another woman in eighteen years, I would injure him most severely.

When Dad finally came home from work, around six-thirty, I could tell he'd had a bad day because he went to the refrigerator and poured himself a tall glass of milk mixed with Hershey's chocolate syrup. This was Dad's way off reverting back to childhood, or back to the womb, for security —

Okay, that's enough. My turn for a while.

It *was* a bad day at work. Aside from Al Sanchez, the strange woman, and all the peculiar feelings, I'd spent the whole afternoon hiring over twenty people, all of whom I had to train starting Monday. When I walked through the door I expected some kind of surprise party. The house was perfectly quiet. I was almost disappointed. It was a relief when Melody appeared on the stairway to watch me drink my milk.

"Hey," I said. "You sure look sharp."

"Dad," she began, "we don't have much time. You have to get changed. Do you mind if I pick your clothes?"

"Pick my clothes? What's going on?"

"It's a surprise. And would you mind wearing the cologne that I bought you last Christmas? The one you haven't opened?"

"Are you gonna tell me what we're doing?"

"Quinn and I are taking you out tonight."

"Quinn? I have to spend my birthday with Quinn?"

Melody's shoulders slouched. "Please, Dad. I've worked really hard to make everything right for tonight. Can you just do what I ask you?" She actually got behind me and started herding me up the stairs.

"What does Quinn care if I wear cologne?"

"The cologne is for me. Now hurry, Dad! Mush! Mush!"

Melody also took the time to comb my hair just right. But this wasn't so unusual. It was a habit she inherited from her mother. For some reason, women have never liked the way I did my own hair. Up until now, I must admit, I did not suspect a thing. How could I possibly believe that my daughter would be so outrageous as to set me up on a blind date?

Dad, this is me you're talking about.

Yes. For a brief instant, I forgot who I was dealing with.

My first clue that something was up struck me when Quinn showed up on the doorstep five minutes before 7:00 and said, "How ya doin', Jim? Happy birthday! You look sharp. So this is the big night, eh?"

Obnoxious little twirp, calling me by my first name. I watched Melody give him a dirty look, as if he'd revealed too much. Actually, what *he* said didn't clue me in to anything. It was Melody's reaction.

"All right, you two. Let's have it. What's going on?"

"We'll tell you in the car," Melody said. "Come on! We'll be late!" She was so certain I'd call everything off that she waited until the very last second.

That second arrived when we pulled into the gutter in front of Sabrina Sorenson's house.

I gave my daughter an icy stare. "You didn't. Tell me that you didn't."

"Somebody had to," said Melody. "You'd have never done it by yourself."

I closed my eyes and pressed a finger to each temple. "I can't believe you did this. How could you do this? I cannot *believe—!*"

"You have to go up and knock on the door, Dad," said Melody. "If you don't, you'll look pretty spineless."

"Melody, this isn't right. I'm not ready for this."

Quinn butted in. "When do you think you'll be ready, Jim? Seems to me, hombre, this is as good a time as any."

I wanted to knock the kid's block off. Then I wanted to stick my daughter in a tower somewhere for life. It was that grin on Quinn's face that gave me the final nudge. Some kind of twisted brand of male competition. If it had just been Melody, I might have canceled the whole thing. It may sound stupid, but I did not want to flake out in front of another guy. Tension curdled in my guts. I hadn't felt such tension since adolescence.

"Never again," I seethed. "Don't *ever* try this again."

"The curtain just flicked," said Melody. "Sabrina's probably wondering what's going on. You better get out."

"I'm going," I sighed. "I'm going."

I opened the car door and planted my feet on the curb. I drew a couple of deep breaths. To an observer, it probably sounded more like gasping. At parties I could now reveal a new "most embarrassing moment." I convinced myself as I trudged up the walk that my only emotion was anger. But looking back, I was plumb petrified. I tried to dry my palms on my pants. Sabrina and I had struck a dozen conversations. We could discuss just about anything. But tonight's conversation would take place in a whole new arena. I suddenly wondered if I could discuss the weather without sounding like an idiot.

All the anxieties of youth rushed back on me, a horrible déjà vu. Why get married if not to escape such anxieties? In spite of my suave reputation, I never really cared for dating when I was young. I was certain I'd like it less as an adult.

You had a suave reputation?

I'll ignore that.

Sabrina opened the door after one knock. "Well hello, Broth—" She scoffed at herself. "I was about to call you Brother Hawkins. Hello, Jim."

Sabrina Sorenson was a good-looking woman. I can admit that now. Her eyes were blue. Her hair was much lighter than Renae's. She'd never worn a lot of makeup. Tonight was no exception. A little eyeliner and lipstick. It was obvious her hair had just been styled. She was taller than Renae. Much more athletic than my wife had—

Sorry. It was hard not to compare every feature and nuance. Just before I spoke, I imagined Renae looking down on us. All at once I felt frightfully self-conscious.

"Yes, Sabrina, hello. You look like . . ."

I'm not sure what I was about to say. Something like, "You look like you just had your hair done," or "You look like you worked really hard to look good for me." Whatever it was, it wasn't thought out very well. Fortunately, I cut myself off. But I still looked like a dope.

Sabrina looked herself over. "That bad?"

"No, no, no," I said. "Like nice. You look nice."

"I look like nice? Well, thanks. You look like nice, too."

"Sorry. You look very nice."

"Happy birthday."

"Huh?"

"Isn't today . . . ? Melody said—"

"Oh, yes! Thank you. My birthday. Yes, it is."

Sabrina stepped out the door and leaned in close to try and stop me from embarrassing myself any further. "Relax, Jim. I'm honored that Melody asked me to be a part of your fortieth birthday. You don't look a day over thirty-five. So what kind of adventure has your daughter planned for us?"

"I have no idea."

"Shall we find out?"

I smiled sheepishly. Putting a man at ease so quickly was a feminine skill I much appreciated. Renae had had that skill—Okay. No more comparisons.

"I think we should," I replied.

She took my arm without reservation. The gesture took me by surprise.

They looked so cute together. Sabrina looked hot. She was wearing this gorgeous white pantsuit with lace on the cuffs and a black belt. And she had on lipstick. I'd never seen her wearing lipstick. She had a beautiful face anyway, and the kind of skin most women would kill for. I could tell she'd gone all out to impress him, without overdoing it, of course. All that evening she worked very hard to make Dad feel comfortable. Dad, on the other hand, was about as exciting as a corpse.

As they climbed into the back, I announced that we were eating at Dad's favorite spaghetti restaurant. I should have known better. When Mom was alive we used to go there about once a month. In the two and a half years since she'd died, we'd only gone twice. But the reason I should have known better had nothing to do with Mom. It had to do with my dad's bizarre sense of frugality.

Generally speaking, my dad is a very generous man. But when it comes to certain things, he can be the ultimate skinflint. He'll drive three miles out of his way to save a penny on a gallon of gasoline. When he shops, he'll go to three different grocery stores. When it came to this particular restaurant, he had no qualms about embarrassing everyone at the table in order to save seventy-five cents.

I think I'd better explain this so it doesn't sound so *unreasonable—*

I doubt it can be done, but go ahead and try.

They had this entree called the Manager's Special, where you could get a plate of spaghetti with two different sauces—a meat sauce and a mizithra cheese. If you ordered either one of these sauces by themselves, it cost a whole dollar less—*a dollar. Not* seventy-five cents. As a family, we always ordered the sauces separately, and then I'd take half of my wife's mizithra cheese and she'd take half of my meat—

And I used to cringe every time they did it. We were in public! The spaghetti would drip all over the tablecloth—

It would not. Why should I have to pay an extra dollar just to have the chef slop a different sauce over each half of the plate?

Dad. Listen to me. Listen carefully. As a family, maybe it was okay—a little tacky, but maybe you could get away with it. But on a date? I could have died. I'm telling you, I could have died!

Sabrina thought it was a good idea.

She thought you were a nerd, Dad. She just didn't want to hurt your feelings.

Well, all right. But hey, I hadn't been on a date in eighteen years! I had the impression the evening was going pretty well. That is, until your boyfriend took out his brains and started rolling them all over the table.

For the sake of those who don't know, this is a lovely expression my father uses for people who try to display their intelligence by saying something stupid.

I wouldn't have responded at all if the kid hadn't been dating my daughter. We were discussing how long the restaurant had been there, and that led to a discussion on the history of Salt Lake, which led to a discussion on the history of the Church.

"Latter-day Saints would have the greatest history of any religion in the world," Quinn said, "if it wasn't for polygamy and denying blacks the priesthood. Those are the two blemishes that make me ashamed to be a Mormon."

Quinn was smirking at me, like a knight who had thrown down the gauntlet. Melody squirmed.

"Those are spiritual issues," I replied. "They have to be discerned spiritually. It's silly to think they can be understood any other way."

"Now, that sounds like a cop-out, Jim. But I guess it's the only possible reply if you still believe the Church is true."

I could feel a prickling heat on the back of my neck. I hated it when someone did this to me. But it was precisely Quinn's objective. "I submit, young man," I said in a voice like an attorney, "that it is a vain thing to judge the mind of God according to man's modern labels of what is morally and politically correct. His ways are not our ways."

"That's a good one," said Quinn. "I like that cop-out a lot better."

Melody dropped her fork on the table. "Quinn! Could I have a word with you in the lobby, *pleeease?*"

When they got back, he was a lot quieter, but I could see his mind spinning, preparing for the next time he decided to take his brains out. Opinions are one thing, and certainly this kid had a right to his.

I only knew that I didn't want him anywhere near my daughter.

Give me a little credit, Dad. I knew he was deliberately trying to get your goat. Stir things up. I cussed him out good for it. He was just flexing his mind muscles. Kids do that, you know. You can't stop them from thinking.

Thinking is fine, as long you don't think in a vacuum—no longer listening. Young people seem to think every controversy they uncover is one that nobody ever pondered before.

Seems to me Mom described you as being that way once.

And then I got married and realized how little I knew. I'm still in that phase, by the way.

The kids wanted to go to a movie after dinner. I explained that I was just too tired. I think Sabrina would like to have gone, but when she heard me decline, she said that she was also very tired.

We drove to her house. I walked her to the front door. I could feel the kids' eyes on my back as we stood in the doorway, but I wasn't about to kiss her goodnight. We shook hands. Sabrina said the obligatory, "I had a really nice time," followed by another, "Happy birthday, Jim."

I didn't respond right away, making the moment very awkward. Finally I heard myself say, "Maybe we could do this again sometime."

I wasn't sure if I really *wanted* to do it again, but I thought it would be a nice thing to say. I think she picked up on the ambivalence.

"Maybe," she responded. "I'll call you."

She smiled and slipped inside the house.

I stood there on the porch a few seconds, feeling exposed. *I'll call you.* That meant the power to make a second date had been stripped from me. It was all in her hands. If I were still a teenager, I'd have felt solidly rejected. As a forty-year-old stick-in-the-mud, I didn't know what to feel. Relieved, I guess. No, that's not quite it. But I didn't want to think about it right now.

The kids dropped me off in front of the house. I told Quinn I wanted my daughter home directly after the movie. I was dead serious, and I think he knew it.

As the car drove out of sight, a pressing loneliness settled over me. I shrugged it off and pulled the keys out of my pocket. As I unlocked the door and stepped inside, an entirely new feeling struck me. How can I describe it? It was as if I had stepped inside a neighbor's house by mistake. But no. It was my living room. It just *felt* different. The house was dark. All the furniture slept in silhouette. Slivers of light from the streetlamp shone through the front window and reflected off the glass in the family portraits. My hand moved toward the light switch, but I hesitated. Something was wrong. I felt a need to study the room while it was still dark. By turning on the light, my eyes would take a split second to adjust. I feared in that split second I might miss something crucial.

It took a moment to realize what was wrong. There was a distinct breeze in the house. A window somewhere had been left open. Or a door. Yes, that was it. The only opening wide enough to create this much breeze was the sliding glass door off the kitchen. Had one of the kids left it open? No. I remembered making myself a glass of chocolate milk when I first came home. It hadn't been open then.

I left the light off and stepped carefully across the carpet until I reached the foot of the stairs. From here I could peer down the hallway and into the kitchen. Sure enough, the back door had been slid back all the way. A mild gust lifted the strands on the valance. I knew our family was not consistent about locking the back door. We forgot it often. Someone had been in the house. Or else someone was *still* in the house.

Just as this thought skimmed over my mind, my eyes turned up the stairway. There at the top I could see a shape. A human shape, standing there, wraithlike, looking down on me. Every muscle in my body constricted. How long had this person been there? Why hadn't I flipped on the light? The instinct to leave it off suddenly seemed foolish.

"Who's there?" I shouted. "What are you doing in my house?"

The shape took flight—in the darkness that's exactly what it looked like. As if a vampire had leaped from the top step just before transforming into a bat. The figure bounded down the stairs, miraculously not tripping, and bowled right into me. The light through the curtains allowed me to catch a glimpse of color before I was knocked to the ground. There was something red, white, and blue shrouding his head—a nylon cap or a ski mask. I think the figure wore gloves.

As I pushed myself to my feet, I managed to see the person crash through the valance strips that hung over the back door and disappear. He (I assumed it was a he) had on a black sweater, jeans, and high-top sneakers.

Still disoriented, I staggered through the kitchen and looked into the backyard. The man had already leaped the fence. He was gone.

A burglar! A man had just robbed my house! But what had he taken? There was nothing in his hands. My wife's wedding ring? I remembered I had left eighty dollars on my dresser.

After switching on every light between the stairs and my bedroom, I began an inventory. All of it was still there: the money, the wedding ring. Apparently I had interrupted the burglar before he could find the loot. I searched every drawer, examined every shelf and desk top. I couldn't discover a single item out of place.

And yet I knew the burglar had been in my room. He had left the light on in my bathroom. A few things might have been moved around, but it was hard to tell. My sink generally wasn't very organized. I thought sure I'd solved the mystery when it occurred to me that my wife's old prescription bottles of Tylenol with codeine were still in the medicine cabinet. Perhaps the burglar was a junkie looking for pain pills. But the bottles had not been touched.

A very inefficient thief, I thought. The money was right out in the open. How long would it have taken to stuff those bills into a pocket of his jeans? Even if he had heard me enter the house, there still would have been plenty of time.

I felt incredibly lucky. So lucky I didn't even think it necessary to call the police. Just some punk caught in the act before he could do any real harm. I was almost tempted to thank him for confirming that my forty-year-old body could still pump adrenaline. Nothing appeared to have been stolen, nothing looked to have been damaged, except perhaps my shoulder, but the bruise would heal. I would, however, call a family meeting about locking that back door. Maybe I'd finally install a deadbolt.

As far as I could tell, only one thing looked as though it might be missing from my bathroom, but since it was an item that my daughters had been known to borrow on occasion, I thought nothing of it.

After all, what would a burglar want with a three-dollar hair brush?

CHAPTER 3

My hectic weekend did not end with the blind date or the attempted burglary. On Saturday my younger daughter, Steffanie, got into a fight during a basketball game and bloodied the boy's nose. It was her third fight that year. As usual, she'd thrown the first punch. She was definitely the most self-willed and opinionated of all my children. Also the loudest trumpeter of injustice and unfair treatment. It drove me nuts sometimes, particularly when I had to answer to some coach or bishop who called to say she'd just decked another kid.

Harry presented a different sort of challenge. Saturday afternoon I got the phone bill and discovered that he and his friends had been calling one of those 900 numbers that advertise on television after midnight. I used to think his friends put him up to this sort of thing. Now I was beginning to wonder if he'd been the instigator all along. It was becoming difficult to talk to Harry. I think he was slightly ashamed of me. His friends happened to have fathers who excelled in multiple sports, from weight lifting to hang gliding. In November, I'd overheard him tell a friend that I'd once played minor league baseball with the Salt Lake Gulls. It tore at my heart. But what was kool about a father who whiled his life away behind a sales desk? It made it difficult to elicit respect when I doled out discipline.

What about me, Dad? I'd hate to feel left out.

I was getting to you.

And then on Sunday, Melody arrived late at sacrament meeting wearing a leather halter top like Madonna.

It wasn't like Madonna. I had a jacket over my shoulders.

If only an earthquake had struck at that moment and buried me. Every head in the chapel turned. The speaker lost his place. Then the congregation looked at *me,* wondering how I could allow my daughter to even *own* such an outfit.

I just used to get so sick of the same humdrum thing every week. Just once, I thought I'd liven things up a little. Be different.

You were different, all right. Several of the high priests nearly blew their pacemakers. I immediately sent her home to change. She didn't come back. I discovered later she'd gone off with Quinn.

I was losing control of my family! That weekend it hit me how neglectful I'd been toward all of my kids. Every gospel basic—family home evening, family prayer, daily scriptures—had suffered deplorably since Renae's death. It had become so hard to rekindle those habits. How could I have allowed this to happen? The passing of a loved one should have brought us closer to God, made us more committed, more spiritual, not torn us apart. These were the years that youth formed testimonies, grounded convictions in truth. I feared I had lost my children. Accountability was mine alone.

On Sunday night, I called them into my room for family prayer. They acted as if I'd spoken a foreign language. "Prayer," I said impatiently. "Do you remember *prayer*?"

It felt awkward, but we got through it. After they left, I knelt again. I prayed for a long time, pleading for help—*begging* for it. Afterwards, I sat at the edge of my bed, feeling just as lost and alone.

On Monday, the strange incidents I'd started confronting the week before continued. That morning I was going over my beard with a Norelco, breathing in the view of snowcapped mountains from my bedroom window, when I glanced down at the sidewalk.

There she was—the small Hispanic woman from the parking lot. She stood across the street, peering up at my window. She wore the same yellow dress, frayed at the hem. She was still smoking.

It was like sighting an apparition. I threw open the window and cried, "Who are you? What do you want?"

Without responding, she fled up the street.

I scrambled down the stairs, half-shaven, the Norelco still in my hand, and burst out onto the front step. Where could she have gone? The interval between standing at my window and reaching the front door was less than thirty seconds. The woman was hiding. But why? Who *was* she? And why was she following me?

The children, seated around a cereal-strewn table, looked up at me queerly as I stood out on the front step, no socks, a shaver in my hand.

"Somethin' the matter, Dad?" Harry asked casually.

I came back inside. "If any of you kids see a small Hispanic woman who smokes a lot hanging around the house, I want you to call me at work right away."

"A small Hispanic woman who smokes a lot?" said Melody dubiously. "What does she want?"

"I don't know," I replied. "I saw her on Friday. I saw her again less than a minute ago."

"Sure you're not seeing things, Dad?" winked Steffanie.

I gazed back up the street. Steff had a point. The apparition theory seemed the only valid explanation.

* * *

"So when do I actually start making money?" asked Alberto Sanchez, kneading his hands like a villain in a melodrama.

"This afternoon," I replied. "You'll get a script and a page of phone numbers right after training."

"Then let's get cracking!"

Al Sanchez had shown up at 9:00 a.m. along with two dozen other applicants, all anxious to realize the company's promise of high commissions. According to our track record, about half of them would last the first week. A fourth would hang on for a month. One or none would remain longer than a year and make a career out of it. Yet they all had to be trained with the same exhaustive attention.

By the end of the workday on Monday, my initial impression of Alberto had mellowed somewhat. I must admit, when he first appeared that morning, I'd wondered if he might be Friday's burglar. But Al was too short. The intruder was close to my height, and his shoulders were filled out. Al still had the lanky frame of a teenager.

Frankly, it was a pleasure to train Al Sanchez. Despite his age, he was the sharpest of the bunch. During training, he volunteered to cold-call a potential customer. I'll be darned if he didn't close a $900 sale on his first attempt. Before lunch, I had all the new telemarketers select a cubicle on the sales floor. Al selected the one right in front of mine.

"Excellent," he said. "Between calls I can lean over the wall and listen to a pro."

I laughed halfheartedly. "You don't need to listen to me, Al. Soon enough I'll likely have all the trainees come over and listen to *you*." I changed the subject. "By the way, you didn't write a phone number on your application."

"I know," he said. "I'll be moving into an apartment in Murray the first of next week. The phone will be hooked up then. Do you need my number that bad?"

"No, it's just—" I shifted in my seat. "It's just for emergencies. There's really no need."

I might have pressed the matter, but I couldn't think of a single instance in the last nine years where I'd been forced to call a trainee at home. If they didn't show up the next day, they just didn't show up.

Something still disquieted me about Al Sanchez, but there was no logic, no rationale for it. Maybe I was intimidated. A guy with his talent could vie for my job in a matter of months. As the days progressed, I thought less and less about my peculiar first impression. The following week, it didn't even occur to me to ask for his phone number. In a way, we'd even become friends. Not buddies or anything, but we got along. The plain truth was, Al was making me a lot of money. As a sales trainer and group leader, my overall commission was directly affected by team success. Odd how money can dull our instincts and consciences.

Things at work came to a head the following Tuesday.

Around three that afternoon, I knocked on Doug Bowman's door. I'd been trying to see the company president since Friday. His secretary kept telling me he was busy and would get back to me as soon as he could. Today I happened to enter his office foyer at a moment when his secretary was out.

Doug's door was open. He was rustling through some papers. "Come in," he said absently. As soon as he recognized me, he abruptly rose to his feet. "Jim! I had a message that you wanted to see me. I was going to have Angie call you in before the day was out. You saved me the trouble. Come in. Come in."

I watched him glance out into the foyer, no doubt wondering why his watchdog secretary was not at her post.

"I wanted to ask you about the Del Greco contract," I said.

"Signed, sealed and delivered," he told me. "Terry is going to start training the Del Greco team this week."

"What I wanted know," I continued, "was what happened with the program I designed."

"Oh," said Doug. "In that case, I'm afraid I have unfortunate news for you. It doesn't look like we're going to be able to use your program. It was a good program, Jim. It just wasn't quite the approach we were looking for at this time."

My breathing became erratic as I tried to contain my temper. "Doug, I worked day and night on that program. Day and night for three weeks. I was counting on those commissions, especially after being transferred back onto the sales floor. Do you know what this is going do to my overall income?"

"I don't see that it will affect it that much. You used to be one of this company's hottest marketers. It might take a while to build up a lead pool again, but I expect you to be back on top in no time."

"Fifteen hundred dollars a month—that's what I was counting on from the Del Greco commissions."

"It just wasn't a workable program, Jim. We had to take it in another direction—more focused on real estate investment."

"I included real estate," I said.

"But not as the central focus. We had to rework the prices and everything."

"You're shooting me in the foot here, Doug."

Doug looked at his watch. "We'll have to discuss this later, Jim. I have a meeting in just a few minutes. Maybe we could set an appointment for tomorrow morning." Bowman noticed that his secretary had returned. "Cynthia! There you are. Pencil in Jim for sometime tomorrow, could you?"

"Tomorrow is impossible, Doug."

Doug grimaced and clicked his tongue. "Sorry about that. Maybe later this week."

Cynthia acknowledged.

Doug led me to the door. "I'm sorry your program didn't work out, Jim. We'll talk about it later."

His door shut solidly, nearly pinching off my nose. Fifteen hundred dollars a month down the drain. But it wasn't going down the drain. It was headed for someone else's pocket.

I immediately crossed the building in search of Terry Sparrow, the designated group leader for the Del Greco team. We called Terry the "Iceman." He was the best phone salesman I'd ever met. Hard to imagine from such a pudgy, mild-mannered soul. Terry and I had been friends for seven years. I had full confidence that he would tell me everything.

"I can't," Terry responded when I asked him if I could see a workup on the new Del Greco program.

"Why?" I asked, bewildered.

"Doug told us he wanted everything kept under wraps until we find out if it will sell or not."

"So Doug designed the program?"

"From what I understand."

"Please, Terry," I pleaded. "Something really rotten is going on. I'm begging you to let me glance over the workup."

Terry's eyes cut around the room. He motioned me to sit inside his cubicle. He didn't even want other marketers on his team to see what I was reading.

"You didn't get it from me," Terry said. "If anyone asks, you found a copy in the garbage or something."

"I owe you big time, Terry."

As I pored over the workup, I became angrier and angrier. Just as I thought, *it was my program!* Some of the external details were different—the price, and some sections of the sales script—but clearly three-fourths of the material had been lifted right out of the workup that I had designed.

I knew it! Doug had intended for that fifteen hundred dollars a month to line his own wallet. Didn't Richard Elms pay him enough as C.E.O.? What financial difficulties might have driven a man like Doug Bowman to steal from his own employee? Had he gotten behind on his swimming pool payments or his time-share condo in the Bahamas?

"Like what you see?" Terry asked.

I didn't hear him. Blood boiled in my ears. I dropped the papers back onto his desk and made a beeline toward Doug Bowman's office. His secretary tried to stop me. She failed. I burst through the door. Doug was seated with two men in business suits whom I didn't recognize. Probably attorneys.

"It's my program, Doug!" I roared. "You *know* it's my program!"

Doug arose. "We'll have to discuss this later, Jim. I'm having an important—"

"What did you think you were doing? Did you think I wouldn't notice? That I wouldn't find out?"

The men in suits watched the exchange with great interest. Doug's face reddened. He walked over to me. "Nothing is set in stone, Jim. Now get back to your team."

"I can't, Doug. This isn't right. I won't go back there unless I get an assurance that credit for that program will be returned to me. If I can't get it, I won't go back. Do you understand? I'll quit. Right now."

Doug's frame relaxed. His lips formed a tight smile. "Well, Jim, you have to do what you have to do."

I stood there, dumbfounded. Doug's eyes didn't even flinch. Cold as steel. I hadn't seen such an expression since I'd looked into the face of a Gadianton robber.

I turned abruptly and walked out. Doug's secretary looked after me pitiably. My mind blanked for the next few moments. I don't remember reentering the hallway or starting down the stairs. I'd done it. I'd actually quit my job. After nine years. One afternoon and it was all over. Just like that.

Something had to be done. Clearly there were grounds for legal action. I couldn't roll over on this one. I had no other source of income and only one paycheck remaining. The answer hit me halfway down the stairs. Richard Elms. I had always considered the owner of the company a personal friend. But how could I reach him? His yacht might be in the middle of the Pacific. Then I remembered Chuck. Chuck Elms was Richard's younger brother. He was also the company accountant. His office was situated at the opposite end of the hall from the C.E.O.

I climbed the stairs again. Chuck was seated behind his computer.

"Hello, Jim," he greeted. "How's life down in the trenches?"

"Hasn't changed much. Listen, Chuck, I need to reach your brother. It's kind of an emergency. Is there any way I can contact him?"

"You're lucky," he replied. "He's visiting my sister in L.A. I can give you that number if you want. What's it concerning?"

"A company matter," I said, not wanting to say much more and risk pitting Chuck against Doug.

I'd worked for the company a long time. If I said I needed to talk with his brother, Chuck trusted that it must be important. He confirmed the number in his day planner and wrote it down on a yellow stick'em note. I thanked him and returned to my cubicle on the sales floor. Al Sanchez was at his desk, scanning numbers on a cold-call sheet. He looked up at me. It was obvious I was distraught.

"You all right, Jim?" he asked.

"I'm fine."

"Anything I can do?"

I shook my head and began dialing the phone number of Richard's sister in Los Angeles. I got an answering machine. After the beep, I left a message.

"Richard Elms? This is Jim Hawkins in Salt Lake. I need to talk with you urgently about a company matter. Please call me at home."

I left my home phone number. Alberto had overheard every word.

"Trouble at the top?" he inquired.

I leaned back in my chair, staring off into space. "Yeah," I mumbled obliviously. "Trouble at the top."

"I'll bet the trouble is with Doug Bowman, isn't it?"

Al earned my full attention. "You're a pretty observant kid, Al. Probably too observant."

Al shrugged it off. "One doesn't have to be all that observant. Everyone knows the guy has it in for you."

"Everyone?" I repeated. "Who's everyone?"

"You must not listen to the office gossip."

"I try to avoid it," I said.

"I heard Doug demoted you."

I decided I'd better end this conversation before I said something inappropriate. None of it was Alberto's business anyway. I gathered up a few essentials: some rough notes I'd penciled in a note pad to prove that the program was mine, my sales leads, a few personal belongings, a small family portrait. As I got up from my swivel-back chair, I took a long look at my cubicle area—my office. I knew that it might be the last time I ever sat in that chair as an employee of Entrepreneurial Marketing, Inc. The only man who might save me now was in California visiting his sister. But in spite of my friendship and nine-year loyalty to Richard Elms, I had serious doubts that he would back me over Doug Bowman. Maybe if I explained it right. I had to be calm and cool. Totally businesslike.

"Hold down the fort," I told Alberto.

He did not reply. His eyes followed me as I left the sales floor.

When I passed the front desk, Angie was on the phone. I was glad. I was in no mood to explain why I was carrying so many personal belongings out to my car. Besides, I still had high hopes that good-byes would be premature.

I paused as I exited the building. Suddenly I felt like a complete idiot. What had I done? How could I have reacted so rashly? I should have thought this out a little better. So childish! I'd been a slave to my temper. Even if I got my job back now, the rift between Doug and myself was permanent. The only stable factor in my life—my job, my income—had collapsed. My world was crumbling around me.

I unlocked my car door and placed my stuff on the back seat. It also occurred to me that my message to Richard hadn't been very well thought out. I had said that I needed to discuss an "urgent company matter." This might inspire Richard to call Doug before he called me. That would give Doug the opportunity to twist things any way he wanted.

I realized I'd left the stick'em note with Richard's L.A. phone number on my desk. I slammed the car door and tromped back toward the building. When I got inside, I stopped again. I was acting totally irrational. Out of control. What did I think I was going to do? Call California every five minutes to be sure I caught Richard the minute he stepped through the door? It could be hours. It could be tomorrow.

No. I'd left my message. Let the chips fall where they may. I could get the L.A. number from Alberto or someone else on my team if I had to. Mostly, I just wanted to get out of there.

Prayer. I had to say a prayer, both to solicit the Lord's help and to calm my spirit. Angie glanced at me questioningly as I turned around and walked back outside. The urge to plead with my Father in Heaven was overwhelming, if for no other reason than to help me start thinking clearly. I made it back to my car and opened the front door. I planted myself behind the wheel, shut the door again, closed my eyes, and bowed my head.

"Señor Hawkins?"

I screamed. I literally hit the ceiling with the top of my head. Someone was inside my car! The short Hispanic woman was crouched down in my back seat! She hadn't been there a moment ago when I dropped off my stuff. She'd climbed inside when I went back in the building!

"What are you doing in here?" I cried.

"Please," she began, her voice creaking. "I must speak with you. Your family is in great danger."

CHAPTER 4

When I demanded to know her name, she told me it was Anna. I did not learn her last name that day. I tried to get her to explain herself in the car. She refused. I couldn't get her to sit up straight. She insisted on crouching.

"We must go away from here," she insisted. "They watch me here. They always watch me. But I got away from them. I got away."

"Why have you been following me? How is my family in danger?"

"They want to hurt you. They want to hurt all that is precious to you."

"*Who* wants to hurt me?"

"I cannot tell you here. They watch me here. *¡Hay ojos en todas partes!*"

I was inches from throwing the woman out of my car. Her clothing was filthy and tattered. No doubt she had worn that same yellow dress for over a week. Her feet and legs were caked in street soot. The stench of body odor and tobacco made my eyes water.

At first I thought she was talking in riddles just to torment me. But as I looked down at her, crouching on the floor of my car, shaking like a leaf, her arms up over her head as if to protect herself from a falling sky, it occurred to me that the woman was mentally ill. I had no idea how severely. Her words were confused and paranoid. I wondered if she spoke these delusions to everyone she met. My first inclination was to drive her to the police station. They would know what to do with a person in this condition. Such an inconvenience on a day when my own nerves were frazzled!

Her next statement cemented my attention.

"They have Garth. They want to kill him. But they cannot kill him. That is why they are here. That is why they want to hurt *you*."

My heart starting racing. "Garth? Garth *Plimpton? Who* has Garth? Please tell me what you're talking about!"

"*No mas*. No more. They can hear me here. They can hear all things." She started making an awful sound in her throat, halfway between a moan and the beep of a red-alert beacon on *Star Trek*.

"Okay. All right." I started the engine. "Calm down. We'll go someplace else. A park. A restaurant. Are you hungry?"

"Oh, *si*. I am very hungry. And I need cigarettes."

She looked famished. Her eyes were sunk deep into their sockets. I wondered if she'd eaten in days.

A Denny's sat just a few blocks away. Once we were inside, once there was food in her stomach, I hoped she'd feel safe enough to talk.

When we arrived at the restaurant, the hostess looked at us with distaste, convinced that I had pulled a homeless vagrant off the street to feed her a meal. She was cordial, however, and asked if we wanted smoking or non-smoking. Anna looked at me pleadingly.

"Smoking," I answered. It was the first time I'd ever given such a reply. The word felt strange on my tongue.

Anna demanded a pack of cigarettes. Any brand. I made the purchase—another first. It felt degrading. But if it would settle her nerves enough to explain herself, I did not hesitate.

The hostess took us to a booth at the back, as far away from all the other customers as possible. I was equally happy with this arrangement—for the sake of privacy. As soon as we were seated, Anna ripped open the pack and balanced a shaky cigarette between her lips. She tore a match from a book she'd obtained at the cash register. It took her several attempts to ignite it. As smoke finally filled her lungs, her countenance relaxed. So sad, I thought, to grapple with an addiction to tobacco as well as mental illness. After her next puff, she grasped out at the air, as if trying to snatch a fly in mid-flight. But there was no fly. The imaginary insect seemed to disturb her a great deal.

Who *was* this woman? Where had she come from? Everything about her betrayed unspeakable horror and abuse. The terror I saw in those eyes was something I'd never witnessed in another human being.

I ordered her a hamburger and fries. She changed it to a New York-cut steak. So she wasn't so ill as to have forgotten the value of good food. As we placed our order, the waitress held her breath, wanting to inhale as little of the woman's stench as possible.

As soon as the waitress left, I started demanding answers.

"Anna, I need you to tell me now. Where is Garth Plimpton? Where is my sister, Jennifer? Who is trying to hurt my family?"

She stared at me blankly, blowing smoke in my face. I leaned away. I felt the urge to get up and leave. This whole affair was so bizarre. Every inch of my tolerance was strained.

She sat sullenly until I said, "I'll cancel the food, Anna. If you don't start explaining yourself, I'll get up right now and leave you alone in this restaurant."

I wouldn't have done it. But I thought the threat might loosen her tongue.

"I should not be here," she said finally. "They know I am here." Again she tried to snatch a fly out of the air.

I took her hand, hoping that human contact might calm her. "Anna, no one knows that you're here. I promise you. You're perfectly safe. I'll protect you. Now, who is 'they'?' What has frightened you so badly?"

She jerked her hand away. "Protect me? It is you who needs protecting."

It was all I could do to keep from leaning over the table and shaking her briskly. "From *who?*"

"My husband," she replied.

My eyebrows shot up. "Your *husband?* Who is your husband? Why does he want to hurt me?"

"Because he hates you. Because you hurt him."

"I hurt him? Who is he? When did I hurt him?"

"Long ago. Before Marcos was born."

"Is Marcos your son?"

"My only son." She began weeping and rocking back and forth, mumbling a prayer in Spanish. After a moment she added, "But now I have no son."

"Did he die?"

"No," she replied. "But it is the same. He is like his father now. They live, but their souls are dead. So is mine."

"Anna," I said, "let's go back to the beginning. What does Garth Plimpton have to do with all this?"

"They have him. He won't tell them anything. That's why they have to hurt you—so that he will tell them everything they want to know. But they don't need you for that. Only one of you. But not *you.* You, they want to destroy."

This wasn't making any sense. Someone I'd hurt a long time ago—this woman's husband—was seeking me out for vengeance. Somehow Garth Plimpton had become embroiled in all this. But Garth was in another land, another time.

"Why have you come to tell me these things?"

"To stop the dreams," she replied. "The terrible fiery dreams. See?" Her hand grasped out at the air again. "They keep coming. I can't stop them. Will you stop them for me?"

I couldn't figure out what she was talking about. Apparently she thought something was tormenting her—a fiery image that appeared and then disappeared as she snatched at it.

"Yes, Anna," I said. "We'll stop the dreams together. But you have to tell me everything. First tell me the name of your husband."

"He is not really my husband. There is no paper. But he took me with him."

"For heaven's sake, *what is his name*?!"

"Jacob Moon. But that is not his *first* name."

Could this get any more confusing? "What do you *mean* it's not his first name? Is Jacob his name or isn't it?"

"It's what he called himself later. Jacob is the name he bought from strangers. A man in an alley. I don't remember Jacob's other name, the first name. It was so long ago."

"Does your husband have any connection with an organization that calls itself the robbers of Gadianton?"

"Gadianton," she spoke dreamily, as if the name rang a distant bell, but not a close one. Not a recent one. "I once heard my husband use that word. He uses it no longer. He is Jacob of the Men of Jacob."

"Men of Jacob?"

"Yes. My husband is the hated one—Jacob of the Moon. The tribes all hate each other, but they will never hate each other as much as they hate Jacob." She buried her face in her hands. "He said he would kill me if I ever told."

This was nuts! There were too many players, too many groups. I pinched my eyes shut to keep it all straight. It was hopeless. Somewhere in this woman's crippled mind existed information that might be vital to my well-being—perhaps vital to the lives of everyone I loved. How could I possibly draw it out?

"Anna, tell me this. Tell me how I hurt your husband so long ago."

"You sent him to that place. That place where I met him."

"Where was this place?"

At that instant the waitress returned. But she did not have Anna's steak; instead, she delivered a message.

"Is your name Anna?" the waitress asked.

Panic swept across her features.

The waitress pointed. "There's a man at the cash register who wants to talk to you."

Anna started hyperventilating. She spun around to look at the cash register, brushing the ash from her cigarette on the waitress's pants.

"Hey, lady! Be careful!" The waitress slapped off the ash.

No one stood at the counter. I could vaguely see the exit door. It was closing slowly, as if someone had just gone through it. The waitress looked equally confused.

"Well, he was there just a second ago." She stepped toward the exit to see if she might spot the man. "Maybe he went to the rest room. I'm sure if the guy wants to talk to you so bad, he'll be back."

Those words struck Anna like a jolt of electricity. He would be back. Anna had no doubt that he *would be back.*

"I must go!" she cried.

I tried to stop her. "Wait! If you're afraid of this man, we should go to the police."

A gurgling scream leaped out of her throat. Her hands thrust out at me like claws, and one of her blackened fingernails drew blood on the right side of my forehead. She slipped past me and broke into a run in the middle of the restaurant. Upon reaching the door, she forced her way outside, looking wildly in all directions. When she saw no one, she took off across the street in a direction she guessed the man had *not* gone. Getting away from the restaurant was the only driving thought on her mind.

I'd pursued her toward the exit door, leaving my car keys on the table. She was still in my sights. I should have gone after her on foot, but I thought it would be easier to pick her up on the street and drive out of the area as swiftly as possible. I went back to the table to retrieve my keys.

But by the time I reached my car and pulled into the street to pick her up, I couldn't find her. I circled the block several times. She'd completely vanished. The short Hispanic woman with the fiery dreams had slipped out of my life as strangely and abruptly as she had slipped in. I never saw her again.

At least, not alive.

CHAPTER 5

I drove home in a daze, wondering which crisis should consume my mind the most—the fact that I had quit my job, or the words of this crazy woman. I decided my job paled in comparison to the danger Anna had portended.

Where had she come from, this tiny, frightened vessel? Why had she hesitated for over a week before delivering her warning? What had compelled her to warn me today? Why had she decided to warn me in the first place? As I understood it—and I fully realized that my interpretation could be wrong—a man from my past, a man who went by the alias of Jacob Moon, had it in his mind to destroy me and possibly my entire family. How had Anna put it? *They want to hurt you. They want to hurt all that is precious to you.* "They" indicated that my enemies were multiple.

It all had to have some connection with the Gadianton robbers. There was no other explanation. Who else would want to hurt me? Who else would carry a vendetta? Eighteen years. Who would have thought that after eighteen years, Gadiantons could drop back into my life?

And yet Anna had not called them Gadiantons. She had called them Men of Jacob. Who was this Jacob Moon—this man from my past whom I had supposedly injured? Was he the leader of a band of Gadiantons? Anna had inferred that the name Jacob was some kind of alias—a name he bought from a stranger in an alley. I had heard of such things. There were people who manipulated computer records to provide a new name and identity for a criminal on the run, sometimes even adopting the social security number of a child who'd died in infancy. Was this what Anna had meant?

She had also mentioned a son named Marcos. No doubt my list of enemies did not end there. Gadiantons were not loners. Like wolves, they hunted in packs.

My first concern was the safety of my family. But how could I protect them? Could I hire bodyguards? Could I place them in hiding? Sequester them like Mafia witnesses? I had to do something. But how would I explain it to my children?—"Kids, we're going to have to pull you out of school for a few weeks, possibly for a few years. Then we'll have to pack up the car and drive around the country, never staying anywhere for more than a few days at a time." Harrison would no doubt be thrilled by such a plan. Melody would have to be dragged to the car kicking and screaming. How would we know when it was safe to come home?

And what about the other shocking information Anna had revealed? She'd hinted that Garth Plimpton was in some sort of danger. What about my sister? Where was Jenny? "They have him," Anna had said. What did that mean? Was Garth being held against his will? If so, where? Here? Or in the past? She had said that Garth "wouldn't tell them anything." This was the reason they had to hurt me. What kind of secret might they be trying to wring from Garth? Did they want to learn where I lived so they could vent their revenge? No. That wasn't it. Anna had found my address easily enough. *What could it be?*

I agonized all the way home. Anna had not provided me with enough information to take any definitive action whatsoever. If I had known whether Garth was still in the past, I might have mounted an expedition immediately. I seriously considered that option anyway. Perhaps in the past I could learn what I had to know. But who would I ask? Where would I go? The world was just as wide in 50 B.C. as it was today—even more so without modern transportation. I had to think.

In spite of it all, I continued to be nagged by the notion that Anna was a textbook paranoid schizophrenic. I might be overreacting to everything she had said. If she hadn't mentioned Garth's name, I'd have already delivered her into the safe custody of the Salt Lake Police.

Could she have pulled the name out of the air by coincidence? It didn't seem likely.

As I pulled into the driveway of my West Valley home, indecision continued to torment me. Before getting out of the car, I glanced in the rearview mirror to see how badly Anna had clawed my face. The scratch was high on the right side of my forehead. Repositioning my hair with a comb, I covered the wound as best I could.

Before I reached the front door, I was accosted by my younger daughter, Steffanie.

"Dad, Harry popped my basketball. He did it deliberately."

Harry was right behind her. "I didn't, Dad. It was an accident. There was a board with nails in the gutter."

"You *threw* it on that board!" Steffanie accused.

"I did not!"

"You *did!* You stood right over it and—!"

"Please! Not now! Not now!" I shut my eyes and passed between them, aiming for the house. They followed me.

Inside, Steffanie continued to whine. "That's just great! Harry gets to do anything he wants. He gets away with murder, as usual!" She stormed up the stairs.

Melody met me in the kitchen entranceway. She was the only one who perceived my distress.

"Dad, what's the matter?" she asked.

Harrison was still behind me. "It wasn't her *good* basketball," he said. "It was the old one."

I wheeled around and faced my son. "You'll buy her a brand new one, Harry. I can just imagine how much of an accident it was. I know you. You wanted to see what would happen if you dropped it on a nail, didn't you?"

"Well . . . I didn't think it would pop."

"No, of course not! Why would it pop? It's just a nail! It's just a basketball! What kind of a stupid thing is that? Are you that much of an idiot? Why can't you get along with your sisters? Why can't we all just get along? Why do I have to come home every night to find everyone at each other's throats?"

Harry's eyes were wide. My tirade had coaxed Steffanie back to the top of the stairs. She did not wear the satisfied smirk I might have expected for coming down hard on her brother. Instead, she looked stunned. Dad had blown a circuit.

Everyone remained still and silent. I studied the surprise and concern on Harry's face. It suddenly struck me how shattered my life would be if that face—if the faces of *any* of my children—were not there to stare up at me. It would be the final blow.

I embraced my son and swept his hair with my hand. "I'm sorry," I said limply. I withdrew from him and shuffled into the kitchen.

Melody persisted. "Is there something wrong, Dad?"

I considered my reply for a moment. "Yes," I decided to confess. But it was only half a confession. "My job . . . I quit today."

Steffanie came down the stairs. All of the children gathered around. "Why?" they asked. "What happened? What are you going to do?"

I shook my head. I wasn't in the mood to explain it all. Especially when there was another matter weighing much more heavily on my mind.

"What would you kids think about spending a few days with your Aunt and Uncle Fenimore in Provo?"

"Provo?" came the objections. "What about school?" "What about practice?"

"It would just be for a few days."

"But, Dad," said Melody. "The Fenimores are in Arizona."

She was right. I remembered. Their son was getting married in the Mesa Temple. Our next nearest relative—my Uncle Spencer—lived in Burlington, Wyoming. I had to think of someplace to send them, preferably someplace close. But I felt strongly that I, at least, should remain in Salt Lake. "I'll think of someplace," I said.

The children's sympathy for me started to thin. "Why do we have to go *any* place?" demanded Melody.

"Yeah," said Steff. "What difference does it make toward your job?"

"Are we planning on moving?" Harry wondered.

"No, I—I'm just concerned about what might happen."

"What could happen?" asked Harry.

I shrugged. I had no explanation.

Melody had baked a tuna casserole. The kids bombarded me with questions throughout dinner. Why had I quit my job? Could I get it back? Did we have enough money for Harrison's scout trip to Lake Powell? Would we have to go on Church welfare like the Blanchards down the block?

"Don't worry," I told them. "Everything will be fine."

"My report is due in history tomorrow," said Steffanie. "Remember? You promised to help me."

"What?" I said absently.

"My report on Quetzalcoatl. You promised to help me write it."

Typical teenager. The world could be ending and they'd still be fixated on trivial things, like whose turn it was to do the dishes.

"Okay," I said. "But not tonight."

"Dad, you're not *listening*. I said it's due *tomorrow.*"

"All right. Relax. I'll help you with it tonight."

Steff looked relieved. "Good. Because I never would have picked this subject if you hadn't suggested it."

"I said I'll help you," I reiterated.

"What's Quetzalcoatl?" asked Harrison.

"Not what. *Who,*" said Steffanie. "He's the ancient god of the Aztecs. Dad says Quetzalcoatl was the name given to Jesus Christ many years after he visited the Americas. But the Britannica doesn't say anything about that. It says Quetzalcoatl means 'Feathered Serpent.' What does a snake with feathers have to do with Jesus Christ?"

"It's symbolic," I said. I shifted in my seat. I doubted if I could concentrate on this right now. Any other evening it might have made for enlightening conversation, but not tonight. Then again, focusing on something else might clear my head. I'd give it a try. "They use the symbol of a snake because of Christ's great condescension to 'crawl' among men. Feathers because of his capacity to soar among the clouds. The original legend is of a white, bearded god who descended out of heaven to teach principles of goodness and truth. He told them he'd return one day. That's why the Indians thought the first Europeans, like Cortez and Pizarro, were gods."

"The encyclopedia doesn't talk about any of that stuff," Steffanie protested. "I wish I could have done my report on the Vikings or Columbus, like everybody else."

A migraine pounded in my skull. "I have other books we can look at after dinner."

It occurred to me to check the answering machine. Sometimes the kids would wait to see whose voice came on the machine before answering it. If it was for me, they often ignored it. The red light wasn't blinking. Apparently, Richard Elms hadn't received my message yet. Either that, or as I feared, he'd called Doug Bowman before calling me. I couldn't help wondering if affairs at work had anything to do with the re-emergence of Gadianton robbers in my life. No, I decided. Doug's soul may have been corrupt, but I doubted that he'd sold it to the devil.

Steffanie dragged me into the study to look at what little progress she'd made on her report. About the time I started to read it, the phone finally rang. I snatched up the receiver. It was Richard.

"Jim? How are you?" His voice sounded tired. Richard always sounded tired when he wanted to make a conversation as short as possible.

I tried to come across very businesslike. I did not want to rant and rave. I hoped I could present this situation with the same detached reserve that I would demonstrate if defending a fellow employee. Normal pleasantries were important. "I'm fine, Richard. And how are you?"

"Fine. Just fine. So what's this urgent company matter? Can't Doug handle it?"

"Unfortunately, Richard, the matter involves Doug directly. All of this is quite delicate. I can assure you, I would not have gone over Doug's head like this if I felt there were any other options."

"Go on," he instructed.

I told him of my demotion to the sales floor. He was surprised; Doug hadn't mentioned it. I told Richard everything. He remained silent until I was finished with my side of the story. This surprised me. Any instant I expected him to interrupt and say, "Doug runs the company, Jim. I turned things over to Doug so I wouldn't have to get phone calls like this!" When I'd concluded, there was a long pause. Finally, Richard spoke.

"Maybe I've been on vacation too long, Jim. Let me see what I can do."

And that was it. The conversation was over. He hung up the phone. I felt conspicuous and embarrassed. I'd never known Richard to be a man of so few words; my call must have irritated him tremendously. A cloud of gloom loomed overhead as I returned to sit next to my daughter on the couch. Somehow I doubted that I would ever hear from Richard again.

To my amazement, less than five minutes passed before the phone rang once more. The voice on the other end was Doug Bowman. He sounded nervous.

"Jim," he began. "I made a mistake this afternoon. I'd like to make things right with you. Could you come out to my house? I'd like to discuss it with you in person. Do you have a pen to take down my address?"

Wow! Richard must have just given him the worst five-minute tongue-lashing of his life, ripping him up one side and down the other. Could it be that my prayers had been answered? Could it be just that simple? In my experience, things only happened this way in dreams and situation comedies.

I scrambled around for a pen. "Go ahead," I replied.

He gave me an address in the avenues east of the State Capitol building. I remembered the house vaguely from a company barbecue held there when Doug was first hired.

"It'll take me about half an hour. Is that all right?"

"Yes, that's fine."

The phone clicked. Strange. My bosses were certainly brief tonight. I told the children I'd be gone for about an hour and a half, and I hinted to them that I might get my job back. Harry cheered and the dreary mood lifted, except for a flash of disappointment in Steffanie's eyes.

"Get as far along in the report as you can," I told her. "When I get home, we'll finish it together—no matter how late we have to go at it." This comforted her a little.

I grabbed a sweater out of the closet. The sun was going down and the April night had taken on a chill. As I slipped the sweater over my head, a chill settled over me as well.

Something didn't feel right about all this. But what could be wrong? Richard had called Doug. Doug had become penitent. I recalled my earlier thought that Doug was a Gadianton robber. Was he trying to lure me into a trap? Lure me away from my family? I shuddered.

I couldn't live like this! I was going to drive myself crazy! Soon I'd become as paranoid and schizophrenic as Anna. Nevertheless, precautions were in order.

"Melody," I said. "I want you to stay home tonight."

"But I was going to meet Quinn—"

"No," I said. "Not tonight. Please."

Rarely did I say please when I made such requests. Melody sensed the gravity in my voice.

"All right," she said. "But can Quinn come over here?"

"Not until I get back. It'll only be ninety minutes, two hours at the most. Can you do this for me?"

"Why?"

I gritted my teeth. Just once I wished a kid could do something for no other reason than because I asked them.

"Melody," I said sternly, "when I leave, I want you to lock every door. If anything unusual happens, I want you to call 911 without hesitation. If I come back and find you gone, or if I find someone else in this house, I'll ground you the entire summer. Don't test me on this. I promise you that I'll do it."

Dad had never talked like this before. The whole evening he'd been acting weird. I knew it was more than just his job. For the first time in my life, I sensed that my father was genuinely frightened. Dad wouldn't tell us anything. I agreed to stay home, and I agreed to not to invite Quinn over to the house. Before Dad got back, I expected to chew my nails to the bone.

* * *

Driving away from the house, I started to relax a little. The neighborhood looked as peaceful as ever. Several neighbors were out primping their yards for the coming season. Brother Petroff, the ward clerk, was playing Frisbee with his son. Life was normal. I breathed deeply and made my way into the city.

I wondered what Doug might say. The only reason I could imagine why he would invite me out to his house was to strike some kind of deal where I'd get what I wanted, but in return, keep my mouth shut.

The details obviously needed to be rehearsed in private. At this point, I really didn't care about arrangements or deals. I'd have been happy enough to get my old job back as Executive of New Accounts and move my stuff upstairs. If this was Doug's intention, I sensed that he wanted to make sure he came out smelling like a rose. Doug didn't want rumors to surface that he had been slammed into his place by Richard Elms. Such news might prompt other employees to circumvent Doug and bring matters directly to Richard's attention.

I exited the interstate at 600 South and turned north on 700 East. It was already dark as I turned onto Doug Bowman's street. I drove along the row of immaculate old houses until I found the right address. Doug lived in a gray two-story manor which had undergone extensive restoration. I remembered hearing him say once that his wife had a thing for old houses. That was just before he and his wife had divorced. She and their two teenage sons moved back to the Big Apple. I was surprised that he hadn't sold the place; it was awfully spacious for a bachelor.

Suddenly I felt sorry for Doug. I'd never thought much about his personal life. It's easy to believe a guy with money is never lonely. Maybe personal pressures had clouded his judgment when he tried to cheat me out of credit for the Del Greco program. Might as well give him the benefit of the doubt. I decided it wouldn't be too hard to forgive him—that is, as long as everything was set straight.

I parked my car in the street and switched off the headlights. Even before I emerged from the car, I could see Doug's front door sitting wide open. The porch light was off, but an inner light illuminated the walkway. As I crossed the yard, I half expected Doug to pop into the doorway and greet me. He did not appear. I reached around and clanked the door knocker several times.

"Hello?" I called out. "Doug?"

There was no reply.

Doug's BMW sat silently in the driveway. Maybe he was in a room upstairs and couldn't hear me. I entered the house just far enough that my voice would carry.

"Doug? It's me! Jim Hawkins!"

The house remained eerily quiet. Somewhere a faucet dripped. Off to my right I noticed the main living room. I imagined that his wife had once furnished it with antiques. Now it was adorned with modern decor, leather couches and chairs. The largest couch had been placed in the center of the room, sandwiched between two ebony lamp stands; before it loomed a big-screen TV. This furniture was sadly out of character with the house's nineteenth-century architecture and trappings. My late wife, Renae, would have shuddered.

The TV was on, but the sound was almost inaudible. The Utah Jazz were playing the Phoenix Suns. A single lamp burned in the corner of the room. This lamp, the television, and the light over my head were the only sources of illumination.

I sighed and glanced at my watch. 8:47. Apparently Doug had stepped out somewhere, maybe next door or down the block to the Circle K. The nerve of the guy to leave, knowing I was on my way. I supposed I could wait in my car for ten or fifteen minutes. I spotted a phone on one of the ebony lampstands. An urge came over me to call home and make sure my family was all right.

And then I saw the shoe.

A beige loafer poked out from behind the leather couch. It was magnified by the crystalline base of the ebony lamp stand. The shoe was attached to a foot.

I strode around the couch. Doug Bowman lay face down on the carpet. At first I thought he'd suffered some kind of seizure. Had Richard's tongue-lashing given the poor man a heart attack? I reached down with both hands to turn him over. The body was heavy and limp. As it rolled, Doug's flaccid arm slapped my leg. His mouth gaped; his eyes were egg wide and frozen. I put my ear to Doug's chest. No heartbeat. When I pulled away, I noticed the redness on my hands. The navy blue carpet was soaked in blood.

Then I saw the two holes in Doug's maroon-colored shirt. The holes looked almost insignificant. They might have been inflicted by a thorn bush in the garden, except that they were seeping. Doug had been shot! Blood glistened on my hands, my shoes, and probably my right cheek where I'd leaned down to listen for a heartbeat. A sickening knot coiled inside me.

Doug's phone on the ebony nightstand started ringing. The noise went through me like a fire alarm. My body remained rigid for several seconds, the air pumping in and out of my lungs. On the third ring, I finally answered it. I did not speak into the receiver. My tongue was still frozen with shock.

"Hello, Doug?" called out the voice on the other end. "Is anyone there?"

It was the voice of Richard Elms.

I recovered enough to reply. "Yes. I—I'm here."

"Jim? Is that you, Jim? What are *you* doing there?"

"Richard, I . . . I—"

"Where's Doug? Do you still need me to speak with him? Or have you worked things out on your own?"

His words didn't make any sense. "Didn't you speak with him earlier? Didn't you call him right after . . . ?"

"I haven't had a chance yet. What's the matter with you, Jim? You don't sound well."

"Richard . . . Doug is dead."

"What?"

A siren moaned in the distance.

I tasted vomit. This did not look good at all. I'd seen too many movies, read too many books. I slammed down the phone. I felt like a cornered animal. Raising up, I considered all the possible escape routes. The front door was closest. I charged through the house, leaped out the doorway, and bounded across the front lawn. As I yanked opened my car door, I hesitated. What was I doing? Why was I running? I was innocent! Running made it look as if I'd done something terribly wrong.

Still, I thought it might be best if I watched from a distance. As I leaned back behind the wheel, something caught my eye. An object lay in the crook of my seat. Black. Curved. It caught a gleam from the moon. I reached down, and my fingers sensed the cold sting of metal. A gun! But how did it get there? In my earlier haste to reach Doug's open doorway, I'd left my window rolled down. Someone must have planted it there as easily as delivering a newspaper. The gun had to be moved. Disposed of. Given to the police. The options swirled like hornets. I lifted the pistol. Was it loaded? Had it been fired? Had this been the instrument of murder?

The air snagged in my throat. I had touched it! I had—!

"Drop the weapon!" a voice commanded. "Don't make a move!"

The police! They had materialized out of nowhere. But how? The siren still pulsed in the distance. I hadn't noticed their vehicles rolling toward me, headlights extinguished. A shock wave rippled through my body. Natural reflexes caused me to drop the weapon as if it were a snake. I turned toward the voice that had shouted. Bright lights stabbed my eyes.

"Get your hands where I can see them! Turn around and face the car!"

Within seconds, multiple fingers were groping through my clothing; handcuffs were pinching my wrists.

"This is a mistake!" I muttered. "I—I just got here. I'm innocent!"

"Innocent of what?" asked the officer whose face I hadn't yet seen. He called to another policeman, "Check the house!"

The officers barked more questions in my ears. I answered them all. Don't ask me what the questions were. Or how I answered. As to what happened over the next several minutes, I don't remember much at all.

In my mind, the universe had exploded.

CHAPTER 6

I sat alone in the back of a patrol car, my only companion the squawk of the police radio. I was shaking like a jackhammer, partly because of the night chill, but only a small part. Half a dozen police had arrived on the scene and were scouring every inch of the property, surrounding it with a line of yellow tape.

The distant siren I'd heard belonged to an ambulance. Its arrival alerted the entire neighborhood. People watched through their curtains or from the top steps of their porches. Most of them kept a safe distance. A pair of boys crept up to my window. They wore the same expressions I saw on children visiting the monkey house at the Hogle Zoo, screwing up their mouths and eyes to try and get the animals to react. An officer shooed them off.

They left me alone there, handcuffs gnawing into my wrists. My perceptions had cleared a little, and I wanted the officer with the notepad to come back. I didn't think my story had been very convincing the first time I told it. Any instant I expected someone to approach the car, open the door, shuffle their feet, and limp out an apology: *"Very sorry, Mr. Hawkins. I'm afraid we've made a terrible mistake. You're free to go home."* This didn't happen. For nearly thirty minutes—the longest half hour of my life—no one approached the patrol car at all.

Finally, the officer who had locked me in cuffs climbed behind the wheel and turned the ignition. By now, of course, I'd seen his face. It was round and puffy—the perpetual teenager. Not at all the hard, chiseled features I'd come to expect from a thousand television shows.

His name tag read "Officer T. L. Huffaker."

As we pulled into the street, he called back to me, "How about those Jazz? Two and 0 now against the Suns. Think they'll make it to the finals this year?"

"I don't know," I replied indifferently. My life was crumbling all around me, and this man wanted to talk basketball.

We drove to the station on 2nd South and 3rd East. To my further dismay, television crews were poised for our arrival. There were trucks from Channel 5, 2, 4 and 13. Cameras and lights assaulted our faces as Huffaker pulled me from the car. I half expected reporters to shout out, "Why did you do it, Mr. Hawkins?" "Wouldn't your boss give you a raise?" "Do you have anything you'd like to say to our viewers before they throw away the key?" But the crews seemed content with the solemn footage of me being escorted into the building in handcuffs. Tomorrow, everyone would know—my children, my bishop, my co-workers—everyone within broadcast range of Salt Lake City, five hundred miles in all directions.

An elevator took us to the sixth-floor—Homicide Division. Two plainclothes detectives were waiting for us. I'd seen one of them at the crime scene—late forties, tall, bushy mustache, a nose that had been broken in several places. The other was a woman, about my age, long blonde hair streaked with gray. Pretty, except that her job and several packs of cigarettes a day appeared to have coarsened her features.

"I'm Detective Riley," said the woman. She made her voice mild and feminine. I might have been deceived into thinking this was her normal tone if she hadn't gruffed at Officer Huffaker.

"Get those cuffs off him!"

Huffaker acted as if he'd been awaiting this command all along. It was a game. Riley wanted me to perceive her as my advocate, my ally. I didn't care. My eyes flashed gratitude. I needed an ally—*any* ally—so badly.

"I'm Detective Walpole," said the tall man politely. "Why don't you step in here?" He directed me into a small gray room. Inside were three chairs, a table in the corner. His hand indicated the chair farthest to the left. "Have a seat. Can we get you anything? Cup of coffee? Cigarettes?"

"No," I replied. "I . . . I don't smoke or drink coffee."

Walpole smiled and grunted. I read his thoughts: *He won't smoke or drink coffee, but he'll kill a man, no problem.*

"Can I use a phone?" I pleaded. "I need to call my kids."

"How old are they?"

"Sixteen, fourteen, and ten. "

"Is the oldest at home?"

"Yes. Please. I have to call them."

Walpole didn't look very sympathetic. "I'll see what I can do." He closed the door. The lock was turned.

I sat in silence and massaged my swollen wrists. I knew now that the cavalry was not coming. I'd been arrested for first-degree murder. They thought I'd shot and killed Doug Bowman. And why not? I'd been apprehended with a pistol in my hands. I could still see bloodstains on my palms. *Oh God,* I thought. *Please, Father, help me!*

I collapsed to my knees and began to pray. The far right wall consisted of a pegboard sheet. I thought they could probably see me praying; most likely there was a camera behind one of those little holes. I didn't care. And I knew my Father in Heaven didn't care.

A setup. This whole thing had been a frame-job. The killer had planned it flawlessly; indeed, he had *wanted* me to be found at the murder scene. He'd undoubtedly called the police himself as soon as I arrived. But how could I get anyone to believe me? Blood on my hands. On my cheek. My fingerprints on the gun. I couldn't have appeared more guilty if I had planned it. But I could explain everything! Surely someone would listen to reason. There must be other evidence—evidence in my favor. How long would it take them to find it?

My children! What would happen to my children?

My prayer to God consisted of disjointed ramblings. Pleas for help, for strength. I couldn't concentrate. I was still on my knees when the doorway opened.

"Am I interrupting?" asked Detective Riley. Again her voice crooned compassion. I wasn't fooled. This woman ate nails for breakfast.

"No," I said, and sat back in the chair.

Walpole was right behind her. The first thing they did was apply a special kind of tape to specific points of skin on both of my hands.

"What's this for?" I asked.

"Gunpowder traces," said Walpole. "If you fired the gun, we'll know it."

Riley watched me to see how I would respond to this. Would I wince with guilt? Actually, it gave me my first inkling of hope. This might be the first evidence in my favor. Then I had a disturbing thought.

"What if I just *handled* the gun?" I asked them. "Would it still leave traces?"

Walpole turned up his eyes and studied me thoughtfully. "Sometimes," he confirmed.

My heart sank back into the abyss.

Riley started reciting my Miranda rights. She paused after each phrase to ask if I understood.

"Yes, yes," I said impatiently.

"Then do you want a lawyer present?" asked Riley.

"I don't need one. I'm innocent. I have to call my children. They could be in danger."

"Danger from who?" asked Walpole.

"From the *real* killers! Don't you understand? I've been framed!"

Riley edged in closer and put her hand on my wrist. "Calm down, Jim. Why don't you tell us again what happened?"

I studied her face. The voice was sonorous, but the eyes were cold. These people had already decided I was guilty. They weren't going to believe me no matter what I said.

They kept me in that room for two and a half hours. They made me tell my side of the story backwards, forwards, and sideways. All I could think about was my kids. By now they had to be going nuts. The detectives tried to trip me up. They said that Richard Elms had called them from California. He had confirmed my motives for killing Doug Bowman. To the detectives, the profile was all too familiar: disgruntled employee knocks off dishonest boss. In his conversation with the police, Richard also confirmed that I was terribly shook up when I had answered Doug's phone.

"Why *wouldn't* I be shook up?" I blustered. "I'd just discovered my boss's dead body!"

"C'mon, Jim," said Riley. "We have witnesses who saw you enter the house just before gunshots rang out."

"That's a lie."

More than once, the detectives stretched the truth about evidence against me. It would make their jobs so much easier if they could just squeeze a quick confession out of me. But I stood firm on every detail.

Then they revealed the clincher. Walpole eased into it by asking me about the scratch on my forehead.

I felt the fresh scab. "That's from this afternoon. A woman in a restaurant. It has nothing to do with any of this."

"A woman in a restaurant?" Riley said skeptically.

Walpole leaned forward. "I think you should know something, Jim. There were strands of hair in the victim's palm. I won't lie to you; I won't tell you we have a positive ID on those strands yet. That'll take our lab several weeks. But the hair is yours, isn't it, Jim? You wanna explain to us how your hair ended up clutched in the victim's fist if he was dead when you arrived on the scene?"

I shook my head in disbelief. "That's impossible. The hair isn't mine."

At that point, Riley's facade of feminine charm collapsed. "Oh, come on! How long do you expect us to buy this garbage? You did it, Jim! You drove out to your boss's house. You hid the gun under your sweater. There was a struggle. He grabbed your hair, scratched your forehead. And you plugged him twice in the chest. Isn't that how it happened? No more games, Hawkins! Tell us the truth!"

I wasn't listening to her tirade. My eyes stared off into space. "The brush," I mumbled.

"What was that?" asked Riley.

I closed my eyes, trying to piece it together. "A week and a half ago, a burglar broke into my home. He stole . . . a hair brush."

"What does that have to do with anything?"

"Isn't it obvious?" I said. "The hair was *planted* on Doug Bowman."

Riley dropped her pen in frustration. Walpole shook his head and suspired.

"Did you report this burglary?" asked Riley.

"No," I said. "I didn't think—"

"You didn't *think?*" Riley huffed. "Well, at least that's consistent with the rest of your behavior tonight."

I leaned over, my elbows on my knees, and put my head between my hands in despair.

"I gotta tell ya, Jim," said Walpole, "your story has more holes than a spaghetti strainer."

"But it's the truth!" I cried. "I swear . . . it's . . . someone's gotta . . . I swear . . . "

"We'll give you a night to think it over," said Riley. "In the morning, we'll just have to hope your memory improves significantly."

* * *

By midnight, my sister and brother had gone to bed. Steffanie slept on the couch, still thinking Dad might arrive home any minute to help her finish her report.

I waited by the phone, pacing the study, chewing what was left of my fingernails. Where could Dad be? Why hadn't he called? He'd never done anything like this before. I knew something had to be terribly wrong.

Quinn called me three different times to see if I was willing to meet him like we'd planned. He didn't understand why I couldn't leave the house. Steff and Harry were old enough to take care of themselves. He said he had something he wanted to talk to me about. It was important, but we couldn't talk over the phone. I told him I couldn't go anywhere until I heard from Dad.

The last time Quinn called was about 11:55. He told me he was coming over. I said it wasn't a good idea. I told him my dad had said to keep the doors locked and not to open them for anyone.

"I'm coming over anyway," he said.

"Quinn," I said sharply, "my dad threatened to ground me the whole summer. He was serious."

"That's ridiculous," said Quinn. "He'd probably just ground you for a weekend."

"Oh, so it's okay if I get grounded for a weekend? That's so sweet of you, Quinn."

"That's not what I mean," he said. "I just . . . I just wanna see you. I have to talk to you. I care about you, Melody. And I miss you."

"I miss you, too. But if my father ever found out . . ."

"I'm on my way," he insisted. "I'll park a couple blocks away. If he pulls up, I'll slip out the back and he'll never know the difference. Whatever you do, wait for me there."

"No, Quinn, I—"

He hung up the phone.

Great, *I thought. I'd never get away with this. Even if Quinn eluded my father, he'd never elude my big-mouthed brother and sister. Maybe it could work. I'd let him in the back and we'd sit in the kitchen. I felt so frightened. Dad couldn't get mad at me for wanting someone to hold my hand through this, could he? Right now Quinn was the best friend I had. Dad had told us he'd only be gone an hour and a half. It had been almost four hours.*

Two minutes after midnight, the phone rang again.

"Melody?" It was Dad!

I was so relieved I nearly broke into tears. "Dad! Where are you? What's happened?"

He sounded as relieved to hear my voice as I was to hear his. "It's complicated, princess."

Dad hadn't called me "princess" since I was thirteen years old, when Boots, my cat, got hit by a car. "What's wrong?" I demanded.

"I've been arrested, honey. Don't worry. Everything will be all right. I'm at the Salt Lake County Jail. It's all a big mistake. A horrible mistake."

It was as if someone had drenched me with ice water. My body went rigid. I tried anticipate my father's next words. He would say, "Just kidding." Please Dad, I thought. Do like you always do and say, "Just kidding."

"Melody, I don't have time to explain everything right now. You have to listen to me very carefully. Where are Harry and Steff?"

"Asleep," I said.

"Wake them. You have to leave the house. Get out of the house right now. I have reason to believe you're all in danger. Please don't ask me to explain. I'll explain it all later. Just do as I ask."

"Wh-where should we go?"

"Anywhere! *Just get out of there. Don't bother packing anything."*

"But you know the alternator just went out on my car."

"You don't need a car. Just find someplace a few blocks away. Someone in the ward. Do you understand what you have to do?"

"Yes."

"Tomorrow morning, I want you to call and tell me where you are."

"What's the number?"

"Uh, it's . . . it's in the blue pages of the phone book—Salt Lake County Jail. By tomorrow, I'll have decided what to do. Until then, don't tell a soul where you're staying. Don't go to school. Don't go anywhere. That goes for all of you."

"Okay," I said. "I'll do it."

"I love you, Melody. Tell your brother and sister I love them, too."

His voice cracked. Tears trickled down my face.

"Okay," I replied.

I hung up the phone. My hands were trembling; I made a tight fist to steady them. It didn't work.

I shook Steffanie and threw the light on in Harry's room. "Get dressed! Dad's been arrested. We have to get out of the house. NOW!"

My brother and sister did as directed, asking a thousand questions. I had no answers for them. I was just following Dad's orders. We walked swiftly to the home of Sabrina Sorenson. She was startled to see us at first, gathered on her doorstep like a litter of orphans. But she and her daughter, Meagan, let us in with open arms. When I finally told everyone what had happened, Sabrina stayed awake with us most of the night, offering whatever support and comfort she could provide.

It was morning before I remembered that Quinn had been on his way over to our house.

* * *

Sterile filth. If such a thing is possible, it sufficiently describes the interior of the Salt Lake County Jail. Ancient grime lay unchiseled in every crack of the tile floor. The dust of lost civilizations caked every air vent. And yet the cinder block walls had been freshly painted in two shades of blue. The place was just clean enough to pass inspection. After all, who would see it? I guess they assumed most of the people escorted through those steel doors were of the same substance as the grime in the cracks.

The booking process took several hours. I was frisked, mug shot, and fingerprinted. They stripped me and took my bloodstained clothes into evidence. I asked them if I could keep my temple garments; they refused without a sideways glance. I was given a pair of antiseptic blue overalls, a comb, a bar of soap, a toothbrush, bedding, and my own plastic drinking cup.

During the remainder of the booking procedure, I spent most of the time seated in a compact waiting area. A television glowed overhead, the volume low. On either side sat several other "catches of the day,"' all looking as if this process were as normal to them as shaving or taking a shower. Not that any of them appeared to have done either for several days. I didn't ask anyone else why they'd been arrested. They glanced at me often. Apparently I didn't look like a member of the club. They knew instinctively that I'd been nailed for something big.

It was during this time, as my paperwork was processed, that I finally got a chance to call home. One of the guards overheard as I ordered my kids to get out of the house. He shook his head and moved on, grinning.

The people who worked here were a cynical breed. I watched them bring in a woman, her face streaked with mascara from crying. I could only imagine what she'd done. Her life looked every bit as shattered as mine. As the arresting officer removed her cuffs, he joked with the booking officer about some new city policy on physical fitness. The plight of the woman was inconsequential.

As I waited, I rolled the image of the stolen hairbrush over and over in my mind. I did not doubt that the police lab would confirm that the hair clutched in Doug's fist was mine. I could explain the blood on my hands, the gun with my fingerprints—I could explain the whole incident with enough conviction to create reasonable doubt in the mind of any jury. But the hair in Doug's fist! That detail might seal my fate. To the detectives, it was more than enough evidence to charge me with murder. For me, it was the final proof that Anna's warning had not been an exaggeration. Somewhere in the world lurked men determined to destroy me. When I faced off with the burglar that night in my house, a plan to frame me had been well under way.

I knew my children were also in danger. If what Anna said was true, my enemies would not rest until they had destroyed everything I cared about. While incarcerated in this dismal place, I was helpless to do anything about it. And they knew it.

But major pieces to the puzzle were still missing for me. If their sole purpose had been my destruction, they might have launched this charade years ago. There had to be another reason why all of this was happening now. That reason involved Garth Plimpton. I shook my head in frustration. If only I'd had more time with Anna!

I wondered if I should hire an attorney. Things were way out of hand, and I wasn't sure I could handle it alone. But wouldn't I look more guilty if I hired a lawyer? My brother in Virginia was a lawyer—not a criminal lawyer, just patents and copyrights. But he might have advice. I'd try to call him tomorrow.

The jailer collected me from the booking area around 2:00 a.m. "Got your room all ready for you," he smirked.

More doors echoed behind me. The spirit of gloom hovered like molasses. I peered into the darkened chambers of the various holding areas where prisoners slept and coughed. The jailer took me to a cell block with three other high-profile felons. One of them roused; I recognized him from the evening news. His crimes were unspeakable. The kind where it would have been better if he'd been drowned with a millstone.

"How do you do?" he said with a greasy smile. I ignored him and stepped into my individual cell. The jailer told me that at 6:00 a.m. my door would slide open, allowing all four of the inmates access to a narrow enclosed area the length of all four cells. I could then mingle with my cellmates up close and personal. I swallowed. Again I tasted bile.

My door echoed shut and I surveyed my accommodations. A toilet and sink, encrusted in lime. A cot with an emaciated mattress. The reek of urine had been ineffectually buried by disinfectants.

Again I knelt to pray, this time dropping to the cement slowly and ponderously. Here in the dank recesses of this judicial tomb, I felt indescribably lonely. Did the Holy Ghost know about this place? As I began to pray, I could only bring to mind the question that Joseph Smith had uttered while languishing in the Liberty Jail.

O God, where art thou? And where is the pavilion that covereth thy hiding place?

CHAPTER 7

"Melody!" cried Quinn. "What happened last night? Where did you go?"

"I'm sorry," I said. "My dad told us to get out of the house."

"Where are you calling me from?"

"I . . . I can't tell you that."

"Why?"

"My father said not to tell anyone. Did you . . . hear what happened?"

"I saw it on the news this morning. I couldn't believe it. I still can't believe it."

"He's innocent, Quinn. I know *he's innocent."*

"Are you certain about that, Melody?"

"Of course I'm certain!" I gruffed. "My father isn't capable of such a thing!"

"Sometimes people are capable of things no one can imagine."

I couldn't believe what I was hearing. "How can you talk like that? Are you against us?"

"No, I'm not against you. I just need to see you, then you'll understand."

I exploded. "I understand everything! It's you who's got it all screwed up! If you knew my father at all, you'd realize this whole thing is ridiculous! You'll see! When this is all straightened out, you'll see!"

"I'm sorry, Melody. Forget I said anything. It was stupid of me."

Quinn continued muttering apologies. I sank down on Sabrina's couch, cradling the phone in my arms while I fought back more tears. My sister Steffanie had vomited in the toilet after she saw my father on the news. Harry had sat in the corner without speaking for almost an hour. As Quinn begged my forgiveness, I could feel my own defenses breaking down. What if Quinn was right? How well did I know my own father? I felt despicable even speculating. I was so confused! Was Dad capable of such a thing? I didn't know! I didn't know!

"I need to see you," Quinn repeated.

"Yes," I agreed.

"Tonight."

"No," I said. "I'm losing it, Quinn. I'm really losing it. I need to see you now."

"I can't see you until tonight. Tell me the address where you're staying."

"I can't. My father thinks . . . he thinks we may be in some sort of danger."

"Why would he tell you that? Danger from what? From who?"

"I don't know. I don't understand any of this, but . . . I have to trust him."

"All right," said Quinn. "I understand. Can we meet somewhere then?"

I hesitated. It was in defiance of my father's instructions. But how could Dad understand all that I was going through right now? What all of us were going through? I needed a friend so desperately—someone to hold me and tell me everything would be all right. Just for a few minutes. Maybe an hour. Then I'd be okay.

"All right," I replied.

"I've got it. The Harmon's Store on 35th South. Meet me in the southeast corner of the parking lot—nine o'clock."

"Yes," I said. "I'll be there."

"I love you, Melody. After tonight, things will make a lot more sense. I promise. We'll get through this together."

"Thanks, Quinn."

"Tonight then?"

"Tonight."

* * *

My cell door opened promptly at 6:00 a.m. One by one, my cellmates emerged from their individual cells. Two of them began pacing the enclosed area, roaming like animals up and down the cell block. I felt like a diver inside a shark cage, except that one of my walls had been removed and I was exposed to the predators. I remained in my bed, hoping they wouldn't notice the new inmate. It was a secret that was impossible to keep. One of them, a tall, shirtless man with bulging muscles, looked in at me, puffing up his chest, letting me know without saying a word that if I crossed him, he wouldn't hesitate to snap my neck. I learned later that his name was Eugene. He'd strangled his girlfriend with her own nylons.

The most social of them was Jason Babbitt, the man who'd spoken to me the night before—the man I recognized from the news. Uninvited, he entered my cell and asked what I was in for. I was tempted to ignore him. Hoping it might intimidate him enough to leave me alone, I looked him in the eye and said, "Homicide."

He wasn't fazed. "Who'd you kill?"

I turned my face toward the wall. "No one. I didn't kill anyone."

"Really?" He took my profession of innocence as an invitation to sit on my bed. "I'm innocent, too. Most of the guys in here are innocent. I'm not saying all, but most. It's a conspiracy. The government hires all these cops and jailers and tells 'em if they don't arrest anyone, they'll lose their job. The conspiracy runs though every level of our society. It's incredibly complex, and it goes right up to the president of the United States. They're all in on it. It leaves them free to break any law they want. Kill anybody they want. Rape anybody they want. Torture anybody they—"

"If you don't mind," I interrupted, "I'd really like to be alone for a while."

Another of the inmates, a bald, stocky Negro named Phil, came to the door of my cell. "You heard the man," he said. "Get out of his cell. Leave him alone." He then advised Babbitt, with a colorful string of profanities, to allow me at least one day before filling me up with all of his ultra-conspiracy nonsense.

Babbitt got up and walked out. Phil glared after him, then looked back at me. After a minute he walked on, laughing huskily and shaking his head. Later, Babbitt told me that Phil had assaulted his neighbor with a tire iron. The man lived, but he was paralyzed below the neck.

Over the last eighteen years, the closest I'd come to a murderer or a rapist was his picture in the post office. Even when I was younger, facing off with such villains as Amaliakiah, the wicked king of the

Lamanites, or Mehrukenah, the Gadianton assassin, they had never considered me one of them. I was never expected to be *chummy.* I groaned within my soul. How could I survive in this place? If someone like Eugene didn't snap my neck, how long would it take my mind to snap? In my ward at home, I'd sometimes heard members refer to themselves as less than celestial. If only they could visit a place like this. They'd know what telestial really was.

When the jailers delivered our breakfast, I declined. I wasn't hungry. Eugene claimed my French toast and bacon without thanks.

"You don't eat breakfast, huh?" he said. "Good. I'm awfully hungry in the mornings."

I remained alone in my cell until almost noon. I tried to think up a plan to keep my children out of danger. Maybe my brother in Montana could take them in. Where was Melody? Why hadn't she called? There was a phone right inside our cell block. She could have called anytime. Maybe she *had* called. Maybe the switchboard wouldn't put her through. I finally built up the nerve to ask Babbitt about the policy on incoming phone calls.

"There is no policy," he said. "We can call out, but no one can call in."

My breathing became short and strained. I thought I was suffocating. I wandered back to my bed and collapsed. Why hadn't this been explained to me? How could I have been so stupid? How was I supposed to reach my children? Where could I look? Who could I call? I rolled onto my back and forced myself to breathe slowly and deeply. I was all right. Everything would be all right. I'd start by calling my bishop. My children had to be somewhere in the neighborhood.

About the time this thought struck me, one of the guards opened the outer door to our cell block. "Hawkins!" she shouted. "Your lawyer's here to see you."

I looked at her quizzically. My *lawyer?* I hadn't requested a lawyer. Why would I be given an attorney without asking for one? The guy must have seen my face on the news and taken it upon himself to claim my case. Then I remembered. Brother Stringham, the executive secretary in our ward, was also a criminal attorney.

"I'm not gonna stand here all day," whined the guard.

She led me into a corridor where inmates sat perched on stools to speak with friends and loved ones through reinforced glass panels. The attorney/client booth was a soundproof chamber at the end of the corridor. The jailer unlocked the heavy wooden door. After I stepped inside, the lock clicked again.

The room was small and claustrophobic. It reminded me of a Catholic confessional. I glanced at the man seated on the other side of the glass. His face was obscured through several layers of grill and mesh. How did they expect attorneys and clients to gain any sense of camaraderie when they could barely see each other's faces? Still, I could perceive enough to know that he wasn't Brother Stringham. The attorney wore a smart black suit and a solid red tie. I took a seat in the small metal chair. We put the two-way phones to our ears.

"I'm Jim Hawkins," I said.

The attorney studied me for a long moment. "Yes, you are Jim Hawkins, aren't you?"

The way he said my name was slurred. He didn't pronounce the "H."

"And your name is?"

"Why, Jim, I'm hurt. Do you honestly fail to recognize me? Look at me closely while I smile."

He pulled the phone away from his ear and outstretched his arms, grinning widely, fingers dancing, like a vaudeville performer.

"What is this?" I demanded angrily. "I was told to come in here and meet with my attorney!"

He replaced the phone and leaned back. "It's just wretched, Jim, the security around here, just wretched. Did you know that just about anyone can walk in off the street, flash a little identification, and everyone thinks he's a lawyer? Nobody bothers to check! Just shameful." The man clicked his tongue in mock reproof.

I strained to see the man's face, but the lousy mesh kept my eyes from registering a clear picture. "Who are you?"

"Then again," the man continued, "I suppose I shouldn't be so surprised. After all, our encounter was so brief. And after all, it was *sooo* many years ago."

I sprang to my feet, about to shout for the guard. The man arose with equal abruptness. "I wouldn't cry out if I were you," he said harshly. "Remember, you're in here. Your family is out there. To use one of your modern phrases, I hold all of the cards."

I sat down slowly. "Jacob Moon, I presume."

The man seated himself as well. "Very good. No doubt you heard that name from the mouth of my miserable concubine, Anna. I don't expect her to tell any more secrets for a while."

"What have you done with her?"

"That's not your concern. You have plenty of your own problems to worry about. And a lifetime to worry about them, I should think."

Again I tried to piece together his face. The long, angular nose. The deepset, owlish eyes. There was something familiar, but I couldn't place it. I couldn't—

And then it registered, like a blow to the stomach.

"Boaz," I whispered hoarsely.

He slapped his hand to his chest. "Whew! Finally! I was beginning to think you'd forgotten entirely."

I might have easily done just that. My encounter with this man, one winter night eighteen years ago, was so brief that it could have easily faded from my memory. That is, the *name* might have faded. Not the face. One doesn't easily forget the face of a man who holds a gun to your head.

"But call me Jacob," the man continued. "I never liked the name Boaz. It was the name of my grandfather, a Christian and a hypocrite. I much prefer the name that I purchased in this century. The birth certificate of Jacob Moon supplied me with a considerable amount of your government's welfare money at a time when I had resigned myself to feed upon stray dogs and rats. But the name wasn't cheap. To raise the money for it, I had to kill a man. No one of consequence . . . a rival drug dealer or some such."

I remembered it all now. I'd heard him called Boaz only once or twice. The name had been spoken by another madman who held a knife to the neck of my beloved wife-to-be, Renae. Mehrukenah's instructions to Boaz that night were very clear. He told Boaz to escort me inside my off-campus Provo apartment and retrieve the Sword of Coriantumr while he remained in the back seat of my car with a blade to my girlfriend's throat.

I'd have eagerly complied with Mehrukenah's request, except for one thing: I didn't have the sword in my possession. Telling Mehrukenah that it was in my bedroom closet had been a bluff to buy more time. When he drove me to my apartment, I realized the bluff had backfired.

Jacob Moon, then known as Boaz, guided me into my bedroom with a handgun. The moment he was distracted, I introduced a small bronze statue to the back of his head. At the same instant, Renae was rescued by Muleki, the son of Teancum.

The police arrived shortly thereafter. Boaz, the Gadianton robber from 50 B.C., was driven away in the back of a patrol car, spewing threats and obscenities. I never found out what happened to him after that. I'd assumed when the police questioned him, he would say many things that would mark him as an insane man. Things about being a citizen of Zarahemla and coming up to this land through a cavernous volcano. Things that would insure his permanent incarceration in an iron-barred asylum.

Jacob Moon confessed that this was exactly what happened to him.

"Eight years of my life. That's what you took, Jimawkins. Most of the time I was in a straitjacket and a padded cell. I may not have been crazy when I went in, but over time I became exactly what they imagined me to be. I thought about you a lot. In a way, that's what kept me going."

"Who is Anna? Why did she try to warn me?"

"Anna is a deeply disturbed woman. I never trusted her; her loyalties were always twisted. I met her in the mental hospital. She was disturbed even then, but I was noble enough to overlook such faults. You see, she was carrying my child. When I escaped, I took her with me. I told her she could live only as long as she took care of the boy. I think the threat helped clear her mind for a while. It was an amazing thing to see—a miracle, if you will." He smiled wryly.

Boaz looked older than I might have imagined after eighteen years. That night in my apartment, I'd have guessed he was very close to my own age. Yet now he was ten to fifteen years my senior. His next statement explained this.

"I went back about two years after I escaped. I took Anna and my son back to my own time. Only it wasn't my time anymore. Decades had passed. People I had known since my youth were described as long-deceased parents and grandparents. You took not only eight years of my life, but everything I'd once known. Fortunately, people still recognized the old signs and tokens. They took me in. The cause of the Gadianton robbers of that generation became my own for nearly twenty years."

So while Jacob Moon had aged twenty years in the past, I'd aged only ten years in the present. The math was confusing. For all I knew, Garth and Jenny were now elderly and decrepit.

"Why did you wait all these years to find me?" I asked. "Why didn't you look for me after you escaped from the hospital?"

"Don't flatter yourself. I had other priorities. In the beginning, it was survival. I was a stranger in a strange land. I couldn't read your language. I didn't understand your society. I've alleviated all those handicaps, however, with my son."

"Alberto Sanchez," I said thoughtfully.

"You see? You're not so stupid—just slow. But my son's first name is Marcos. He used his middle name, Alberto, for your benefit. Marcos was born here, in this century. He came back here some years ago with his mother. Over half his life has been lived here. He understands all the intricacies. In fact, he bought me this suit. Do you like it?"

Now I understood why I thought I knew Al Sanchez the first day I met him. His face was very similar to his father's from eighteen years before.

"I still don't get it," I said. "Why now?"

"Let's just say the timing is right."

"If you hate me so much, why all of this? Why didn't you just kill me?"

He looked deflated. "Oh, Jim. You have so little imagination. In my mind, I must have killed you a thousand times. After so many years, death just seemed . . . too clean. Don't you think this is more creative?" He leaned forward, his eyes exuding pure hatred for the first time. "I wanted you to know what it feels like to rot inside a place like this. I wanted you to know what it means to lose everything. When I was child, we found a monkey in the woods. The monkey was deformed, outcast by its own. We took such delight in tormenting that monkey. When it died, it wasn't from any injures we had inflicted. It had simply had enough and keeled over. That's the kind of experience I wanted you to have."

I shook my head in consternation. "You're crazy."

His face lit up, as if this was a new revelation. "Do you think so? I've lost entire nights of sleep wondering exactly the same thing. Do you think I should seek therapy?" He acted as if awaiting a serious response, and then broke out laughing. The sound was sickening.

My eyes narrowed. "Where is Garth Plimpton?"

He perked up again. "Funny you should mention him. I find myself faced with a peculiar dilemma at the moment. Maybe you could help me solve it. A certain man I know—and coincidentally, you know him too—possesses certain information. The information, it turns out, would help me enormously in my service to humanity. We've asked this man, politely, if he might give us this information; but in spite of our kindness, he persists in being difficult. Put yourself in my position, Jim. If you were me, how would you go about coaxing this man to tell you everything you wanted to know?"

I struggled to suppress my rage. "I wouldn't have the slightest idea."

Jacob sighed. "It *is* a dilemma. But I wouldn't worry yourself about it; I have a feeling we'll shortly have the situation under control. I do wish you could see my empire, Jim. Even now, I've laid the foundation of the greatest city in all the ancient world!" His eyes filled with fury. "I am King Jacob of the Moon, the most feared and hated man among all the tribes—Nephite and Lamanite! And after we have conquered all the lands northward and southward, we shall come back here, and our campaign of lightning will begin again." His face fell back into repose.

He glanced at his watch. "Well, I'd love to stay and chat more about old times, but I have more important matters to attend to." He started to rise. "This has been wonderful for me, Jim. And to think I almost let you stew in the dark for the rest of your life, wondering who had inflicted your misery. Call it a weakness. . . I just couldn't resist."

My rage broke loose. I slammed my fist against the glass. "If you lay a hand on any of my children—!"

"Why, Jim, that almost sounds like a threat. Is it?"

I shrank away. Threatening him accomplished nothing. Jacob Moon had me exactly where he wanted me, and he reveled in it. My heart shriveled. I nearly dropped to my knees, groveling. *"Please,"* I begged. "You've succeeded in destroying my life. Leave my family out of this. Leave my children alone."

"I'll consider your request. I promise. In the meantime, take care of yourself, old friend. I understand a crime like yours often warrants the death penalty. In my day, such a sentence was truly disheartening. But today there's no real cause for alarm. It'll take them at least ten years to carry it out. Good luck to you, Jim. I can't tell you how gratifying it's been to see you again."

He stood and set the phone on the counter, then he opened the door and spoke briefly to the guard. I heard his words faintly over the phone line.

"Totally hostile and uncooperative. I'm afraid Mr. Hawkins will just have to find himself another lawyer."

CHAPTER 8

In my lifetime, I'd met three men who epitomized evil. When I was twenty-two years old I encountered Mehrukenah, the old and wizened assassin. But Mehrukenah's talents were limited to his ability to kill. He was a killing machine, and, like any predator, his focus did not waver until the prey was cold. But he was no politician, no mover of men. He couldn't have inspired loyalty and passion in others. Mehrukenah was at his best when he worked in the shadows.

Amaliakiah, on the other hand, was a mover of men. I was only thirteen years old when his eyes had frozen something inside me. But I had the impression that Amaliakiah didn't really relish his conquests so much as the pursuit of power. His lust for it was like an itch under the flesh, tormenting and gnawing, driving him on. That itch would have tormented him forever, no matter how much power he attained.

Jacob Moon was something different altogether. When I'd first met him in my early twenties, he'd seemed naive, even clumsy. The clumsy boy had come far. I'd never met a man who took such pleasure in plunder. He rivaled my image of Satan himself, relishing every moment of his evil conquests, diabolically energized each time a new enemy was crushed under his feet. Here was a man who would never grow weary of inflicting misery. If God did not directly intervene, how could such a creature be defeated? In an unrighteous world, a man like Jacob would reign in blood and horror, virtually unchallenged.

I could only hope Jacob and Satan possessed the same fatal flaw—a hopelessly myopic view of the universe, a mental block that prevented them from seeing the beginning from the end. The time bridge inside Frost Cave had given Jacob the opportunity to wreak havoc upon two separate generations of God's children—past and present. He could become history's ultimate anti-Christ. For the sake of both generations, I could only hope that deep inside the psyche of Jacob Moon were sown the seeds of his own destruction.

But for myself, confined inside the cinderblock walls of the Salt Lake County Jail, such hopes seemed inconsequential. As far as my own fate was concerned, Jacob Moon had won. He'd defeated me even more decisively than he could have expected. In a few months, I would be tried. For my jury, it would be a remarkably short deliberation. I'd be convicted of first-degree murder and sentenced to life in prison or death by execution. My life was over. My children's lives were ruined. The horror pressed down on me, pinning me to the mattress as I lay in my cell.

But the most deflating moment was yet to come. Around four o'clock, I was told I had visitors. My children had been brought to the jail by Sabrina Sorenson. Appropriately, Sabrina and her daughter did not accompany them to the visitors' area.

At first I was angry with Melody. "I told you not to go out! Do you realize the danger you might have put yourselves in?"

"Please don't be angry," she pleaded. "We had to see you. We had to know if you're all right."

I regretted my outburst almost immediately. For most of the thirty minutes we spent together, our faces were streaked with tears and our hands pressed against the glass, trying to draw strength from one another's touch. My children could sense the hopelessness. I told them repeatedly that I was innocent, that everything would be all right, but I wasn't sure if they believed me on either account. I knew they *wanted* to believe me, and for now, that seemed enough.

"I've called your Uncle Judd and Aunt Crystal in Billings," I informed them. "They're going to drive down tomorrow to pick you up. You remember your Uncle Judd, don't you? And your cousins, Emily and Michael?"

"Yes, and I hate them," said Harry, wiping back another tear.

"Please." My voice sounded drained. "I'm doing the best I can. You have to leave Salt Lake for your own safety."

"Why won't you tell us why?" demanded Steffanie. "Why can't you explain it?"

"We have a right to know," said Melody.

I shut my eyes tightly. "It's complicated. You have to trust me—just this one last time. I promise you, I know what I'm doing."

The children nodded their consent, however reluctantly. I felt certain they only agreed because of the circumstances of the moment. As soon as they left the jail, I feared each of them would stubbornly proclaim that they weren't going *anywhere.* Partly because they didn't want to leave home, partly because they didn't want to leave me. After all, I was all they had. Their mother was gone, and now the fate of their father looked unalterably grim. Could the world of a child or teenager be more effectively devastated?

I told them several more times that everything would be all right and not to lose faith. I told them to fast, and I told them to pray; they all agreed to start that process immediately. I watched them leave the visiting area. After they were gone, my soul sank back into the void.

But if I believed things couldn't get worse, I was wrong.

Around 8:00 p.m., Detective Walpole came to the jail, slapped on the cuffs, and fetched me back to the police station on 2nd South. He and Detective Riley had been working late, he said. They'd invented a few more questions. He intimated that he wanted to finish up as quickly as possible, as there was some sort of office party at the Red Lion at 9:00. I certainly didn't want to spoil his recreation, I thought sarcastically. Walpole did not elaborate on his questions until he and Riley had me squarely seated in that pale gray room on the sixth floor.

Riley slapped a photograph under my eyes. It was a woman—a dead woman. Her skin was pallid, and her hair and clothing were soaked, as if she'd been fished out of the water. A red scar encircled her neck where she'd been strangled with a wire garrote. I turned away in despair.

The woman was Anna.

"Some kids spotted her body floating down the Jordan River near 33rd South around nine o'clock last night," said Walpole. "Nobody knows who she is, but according to the coroner's best estimate, she was killed yesterday between 5:00 and 6:00 p.m."

"Funny thing," Riley continued. "This photograph was broadcast tonight on the evening news right after the story on you. Right away our office gets several calls from viewers who claim they saw you and this woman at a Denny's restaurant in Murray. Now, why do you suppose anyone would make such a connection?"

"Her name is Anna," I confessed. "I only met her once, yesterday afternoon around four or four-thirty."

"Witnesses claim you two had an altercation in the restaurant, that she ran out in a hurry, and that you went after her."

"She was frightened," I explained. "Someone had followed us to the restaurant. I tried to stop her from leaving. When I went to look for her, she was gone."

Both detectives looked incredulous.

I squirmed in my seat. "What are you suggesting? That I killed her, too?" I laughed feebly. "You've gotta be kidding! This is too *much!* Tell me you're kidding!"

The detectives glared at me hard.

"There's another matter we want to discuss with you," said Walpole. "We'd like to talk about a missing persons report that's been on our docket for some time. The missing persons happen to be related to you. Maybe you know them—Garth and Jennifer Plimpton."

My mouth fell open in astonishment. Were they now suggesting that I had murdered my own sister and brother-in-law? This was unbelievable! They were looking at me like I was some kind of maniac!

"It's time to come clean, Hawkins," said Riley. "Time to start telling the truth."

I smiled grimly. The truth. No, the truth was the *last* thing these people wanted to hear. Yet I was so tempted to blurt it out: *The killer is a Satanic madman born over two thousand years ago! He came forward in time to get even with me for events that occurred eighteen years ago!* The *truth* would have landed me in the loony bin! Then again, the way things were going, a plea of insanity was fast becoming my best defense.

"It's just getting deeper and deeper, Hawkins," said Walpole.

"You've got three children," said Riley. "Do you care about them?"

"Of course I do."

"Then think about *them.* Don't make this any worse for them."

I couldn't believe she'd resort to such sleazy manipulation. But the detectives were right about one thing: it was getting way too deep. Things were spinning out of control! There was nothing more I could say. It was time to invoke my Miranda rights. I didn't care how it made me look; they both thought I was guilty anyway. Nothing I said would change it now.

"I want to talk to a lawyer," I announced.

The detectives didn't flinch a muscle. They glowered at me from across the table, as if I'd just spit in both their faces. Any hopes of neatly wrapping up this case tonight had just been dashed. For all I knew, I'd just blown somebody's promotion.

Walpole slapped his knees and glanced at his partner. "Well, that's it."

"Take him back 1019," said Riley, disgusted. "Get him out of my sight."

Walpole pinched the cuffs on my wrists, tighter than before. Riley remained in her seat, looking morose and exhausted. They spoke to each other now as if I wasn't there. I'd become an inanimate object.

"We can still make the Red Lion," said Walpole.

"Fine," said Riley. "See if there's a uniform available. We can be out of here in ten minutes."

They planted me in a chair beside the elevator while Walpole picked up the phone and requested dispatch to send an officer to escort me back to jail. Neither detective spoke to me again. Within five minutes I heard the elevator arrive. As it opened, I did not look up. What did I care who took me back to jail? Back to my hell-on-earth.

"Here to collect the prisoner," said a mild, resonating voice.

Walpole gave a wave of his hand, barely looking up from the paperwork he was eager to complete. "He's all yours."

At last I looked up at the policeman's face. Our eyes locked. He was a little older than the average street cop. Early fifties maybe. His hair was platinum white, like that actor on the old *Mission Impossible* series. His face had been chiseled with deep lines, like an old salty sailor or a desert cowboy. He just stood there, his eyes not wavering from mine. It was the kind of stare that normally would have made me look away to break up the intensity. But I did not look away. An unusual feeling settled over me. I wondered if I'd ever seen a more distinguished face. I felt silly. After all, in about five minutes this man would deliver me into the hands of my jailers. I'd probably never see him again. It was those eyes. They went on forever, like mirrors in a temple.

When I finally looked away, I felt dizzy and frightened. For some reason, I did not want to be released into this man's custody—not even for a brief ride to the jail. I glanced at Riley and Walpole, their noses still buried in paperwork. My mouth opened to protest.

Before I could speak, the uniformed officer took me by the shoulder. His grip was firm, but not harsh. Immediately, my spirit calmed. How was it possible to feel such calm? I'd just been accused of being nothing short of a serial murderer. Yet every shred of tension rushed out of me like a whoosh of air.

"Let's go," the officer said to me.

He helped me to stand. We climbed into the elevator. Riley glanced at us as the doors were closing, then turned away. At the last second she did a double take, as if something struck her as odd. I wondered if she'd looked into the policeman's eyes and experienced the same bizarre sensation.

As we stood side by side in the descending elevator, I noted that everything about this man's uniform appeared to be normal—belt, holster, radio, etc.—but one thing was missing. There was no name tag over his left breast pocket.

For several seconds I debated if I should ask him about this. Finally I heard myself say, "What's your name?"

His eyes remained forward and focused as he replied, "Jonas."

The elevator doors opened. Officer Jonas led me into the stairwell that took us out the back door of the police station. He did not glance over at me again. It was all business now; I was on my way back to jail. Depression crept back into the pit of my stomach. I started to doubt whether there was anything unusual about this man at all. My brain had probably just released an odd chemical or hormone.

We stepped out into the cool night air. It was after hours, and the station's parking lot was virtually empty. No one in sight. I couldn't see any patrol cars. I wondered where Officer Jonas had parked his vehicle.

"Walk over here," he directed me.

We crossed behind the dilapidated annex building a dozen yards to the east. Here, behind the entranceway to an old sealed garage, we stopped. The shadows were thick. No one in an upper story of the police station could have spotted us. Again, I became entranced by the eyes of this strange white-haired officer.

"What's going on?" My voice sounded hollow, a million miles away.

"Turn around."

I did as directed. Within seconds, my hands were free as the cuffs dropped off my wrists. For the first time in twenty-four hours, my arms were not pinioned behind my back as I stood out in public. I'd wondered if my hands would ever be free again in the fresh air of night. I faced my liberator, open-mouthed.

Jonas was smiling now. The smile was full of pain, and also compassion.

My breath came in short gasps. "Wha—what are you doing?"

His expression tensed. "They need you. Go to them."

I didn't have to ask what he meant. My family. He was telling me to go to my family.

"You're setting me free?" I asked stupidly.

Jonas grinned. There was laughter in his voice. "Yes." And then his expression saddened. "But I can only help you once. I can't help you again."

A tear fell down my cheek. "Why are you doing this?"

He tilted his head, almost bashfully. "Because . . . I owe you."

This baffled me. I thought I'd heard him wrong. Did he just say that he owed me?

"I've owed you for a very, very long time, Jim Hawkins."

What was he talking about? I'd never met this person before in my life; I was certain of it. I'd never have forgotten that face. My mind raced back through time. I sorted through dozens of faces from my sojourn among the Nephites when I was thirteen years old. Was Jonas a child I'd helped and forgotten? I couldn't remember any particular incident where I'd saved a child. When had I earned such a remarkable favor?

"But I don't know who you are," I protested.

"That doesn't matter now. You have to go. And so do I."

His voice was urgent, as if someone might appear at any moment—as if it might finally occur to Riley that she did not recognize the policeman who'd taken me into the elevator. Why was I questioning this at all? It was happening! Wasn't that enough? And yet I lingered a moment more. I did not want to leave this man's presence. It was like being in the presence of an angel. I wondered for an instant if that was exactly who he was.

Suddenly Jonas grew vehement. "Go now!" he whispered harshly. "You have no time to spare!"

A surge of adrenaline rushed warmly in my veins. I gazed one last time into those eternal eyes. The lump in my throat was like a golf ball. Jonas read my inexpressible gratitude and nodded.

I dashed toward the northwest end of the parking lot. Along the north and west boundaries stretched a chain-link fence, six feet high with green plastic privacy strips woven into the links. I grabbed the top bar of the fence and prepared to hoist myself over. At the last second, I turned back.

Jonas no longer stood at the garage door behind the annex. I looked around, but I couldn't see him. The white-haired man had faded like a guardian spirit into the April night.

* * *

My brother and sister and I sobbed most of the way home from the jail that afternoon. Seeing my father in that awful prison uniform, unable to hold us or touch us through the glass, was too much.

The gloom persisted long after we'd safely returned to Sabrina's house. At one point, Steffanie suggested we rent some videos—preferably comedies. Anything that might divert our minds from reality. I reminded her of Dad's warning not to go out for any reason. What a hypocrite I was, because at 8:30 that evening, I secretly slipped out the back door to keep my appointment with Quinn.

It was only a fifteen-minute walk to the Harmon's supermarket on 35th South. I knew I'd be early, but I also knew if I hadn't gotten out of the house when I did, I might not have escaped unseen. In any event, I knew it wouldn't take them long to realize I was gone. I left a note on my pillow in the guest bedroom saying I'd gone for a walk and that I'd be back before ten. I thought I might get back before the note was even discovered. Maybe I could tiptoe back upstairs without anyone knowing. But I knew this wasn't likely. Steffanie and I slept in the same guest bed. When people get as depressed as us, the first priority in life is sleep. I doubted Steff would stay awake until ten. I wasn't sure how I'd explain myself—and at the moment, I didn't care.

The sky faded fast as I continued toward Harmon's. It was a cold night, and I was only wearing one of Sabrina's thin sweaters. Every stitch of clothing I had on belonged to Sabrina. Same with Steff. Meagan offered Harry some of her clothing, but Harry decided he'd rather wear his own clothes another day. I contemplated dropping by the house on the way back to grab some underwear and shirts for all of us, then I decided not to chance it. What I was doing at the moment was stupid enough.

You got that right. What you were doing was so *incredibly* stupid, if I had known you were planning it, I'd have made certain that Sabrina locked you in a closet!

How could you not know? Why couldn't you have trusted me?

I know, Dad. I know. And I'm sorry. I'm so *sorry. I can never say it enough. I'm not sure what was going on in my head. I hadn't been thinking straight for the past twenty-four hours. All I knew was that my aunt and uncle from Billings were driving down the next day to take us back to Montana. It might be the last time I saw Quinn for weeks. I wanted to at least say good-bye.*

I've played what was about to happen over and over in my head a thousand times. I had no idea Quinn was capable of something so horrible. He said that he loved me. How could I have known?

I arrived at the Harmon's parking lot about a quarter to nine. I didn't expect Quinn to be there; I expected to wait in the store lobby and watch for him. But his silver RX-7 was already parked in the southeast corner. I could see him seated behind the wheel, waiting. The engine was running to keep him warm.

He looked startled when I opened the passenger door.

"Melody! You're . . . early."

I reached out for him and began to cry like a dope. He held me for several minutes, letting me exhaust my emotions. Then he took me by the shoulders.

"Are you okay?"

"We're leaving tomorrow, Quinn."

"Who's 'we'?"

"My brother and sister and I. We're going to Billings, Montana with my aunt and uncle."

Quinn considered this a moment. Then he nodded, as if giving his consent. "That should be good for you."

This surprised me. "What do you mean? It's the last thing I want. I don't want to leave you. I don't want to leave my father."

"Maybe you'll feel it's the best thing for everyone, especially after what I have to tell you."

I cocked an eyebrow. I had come here tonight expecting only Quinn's comfort. What did he think he had to tell me?

"I don't understand," I said.

"It's about your father."

"My father? What could you . . . ?" I shook my head, perplexed.

Quinn took a deep breath. "I love you, Melody, and I don't want to hurt you. But there are things you should know. I'm glad you came early. This gives me a chance to prepare you."

"Prepare me for what?"

"There are things your father has never told you about himself."

My confusion was turning into frustration. "What are you talking about?"

"Two days ago," Quinn began, "I met a man. He knew my name. He knew you. He told me that something terrible was about to happen in your life. At first I brushed him off, but the man was joined by four other men. They more or less forced me to listen."

He approached his next statement gingerly. "Melody, the man your father shot yesterday is not the first man your father has murdered."

My breath snagged. The air wouldn't go into my lungs. Quinn tried to embrace me. I resisted him and shrank into the corner.

"I don't blame you for reacting like this," said Quinn. "I'm sure I'd react the same way. I didn't want to be the one to tell you, but now I'm glad you'll hear it from me first. Your father is part of an organization, Melody—an organization whose sole objective is the plunder and murder of anyone who gets in its way. This man told me things about your family that no stranger could have known. But still, I'd have never believed a single word if your father hadn't been arrested the very next night—just as this man had predicted! Suddenly everything he said started to make sense."

I couldn't listen to this anymore. I reached for the door of the car, but Quinn grabbed my arm.

"Melody, hear me out. Your father has been living a lie for eighteen years. I know he portrays himself as this stalwart, upstanding Mormon. But it's all a front, Melody. Every bit of it. Your father is an assassin. He works for this organization. The man I spoke with is a special agent with the government, a branch I'd never even heard of before. It's called the Brimstone Agency. Its function is to investigate Satanic organizations. He's been tracking your father for years."

"You've lost your mind, Quinn! This is the most insane nonsense I've—!"

"Think about it, Melody! What about your Aunt Jenny and Uncle Garth!"

My mouth fell open. I had never told Quinn about Jenny and Garth, except to say that I had an aunt and uncle who were traveling the country. I'd never mentioned their names!

"He killed them, Melody. They found out who he really was, so he rubbed them out. He had to! It was the only way he could continue his masquerade of murder and mayhem."

At that moment, a Chevy van pulled up hurriedly in front of Quinn's RX-7. A Lincoln Continental parked behind it.

Quinn kept talking, as if the arrival of these cars had been anticipated. "I probably shouldn't have told you. They wanted to tell you themselves. They wanted to do it last night, but then you disappeared. I was just supposed to get you here, but they knew you wouldn't come if I told you the real reason—"

I started to panic. The lies someone had spun in Quinn's mind were incredible, but the shock of his words did not outweigh my dread as I recalled my father's warning.

I threw open the car door and yanked free of Quinn's arm. He tried to grab me again, but I flailed my arms and accidentally stabbed my finger into his eye. He shrieked in pain. I fell out onto the pavement and pulled myself up using the car door. At that moment, people sprang from every door in the van and the Lincoln.

I tried to scream for help. The parking lot was packed with cars. I could see people stuffing groceries into their trunks, more people coming in and out of the store entrance. But no one was near the southeast corner, even if anyone had half considered rushing to my rescue.

A man from the Lincoln lunged at me. His face was hideous, with gaping holes in his cheeks and at the corners of his mouth. He flashed a smile, and I could see teeth through every opening. There was plenty of space to slip by him, and I felt certain I could escape. But something flashed in the man's hand. As he thrust it toward me, I remember seeing a streak of blue light and feeling an electric shock rip through my body. Bright colors started swimming in my head.

After that, there was only blackness.

CHAPTER 9

A phone.

I had to find a phone. I had to call Sabrina Sorenson. How would she respond when she heard my voice? Would she hang up? Would she call the police? I had serious doubts that our single date had earned me any romantic loyalties. But if I revealed that I had escaped, and then if she failed to notify the police, she'd be breaking the law—aiding and abetting a fugitive. Mixing her up in all this was unpardonable, but I had nowhere else to turn. Literally, nowhere else to turn.

Yet my first problem was not what I'd say to Sabrina. It was how I would obtain a simple quarter to make a phone call. Then I would have to locate a pay phone. I didn't have time to be wandering about the streets searching for these things. "S. L. Co. Jail" was printed on the back of my overalls.

After climbing the fence, I moved swiftly down the block to 1st South. Fortunately, there were many shadowy trees and dimly-lit sidewalks. A 7-11 sat on the corner of 1st South and 3rd East. A bank of phones hung left of the door, but I couldn't use them. I was still less than a block from the police station. I don't think they knew yet that I was missing, but a passing patrol car might recognize the orange uniform.

I turned east on 1st South, keeping near the shadows. Cars whirred past; no one slowed down. I lowered my head and walked briskly, steadily. Passersby might think I was a painter or a car mechanic.

On the corner of 4th East stood an LDS chapel. It should have been a perfect sanctuary. Free local calls might be made from the lobby. But no lights burned in any windows; no bishops worked late consoling the penitent or distressed. I noted a garbage dumpster in the rear.

On 5th East I located a Top Stop convenience store. Two cars were filling up at the pumps, two more were parked right of the door. Teenagers surrounded the parked cars, some poking their heads out the windows like turtles, others leaning on bumpers and hoods.

I spotted two banks of pay phones. The first stood out in the open, near the street corner; the other hung on the wall just right of the teenagers. I approached the teens. They gave me a once-over, then turned back to their gossip and laughter.

"Excuse me," I said.

A young man with gold earrings raised his eyebrows.

"Do you have a quarter?" I asked.

"I don't," he replied. He turned to his friends. "Anybody got a quarter?"

"Sure." A girl poked her head back inside the car and sorted through some coins in the ashtray.

"When you gonna pay it back?" asked another kid. Smart aleck.

"Be sure and get his address," jibed another.

They teased me about interest accrued by the hour. Then by the minute. I grinned and nodded, eager to assure them all that they would make great comedians.

The girl flipped the quarter at me with her thumb. I reached out and caught it in my left fist. The kids applauded.

"I appreciate it." I backed away awkwardly, trying not to display the words on the back of my overalls. The kids tuned back into their own world.

I didn't know Sabrina's number. The plastic folder beneath the pay phone was empty. Someone had stolen the phone book. What next? I ventured around to the phone on the corner, keeping my back faced away from the Top Stop. Anyone on the street, however, could have read it plainly. I searched the phone book. Cars paused at the corner stop signs and drove on. Any one of them might have been a patrol car. I found Sabrina's number. Repeating it under my breath, I returned to the other, less exposed bank of phones.

As Sabrina's line began to ring, I looked all around. No one seemed concerned that I was there.

"Hello?" said the voice on the other end.

"Sabrina?"

"Jim? Is that you?"

"Yes."

I paused. How could I start this? Sabrina surprised me by speaking first.

"Jim, Melody is missing."

I was disconcerted for a second. "What do you mean, 'missing'?"

"Gone. Steffanie found a note on her pillow. She said she was going out for a walk."

I felt a surge of rage. I almost jumped down Sabrina's throat, but I caught myself. "How did she—? How could she—?"

"Nobody saw her leave. She snuck out."

I knew the reason immediately. Quinn. She'd gone to meet her bozo boyfriend.

"The note said she'd back before ten," Sabrina continued. "It's only about twenty after nine. I was about to go out and look—"

"Sabrina, listen to me," I interrupted. "I'm out of jail."

"What? How?"

"The police set me free." Which was true, in a manner of speaking.

"What happened? Did they find the killer?"

"Not exactly. It's a long story. But none of it really matters now. I'm free!"

"I can't believe it!" Sabrina started weeping. "Oh, Jim, I'm so glad. I never believed you were capable of the things they accused you of. Thank heavens the police came to their senses."

"Yeah," I said insincerely. I had no right to mislead her like this. But how could I tell her the truth? I barely believed it myself!

"The children will be ecstatic!" said Sabrina. "They've been fasting—"

"No! No!" I insisted. "Don't tell the kids yet. Please. I want to surprise them. I want to explain everything in person."

Her weeping stopped. Her next words sounded thoughtful, almost apprehensive. "Are you all right, Jim? Is something wrong?"

I scolded myself for speaking so impetuously and tried to smooth it over. "I'm fine. I'm just frightened about Melody. I'm afraid she might be in trouble. We have to find her. I'm hoping she just stepped out with her boyfriend."

"Quinn?"

"Yes. We won't find Melody unless we find Quinn's RX-7."

"RX-7? I'm not sure what that is," said Sabrina.

"Never mind. I'll help you find it. I need your help, Sabrina. I know you don't really know me from Adam, but I need your help desperately. Could you come and get me?"

There was a pause. "Where are you, Jim?"

"At a pay phone near the police station. Pick me up at the LDS chapel on the corner of 1st South and 4th East. Drive around back to the parking lot. I'll be watching for you. And don't bring the kids. Leave them there in case Melody comes home."

I shut my eyes and bit my lip. Was she buying this? Oh, please. She *had* to buy it. I couldn't think of a single soul on this earth I could call if she turned me down.

"1st South and 4th East?" she repeated.

"Yes."

The phone clicked. The hangup had seemed rather abrupt. Her intentions were not wholly clear. Would she call the police to verify my story? Would she discover that I'd escaped? Would she report me? I hung up the phone. I had no choice but to trust her.

Surreptitiously, I crossed the street and backtracked toward the chapel. A plaque beside the front doors, green with oxidation, read "South Thirteenth Ward—est. 1951." I made my way around back and located the dumpster. It was encased on two sides by a cement containment wall. I waited in the space between the wall and the dumpster, my fate in the hands of the first woman I'd dated in eighteen years. I guess now I'd really learn how well the date had gone.

As I crouched in the darkness, I thought about Melody. When we found her, I'd promptly strangle her. Oh, how I wish there was a way to freeze a child's age at four or five years, when the worst they could do was spill a glass of milk or color on the wall. I concentrated on something Jacob Moon had said when I asked him about Garth Plimpton: *Put yourself in my position, Jim. If you were me, how would you go about inducing this man to tell you everything you wanted to know?*

The words had taken on a kind of eerie resonance. The answer hit me, and it chilled my blood. If Jacob's efforts to make Garth disclose crucial information had failed, the best way to loosen Garth's tongue would have been to threaten the life of someone he cared about very deeply. The obvious first choice would have been Jenny, his wife. But if Jenny had been available, why would Jacob have said this to me? Somehow, Jenny was *not* available to Jacob Moon. Was my sister dead? Ice shot up my spine. I could only hope Jenny had somehow eluded Jacob and was now in safe hands.

So who would have been Jacob's second choice?

The answer to this question made it clear why Jacob had come back to this century. It also revealed why he'd at long last sought me out for revenge. It wasn't just to ruin my life. It was an effort to get me out of the way. Jacob's hatred would have disqualified me as his second choice. So much better to obtain one of Garth's young nieces or nephews. Someone weak and vulnerable. Someone with their whole life ahead of them.

And so I did as Jacob had asked and put myself in his place. If I were a villain like Jacob Moon, I would kidnap a child whom Garth loved and take them back to ancient America. The child would be made to stand before Garth Plimpton. Jacob would threaten to kill the child then and there if Garth didn't talk. It was Jacob's only logical alternative. I'd denied this horror for several hours, clinging foolishly to the hope that Jacob's promise to leave my children alone had been sincere. How stupid could I have been? Capturing one of my children had been Jacob's intention all along!

Please, God, let Melody be with Quinn. Compared with the alternative, an evening with Quinn was suddenly a parent's dream come true.

Headlights swerved into the parking lot. The car rolled slowly. At first I was certain it was a patrol car, then I caught the shape of Sabrina's Honda Civic. I emerged from my hiding place behind the dumpster. Sabrina hit the brakes. Hastily, I climbed inside the passenger door.

"Thank you for coming," I said.

Sabrina did not reply. She gaped at me. My appearance from the shadows had bewildered her. Her eyes scanned my prison overalls.

"Where are your clothes, Jim?"

"I . . . don't have them yet," I said limply.

Her hands began shaking on the steering wheel. "Why were you hiding back there?"

I didn't answer. I decided to let the reality of the situation sink in, and I watched intently to see her reaction.

"They didn't really let you out, did they?" she said carefully. For a moment, I thought she'd digested this remarkably well. Then her hand flew over her mouth. Her eyes filled with tears of terror. "Oh my gosh! You've escaped!"

I reached out to touch her hand. She stiffened and recoiled.

"I'm not going to hurt you, Sabrina. I swear it. I would never hurt you. Don't be frightened."

"How did you do it?" she whimpered.

I spoke slowly, trying to sound pacifying. "I had help. People who know that I'm innocent helped me to escape."

She muttered to herself. "What am I doing? What have I gotten myself into?"

"Sabrina, listen to me carefully. The man who helped me escape told me that my family was in danger. He said that I should go to them. Do you understand?"

She continued rambling. "I could go to jail for even speaking with you here."

My shoulders slumped. Calling Sabrina appeared to have been a mistake. "You're right," I said. "I shouldn't have involved you. I won't ask for your help. I would never ask you to do anything against your will, Sabrina. If you want me to get out of your car right now, I'll go."

This mollified her a little. She worked up the nerve to speak again. "Where would you go?"

I shook my head. "I have no idea." Encouraged, I leaned toward her again. "You told me on the phone that you didn't believe I was capable of the things they accused me of. Do you still believe that?"

She took a moment before answering. Finally, she closed her eyes and began to nod. "Yes," she whispered, assuring herself as well as me.

"Don't turn me away, Sabrina. I have nowhere else to go. We have to find my daughter. There are men who might harm her if they find her first."

"Who?"

"The same men who framed me for murder."

Sabrina faced forward, her eyes still closed. "I'm not sure I can deal with all this, Jim."

"All right." I blew the air out of my lungs. "All right, Sabrina." I reached for the door handle. "I understand."

"Wait!" Her eyes were still closed. She opened them and looked at me for a long moment. She laughed. It was a self-deprecating laugh, as if she were chiding herself for the kind of men she became involved with. Losers, abusers, and now accused murderers. She looked toward the ceiling and regained her self-control. Then she said, "Do you know where Quinn lives?"

"Yes," I replied. "I found Melody at his place two weeks ago after she skipped church."

I watched the wheels spinning in Sabrina's mind. She nodded to herself. My statement about fetching Melody after she skipped church seemed to reaffirm that I was a normal person—a normal father with normal problems. I struggled to think of something else to say that might make me appear normal. Less like a murderer. But it wasn't necessary. A light switched on in Sabrina's eyes. She began to look at me with all the sympathy that a man in my predicament deserved. Her hands stopped shaking and she gripped the steering wheel tighter. "I'll help you find her, Jim. But that's all I can do."

"I won't ask you for any more," I said. "I promise."

Sabrina's foot pressed on the gas pedal. We turned the car around and aimed it back toward West Valley.

CHAPTER 10

Quinn lived in West Jordan with his family. His room was a converted single-car garage at the left side of the house. This made for a separate entrance, like a mother-in-law apartment. I couldn't help wondering if the parents of this obnoxious kid preferred it that way.

We stopped at a pay phone before driving out to West Jordan. Sabrina wanted to call home and make sure Melody hadn't shown up. Her daughter answered. Meagan informed her that everyone was frightened. They wanted to know what was going on. Sabrina told them to hold tight, and she'd be home shortly. My children still didn't know I was free. For now, I preferred it that way. Better to explain in person.

We arrived at Quinn's home in West Jordan around 9:45. Quinn's RX-7 was in the driveway. The main part of the house was dark; his family was asleep. In the converted garage, a single lamp burned. Quinn's face flashed in the window as we cut the engine, then it disappeared. The boy's expression had looked surprised, even startled. I became hopeful. Such an expression could easily mean that Melody was inside; Quinn had gone to warn her. I'd still wring my daughter's neck, but only after throwing my arms around it in relief.

For obvious reasons, I asked Sabrina if she would be the one to knock on Quinn's door. Reluctantly, she agreed. She climbed out of the car, and I watched her approach the house. Her rap on the door was very light so as not to disturb the rest of the family. She waited. No one answered. Sabrina glanced back at me and shrugged her shoulders.

I knew Quinn was in there. I strongly suspected my daughter was, too. I climbed out of the car and marched up to the garage. At the moment, I didn't care that Quinn's family might look out the window and recognize me. With Sabrina at my side, I pounded harshly on the wood. Again, no one answered.

My patience was running thin. I twisted the doorknob. It was locked.

I turned to Sabrina. "Do you have a credit card?"

"In—in my car," she replied.

"Can you get it for me?"

She rushed back toward the Civic. For an instant, I thought she might start the engine and screech away. Instead, she returned promptly and gave me her Visa. It occurred to me that it might be better if she stayed outside. I doubted if anyone had seen her yet, or if they had, I doubted if she'd been recognized.

"It might be better if no one saw us together," I said.

"I'll wait here, behind the door," she insisted.

It only took me fifteen seconds to jimmy the lock. I'd had quite a bit of practice. Last spring I'd lost the shed key, and had to open it this way all summer.

The door swung open. At first the place looked empty, then I noticed Quinn in the corner, cowering behind his bed, sweat beaded on his forehead. He clutched his pillow like a life preserver. The boy looked terrified.

I stood over him. "Where's Melody?"

"I—I—" Something had shaken him up so badly he could hardly talk.

I repeated the question more severely. "Where is my daughter?"

"Sh—she's gone," Quinn managed.

"Was she here earlier?" I said impatiently. "Did you take her home?"

Quinn shook his head. He found it hard to look at me. Each time he did so, he looked like a child trapped by a monster. I decided to use this to my advantage. I gripped his shirt collar and leaned in close.

"Tell me what happened to her."

"Th—they took her."

I stiffened. "*Who* took her?"

"The Brimstone Agency. At least, that's who they said they were. I don't know anymore. There were six of them. They said they just wanted to talk to her. They said . . . They said . . ."

I shook Quinn. "Where did they take her?"

"I don't know! They tried to take me, too. I punched the gas and got away."

"When?"

"A half hour ago. Forty-five minutes maybe."

"Where did this happen?"

"The Harmon's on 35th."

I suddenly had a clear picture of what had occurred. "You led them to her, didn't you?"

Quinn tried to reply, but nothing came out of his mouth.

It took incredible restraint to release Quinn with little more than a shove. His father appeared in the doorway leading into the main part of the house.

"What's going on?" the father demanded. He glared at me. When it registered who I was, his face went pale. I got out of there rapidly.

* * *

Two patrol cars, sirens blasting and lights flashing, sped by us as we turned onto the Bangerter Highway. I crouched down in the seat. The police raced away in the general direction of Quinn's house. If they were looking for us, Quinn's father hadn't given them a usable description of Sabrina's car.

At first Sabrina and I spoke very little. I tried my best to look poised and self-assured. But my teeth were grinding. Once Sabrina glanced at my trembling hand. She knew that I was dying inside. That I was devastated with terror for my daughter's life.

Sabrina had grown unexpectedly cool and collected. She had heard every word of my conversation with Quinn. The boy had unwittingly confirmed my innocence. The threat to my family had been verified. Sabrina drove a little too fast, however, and I had to remind her to slow down. Finally, she began to ask some pointed questions.

"I don't understand," she said. "*Who* took Melody?"

"I told you. The same people who framed me for murder."

"But why? Why are they doing this?"

"They're an organization that *specializes* in doing things like this."

"Terrorists? Gangs? The Mafia? *Who?*"

"All of the above," I replied.

"What could they want with Melody? She's only sixteen! She's just a kid!"

"I wish I knew." Actually, I *did* know, partially at least. But I was too distressed to discuss it.

A sob escaped Sabrina's throat. "If only I'd kept an eye on her. How could I have known she would try to leave the house?"

"You *couldn't* have known," I said. "It's not your fault. It's not anyone's fault. If they hadn't gotten her tonight, they'd have tried again tomorrow. They'd have kept on trying until they succeeded." I spoke thoughtfully. "I think I may know where they took her."

"What are you going to do? You can't go to the police."

"I know," I said. "I'll have to find her myself."

We got off the Bangerter Highway at 41st South and turned west toward Sabrina's home.

"What about Harry and Steffanie?" she asked.

"I . . . I'm not sure yet. I've asked my brother in Montana to take them, but . . . No, I can't endanger his family. I'll have to take them with me, at least part of the way. There are good people at the place where I'm going. I hope I can persuade these people to take care of them. I hope I can also persuade them to help me."

"Where is this place?" asked Sabrina.

"Please don't ask me that," I pleaded. "It's safer for you if you don't know."

She looked hurt.

"Oh, Sabrina, I wish I could tell you. You've been such a great friend. An *exceptional* friend. I hope someday I can tell you everything. But right now, I'll have a hard enough time explaining it to my children. I'll tell them along the way."

"How long will it take you to get to this place?"

"Several days, I think."

"Do you have a car?"

I frowned. "No. I'm sure they've impounded my Pontiac."

"There's an old Subaru in my garage," said Sabrina. "The driver's side window won't roll up and the radio doesn't work, but I think it runs okay."

I looked at her in all soberness. "Sabrina, you realize that if they catch me, they'll trace the car to you. They'll know that you helped me."

Sabrina watched the road. Tears pricked at her eyes again. "So avoid getting caught."

"I don't know how to thank you."

"Jim, this is all so crazy!" she exploded. "What if something happens? What if I never see any of you again? It would help if I had some idea—*any* idea—how long you'll be gone."

"I wish knew." I gazed out the Civic's passenger window toward the starlit skies of Wyoming. "I wish I knew."

* * *

I saw myself standing in the midst of a thick wood. I could hear birds all around me and a babbling brook. A voice had called my name. I searched in all directions looking for the source. It had been a woman's voice. I realized that she was hidden behind some leaves, obscured by shafts of sunlight. I could feel the sunlight. It wasn't just warmth. It was security. Nothing could hurt me here.

"What a beautiful girl you've become," said the voice, soft and melodious.

I struggled to push my way through the leaves, soaking my arms and face in cold dew. I tried to shield my eyes from the shards of light that pierced through the branches and brambles. For some reason, my hands wouldn't work right. They wouldn't raise up to move all the branches aside. I started to cry in frustration.

And then the branches parted by themselves. The blinding sunlight became subdued through a fog. The woman who had called my name stood directly before me in the mist. The light source behind her head silhouetted the features of her face. Still, I could see enough to know that she was incredibly beautiful. Her hair was long and black, reflecting a kind of light all its own. Her dress was whiter than any white I had ever imagined.

"You're as beautiful as an angel," the voice continued.

Tears leaped out of my eyes. "Momma? Momma, is that you?"

She smiled at me warmly. I could hardly see her through my tears.

"I miss you, Momma," I cried. "I miss you sooo much."

"I'm with you, my child. As often as I can, I will be with you . . . "

She said something else, something I didn't quite understand. My mother disappeared in the fog. She disappeared in the midst of my tears. I began sobbing uncontrollably.

And then my eyes opened.

I started to become aware. But my mother's spirit remained with me; I'm certain I felt its presence for almost a full minute after I awakened. I continued to cry, but my sobs became less intense. As I remembered my circumstances—and the horror—I stopped crying altogether.

It was dark. Though my eyes were wide open, I couldn't see a thing. The floor was rumbling; there was rumbling all around me. I was lying on my side. I couldn't move my arms and legs apart! My hands had been locked in front of me, and my ankles had been manacled as well. The metal hurt, especially my legs. I rolled onto my back and felt the ceiling. Now I remembered where I was.

The stun gun had only knocked me unconscious for a minute or so. Vaguely, I remembered them shackling my hands and feet and dropping me into the trunk of the Lincoln Continental. After that I blacked out again, this time from sheer terror. I was still inside the trunk, shivering. It was cold.

I started gasping. I'd always hated closed-in places. Once, as a little girl, I wandered inside the coat closet and shut the door on myself. The inside knob had been broken off. I screamed for help, but Mom and Dad were in the backyard. They told me I was only in there for two or three minutes, but it felt like an eternity.

I choked out a word. "Help!" But who did I expect to help me? Only those awful men could have heard my cries. Why were they doing this? Where were they taking me?

"Help!" I screamed again. "I can't breathe!"

I felt the car begin to slow down. Gravel crunched beneath the wheels. The car stopped, and I heard the driver's side door open and close. The trunk flipped up. A starry sky filled my vision, and the silhouette of a man. I heard another car pull up behind us. It was the van that had been with the Lincoln at the parking lot. I winced as a flashlight shined in my face.

"What's the matter with her?" a voice demanded. It came from up front, someone calling out the passenger window.

"Are you all right?" asked the man with the flashlight.

"Can't breathe," I panted. "I'm so cold. "

He lowered the flashlight and called back to the man in the car. "She says she's cold and she can't breathe."

"She's been breathing fine for three hours," said the man in the car. "She probably just woke up and started to panic, that's all. Close the trunk, Marcos, and let's get going."

"What if we let her ride in the back seat or in the van?" Marcos inquired.

"No! Now get back in the car! I want to get there before the sun rises."

Marcos lingered over me another moment. I could see his face a little. He wasn't much older than me—eighteen or nineteen. He started to remove his coat.

"Here," he said. "I won't need this." Marcos laid it gently over my shoulders.

"Where are you taking me?" I asked, my voice pleading.

Marcos did not reply. He reached up and slammed the trunk. Once again I was surrounded by darkness. I shut my eyes tightly, clenched my fists, and braced myself for a wave of panic. I will survive this, I told myself. I can make it. Strangely, the wave of panic never arrived. The words that my mother had spoken in the dream came flooding back. "I'm with you, my child. As often as I can, I will be with you . . ." And then I realized the last words she had uttered before melting into the fog.

"But your Savior will be with you always."

CHAPTER 11

It looked as though Harry and Steffanie had finally dropped off to sleep, their bodies bundled up in two Mexican blankets that Sabrina had loaned us. I'd been operating the Subaru's heater on high since we left Salt Lake City. Still, it was difficult to retain any heat on account of the broken driver's side window. The inside temperature was only a little better than the snow-encrusted plains between Evanston and Rock Springs, Wyoming. My face had been numb for several hours, but at least my body was warm.

Before we had left Salt Lake, I was able to shed my jail overalls. It was too risky to drop by our house for clothing, but Sabrina managed to find me a sweatshirt and an oversized sweater left by her first husband. She also dug up a pair of pink sweatpants that came halfway up my shins. I vowed not to step out of the car until we reached the summit of Cedar Mountain in northern Wyoming—partly as a precaution, and partly so I wouldn't have to display those embarrassing sweatpants.

I'd forever remember the expression on Harry and Steffanie's faces as I walked through Sabrina's doorway. They had known about my escape before we got there, as local television and radio stations had interrupted their regular broadcasts to announce my disappearance. First reports speculated that I'd overpowered a police officer while in transport back to the county jail, but officials couldn't yet release the officer's name. *And they never will,* I thought.

As I embraced my children, I thought of the reunion between Alma and the sons of Mosiah in the land of Gideon. Ammon had felt joy to the point of exhaustion. I understood now, in some small part, what that scripture meant. But our joy was incomplete. Melody was still missing. Our joy was also diminished by my announcement that we were leaving town within the hour. I couldn't say when we would return.

Harry and Steffanie wanted to know where we were going. I hesitated giving them an answer. I'd explain it all along the way, I promised. I also became quite anxious as I recalled our destitute finances. I suggested to Harry that he might sneak into our house and retrieve the First Security Visa from the top drawer of my dresser, but Sabrina quashed the idea. By now, she reminded me, the police were surely circling our house like vultures. Her daughter, Meagan, reported that cops had been patrolling the neighborhood like sentries for the past half hour.

Sabrina handed me her only Visa and gave me her code for accessing a cash machine.

"It's close to the limit," she said. "There might be three hundred dollars left. Considering I already owe twenty-seven hundred, another three hundred doesn't sound like any big thing."

"I don't know when I can return this," I told her.

"It's probably better if you don't."

I embraced Sabrina. This woman had restored my faith in unconditional friendship. Harry and Steffanie embraced her as well. As an afterthought, I asked her if I could borrow the Book of Mormon on her coffee table—a blue missionary-style volume with the subtitle "Another Testament of Jesus Christ" emblazoned in gold foil. She agreed, thinking I needed it for spiritual support. She was right. But how could I have explained that it might also come in handy as a kind of tour map?

We piled into Sabrina's Subaru. After one final wave to her and her daughter, we were off.

We took a side street to 35th South, avoiding a patrol car as it crossed in front of us, and continued down a side street. Sabrina had overestimated the amount left on her credit card. The First Interstate Bank cash machine would only give us $240. I used fifteen of that to fill the tank with gas; my son pumped while his sister paid the bill.

Harry wondered if he and Steff could break their fasts and buy soft drinks and munchies. After all, I was out of jail, so the point of their fast had already been achieved. I asked them if they might continue until morning. "Only now," I said, "direct it toward Melody's safe return."

Anxiety coiled inside me as we approached Parley's Canyon. What if the police had set up a roadblock on I-80? To my relief, if such a plan was in the works, it had not yet been implemented. Our escape from Salt Lake City went smoothly. No hitches. My son didn't think Harrison Ford's character in the *The Fugitive* could have done any better.

Just outside Park City, the kids finally began demanding some answers. Was Melody all right? Had she been kidnapped? Had the kidnappers requested a ransom? Would they hurt her? Did I know where they were taking her? Would we catch up with her tomorrow? Was there a chance that we might never see her again?

I couldn't put off telling them our destination for much longer. It was time to resurrect all their whimsical fantasies—the ones every child seems to abandon around five years of age—and speak of lost worlds and secret underground passages as casually as one might rehearse tales from high school or boot camp. But I was tired, and I knew my children were tired. When I finally revealed my secrets, I wanted everyone as alert as possible. So I told them to go to sleep, promising that after tomorrow, they would understand everything. Reluctantly, Steffanie and Harry did as I instructed, pulling the Indian blankets over their faces to keep warm.

We turned off the Interstate just a few miles short of Green River and began the trek north. About the time we reached Farson, Harry started to stir in the seat beside me. He poked his head out from under the blanket and gazed off toward the jagged silhouettes of the Wind River mountains.

"We must be screwing up big-time, huh, Dad?"

I looked at him curiously. "What do you mean?"

"The way we live. The way we *are.*"

I drew my eyebrows together. "I still don't follow. Are you saying you think we're being punished?"

"Well, it only makes sense. After all, we're not a very righteous family."

This hurt most coming from my son.

"Righteousness is a direction," I replied, "not a position. I think we're at least headed in the right direction, don't you?"

"Nah. If we were headed in the right direction, God wouldn't punish us so much."

I sighed. These were perfectly logical conclusions for a ten-year-old. Heck, they were logical for most adults. The way things looked, nothing in our family could ever be the same. Even the freedom we felt at this moment, the strength we drew from one another, seemed fragile and fleeting.

"Bad things happen to good people," I said, running for cover behind the cliché.

"Then everything they say in church is a lie."

"What do you think they say in church?"

Harry's voice became singsong. "If you do this, you'll be blessed. If you do that, you'll be damned. It's like a game. If you do everything right, nothing bad is ever supposed to happen. I know I don't do everything right. Maybe that's why so many bad things are happening."

"You've got it all wrong," I said. "It's not always your fault when bad things happen. Remember, the most righteous man who ever lived endured the most terrible things a man can endure. He was crucified by the very people he came to save. The occurrence of bad things is all part of the eternal plan. It helps us grow. It helps us learn and become stronger. Afflictions may in fact be blessings in disguise—blessings that we earned *because* of our righteousness."

"So you're saying that wicked people might not have as many bad things happen to them?"

"No, that's not what I'm saying. Sometimes it might *seem* that way, but—"

"So maybe if we'd been wicked all our lives, you think Mom might still be alive? You think you might have never been arrested? And that Melody might have never been kidnapped?"

"I don't know, Harry. But I think—"

"So maybe, in a way, it's *better* to be bad."

How was I failing to communicate this principle so miserably? This was so typical of Harry. At certain moments he seemed to enjoy wallowing in misery. Part of the fallout, I supposed, from his mother's death.

"Harry, I think bad things happen to everyone, no matter who you are, and no matter what you do."

"Even as bad as this?"

"Sometimes worse. At least the three of us have each other. Everything happens for a reason, son. Sometimes we may not know the reason, and we might not find out until after we die. But we *will* find out, and then we'll realize that suffering and affliction gave us the opportunity to become better people."

Harry crinkled his nose. "Do you really believe that stuff, Dad?"

"I do," I replied. But of course, I was well aware of how easy it was for a person to *forget* that they believed it.

"So you think when I flushed my Spiderman and we had to call a plumber, that was good?"

"Well, hopefully you learned responsibility. I know I certainly learned patience . . . "

"And when I broke my wrist on the Pittsingers' trampoline, that was good too?"

"Now that it's healed, you appreciate it a lot more, don't you?"

"And you think everything that's happening now—all these terrible things—you think they'll make us better in the end?"

I opened my mouth to answer. Then I closed it. I sighed and gazed off into the night sky ahead.

"I do," I said finally. "I know it doesn't make sense. But I believe it with all of my heart."

"How is this supposed to make us better?" Harry challenged.

The clouds over the Wind River mountains had twisted into a gloomy whirlpool, smothering the light of the crescent moon.

"You keep asking yourself that question, Harry," I replied. "I'll keep asking it, too."

* * *

I was in the trunk of the Lincoln for another six hours, give or take half an hour. I'm pretty good at estimating the passage of time, even when I'm not wearing a watch—even when I'm at my wits' end with fright. But I couldn't have guessed which direction we were traveling. For all I knew, we were now in any one of six different western states.

When the sun rose, none of its light seeped inside the trunk. Still, I could sense that it was lighter. Toward the end of the trip, the car turned onto a rough gravel road and my body was jolted back and forth. The Lincoln began climbing what seemed like switchbacks on a mountain. Was I to be imprisoned in some remote mountain cabin?

I'd exhausted every speculation about where they were taking me or why I'd been kidnapped. I decided it couldn't be for money; surely they knew that my father was in jail. Only one thing seemed obvious: these men were somehow connected with my father—enemies that he had never told us about. My father may have been innocent of murder, but he was still a man of many mysteries. I no longer knew him. Not that this mattered. It looked unlikely that I would ever see him—or anyone else in my family—again.

At last the car rolled to a stop on the rocky surface. I heard another vehicle—the van—pull to a stop behind us. Both engines cut out. Car doors opened. I heard muffled voices. Finally someone shouted, "Unload it all! All of it!" Then the trunk flipped up, spraying morning sunlight into my face. It couldn't have been much past 7:00 a.m.

Marcos looked in at me. His face was more discernible now. I couldn't quite place his nationality. The complexion was dark; I could only guess Mexican. His eyes were vividly clear, but the wrinkles around them were deep, despite his young age, as if he'd spent a lot of time squinting at the sun.

At first he acted sympathetic. "How are you?"

I answered timidly. "Okay."

His expression stiffened, as if he'd remembered that it was pointless to show me any sympathy. In his hands he held a key. Reaching toward my ankles, he unlocked the manacles and removed them. He was about to unlock my hands when another face appeared—an older man. His nose was long and sharp. The dark leather of his face tightened and rippled on his skull.

"Leave her hands until we get inside the cave," he commanded.

"But she might trip and injure herself," said Marcos.

"She's your responsibility," said the man gruffly. "If she injures herself in any way that hinders her ability to travel, she will be killed, and so will you."

"Yes, Lord," Marcos replied submissively.

Lord? *Such a lofty title. Or maybe it was just his name, like Lord Byron or some such.*

Marcos helped me out of the trunk. The blood rushed back into my legs and I leaned on the car for support. We were on a mountain top. I didn't recognize the location. There were six other men besides Marcos and "Lord." I recognized one of them—the man with the gaping holes in his cheeks. At first I thought he'd been affected by a kind of leprosy . . . surely someone wouldn't intentionally inflict such wounds. Then I realized there were also gaping holes pierced in his nostrils and ears, as if to support heavy jewelry. Through the holes under each corner of his mouth I could see through to his teeth, even when his lips were shut. Eating oatmeal must have been a very messy affair for this guy.

The men unloaded supplies from the van—backpacks, flashlights, food, canteens, ropes. I asked Marcos hesitantly, "Are we going on a hike?" He ignored me and gathered up one of the backpacks. Four of the other men did the same. The remaining two men approached "Lord" and knelt before him. Did I say knelt? These guys practically kissed the dirt at his feet! They wouldn't look at his face. Their arms stretched out before them. Their noses nudged the soil.

They said in unison, "Lord, my Lord, my great Lord Jacob, son of the great moon goddess, earthkeeper of the keys of the heavens and the underworlds . . ."

"I grant you permission to depart," Jacob said, hurrying them along. "But mark my saying: I will return. And when I return, you will have the honor of serving me forever. Watch for the signs in the heavens."

"We will watch for the signs, Lord Jacob," said one of them.

"Now go."

I'd never seen a more ridiculous display—two grown men in jeans and sunglasses behaving like primitives! And this man, this Lord Jacob, was lapping it up. These were very weird people. Images of Charles Manson, Jim Jones and David Koresh flashed in my mind.

The two men glanced at Marcos and nodded their good-byes. One of the men climbed into the Lincoln, the other into the van. The vehicles wheeled around and crept back down the mountain.

Jacob, weighted down with nothing but the clothes on his back, started toward a cliff line along a promontory of the mountain. The others fol-

lowed without uttering a word. Marcos took me by the arm. Walking was awkward with my hands locked in front of me, and Marcos held me up with difficulty. According to Jacob, it would mean his life as well as my own if I sprained an ankle.

We came upon the rotting remains of a wooden walkway. We walked beneath it. The hillside was very steep; if I was to injure myself, this was the place to do it. Marcos kept me from losing my footing. A flight of moss-covered stairs had been cut into the rocky cliff. We rounded a bend and descended onto a stone platform. Facing us was the gaping mouth of a cave, its entrance barred by a steel gate with peeling red paint. The man with the holes in his face removed a key from his pocket. He muttered something under his breath as he unlocked the padlock on the chain. I couldn't hear the words, but it struck me as some kind of chant, as if the cave had some kind of religious significance.

The men proceeded inside. Marcos nudged me along. After one step, I stopped cold, prepared to collapse if Marcos tried to force me.

"No!" I cried. "I'm not going in there—not until someone tells me what's going on! Not until someone—!"

Reaction was swift, like a serpent's strike. The man who had unlocked the gate struck me across the face. I fell on the stones. No one had hit me in the face since Alyssa Mosbacker in the second grade. For a moment I was too stunned for tears, but then the tears came.

"No one speaks in the presence of His Majesty, Lord Jacob of the Moon, without first receiving permission!" the miserable little man barked.

Now it was "His Majesty"! This man was a king, a Lord, a keeper of the heavens and the underworlds. The only title I hadn't heard applied to him was "Mr. President."

Marcos looked as though he wanted to help me, but he didn't dare. Lord Jacob himself stepped toward me.

"You'll make no demands here, Melody Hawkins. Your old life has ended. If you do what you are told, you will eat. If you speak when you are spoken to, you will drink. If you disobey, you will be punished swiftly and harshly. Understand?"

I refused to lift my eyes. "Yes."

The man who hit me spoke again. "You will answer King Jacob in this manner: Yes, Lord, my Lord, my great Lord."

I looked up. My eyes pressed into those of King Jacob. It seemed as if another person—certainly not me—replied, "Then do what you're going to do. Get it over with. Because I will never *call this man Lord."*

Eyebrows shot up all around me. I have no idea where I found the courage to say such a thing. The words spoke themselves from deep inside my soul.

Incensed, the miserable little man with holes in his face raised his hand to strike again. Marcos caught his arm.

"No more, Balam," said Marcos. "You'll make her too ill to travel. We did not come all this way and endure all that we have endured to leave her dead along the trail—especially when we are so close to the prize."

Balam looked at Jacob, whose eyes had narrowed to the size of coin slots. Jacob pressed his nose in Marcos' face, challenging him to make some unwise gesture. Abjectly, Marcos lowered his eyes. Jacob backhanded him in the mouth. The blow did not seem even as violent as the one I'd received, but Marcos fell backwards. Out of courtesy, it seemed.

I felt what Marcos had said was true. I still didn't know why I'd been kidnapped, but it didn't seem logical that they should go to such pains and then so casually threaten my life. The threats were empty. My life was secure, at least until we got to wherever we were going.

Jacob blustered at Marcos. "You will teach her the proper ways, or the gods will drink your blood as well."

"Yes Lord."

"Do not think that because you are my firstborn son, you are inviolable."

"Yes Lord."

"If you have to carry her all the way to Jacobugath, so be it."

"Yes, great Lord."

And with that, Jacob and the others descended into the cave. Marcos looked at me longingly, wondering if I would, in fact, force him to carry me. I stood up awkwardly and felt my left ear. There was a little blood, and the earring was missing. I wondered if the pierce had been ripped clean through, but the injury didn't seem quite so bad. Just a scrape. I ventured into the cavern on my own accord. I did not want Marcos, or any of these other ogres, to touch me. But that wasn't the only reason I decided to cooperate. I did not miss the emphasis Jacob had used when he said "the gods will drink your blood as well."

Although I prayed I'd misunderstood, it appeared as if the principal victim he'd been referring to—the one whose blood was already listed on the divine menu—was me.

CHAPTER 12

It was all I could do to keep from rocketing across the lonely Wyoming landscape at ninety miles an hour. But I couldn't risk alerting a radar gun, so the speedometer never rose a single notch above fifty-five. Until I reached the cavern entrance on Cedar Mountain, I would do absolutely nothing to draw attention.

Despite all my efforts, we picked up a patrol car as we passed through the tiny municipality of Shoshoni. I looked around for a speed limit sign, fearing I'd missed one. Perhaps I'd accelerated too fast when I left the city limits. The sun had barely crept out from behind the hills, and as far as I could tell, I was the only other vehicle on the road. The policeman seemed to be following us out of sheer boredom.

Five miles later, the patrol car continued its steady pursuit. I kept my speedometer around fifty-three, my heart pumping wildly. Was I driving too slowly? By reputation, the speed limit along this stretch of highway toward the Wind River Canyon was the most abused in the state. Anyone driving less than seventy was considered abnormal. At last, the patrol car finally pulled onto the shoulder and flipped a U-turn.

Around 9:00 a.m., we entered the city limits of my old hometown, Cody, Wyoming. I hadn't been back here since my mother's funeral, a very tense weekend. My wife had been hospitalized only the week before; I'd flown in that morning and was back at my wife's bedside by evening. Because of the circumstances, I felt I'd never really had a chance to properly mourn my mother's death. Such were my thoughts as we passed before the houses and storefronts that had changed so much and yet so little since my boyhood.

We pulled into the Wal-Mart on the West Cody strip. Until now, I'd procrastinated offering Steffanie and Harry any explanations. Even Steff, the more solicitous of the two, had abandoned her efforts to leech information out of me, granting that when I was ready to talk, I'd talk. I suppose I was afraid that if I told my children we were about to climb inside a cave and emerge back in ancient America, they'd decide Dad really *was* insane and spring from the car the instant we hit a stoplight.

I wrote up a list: flashlights, canteens, matches, candles, rope, and at least two cheap backpacks. The list included a change of clothes for each of us, preferably denim jeans (I listed my sizes) and enough food to survive three days. Nothing too bulky. I suggested trail mix.

"Are we escaping into the mountains, Dad?" Harry asked.

"Close enough," I replied.

Fearing I might be recognized, I sent the children into the store without me. I hoped Sabrina's $240 (minus $25 for gas and $7 for a mini-mart breakfast) would stretch far enough to buy everything we needed.

I avoided eye contact with people walking in and out of the store. Almost thirty minutes after the kids disappeared inside Wal-Mart, a white pickup planted itself in the stall next to mine. The driver, a man about my age wearing a Colorado Rockies cap, glanced at me, nodded, and walked on. Then he did a double take.

"Jim? Jim Hawkins? Is that you?" He edged up for a closer look. "I don't believe it! It *is* you!"

I hadn't seen Greg Shelby in thirteen years—not since our ten-year high school reunion. All I remembered about him from the reunion was that he was the first one to get drunk and pass out. My fondest memories of Greg Shelby went back to the seventh grade, the very day that I befriended Garth Plimpton. Garth was sort of a nerd back then, and Shelby insulted me for being seen with him. His final statement suggested that Garth and I were "made for each other." This made it necessary for me to give him the shiner of his life in the parking lot of the Cody Bowling Alley.

"How are you, Shelby?" I said reservedly. Amazing how after twenty-seven years, he was still "Shelby" to me. I couldn't remember ever having called him Greg.

"What brings you to town?" He didn't wait for me to answer. "I heard about that trouble you got yourself in out in Salt Lake."

Obviously Cody, Wyoming, was still in the broadcast range of Salt Lake's news channels.

"Sounded like a bum deal," he continued.

I nodded. "It was."

We stared at one another for an uncomfortably long moment. In an instant I realized that Shelby had been following the whole story. He knew everything, including the report that had no doubt jammed the broadcasts since last night.

"So, do you need anything?" he inquired, pretending we were old and bosom friends. Actually, we'd had very little to do with each other since that day at the bowling alley. In high school, we nearly had it out again outside the gym during our Junior Prom.

"No," I replied. "Thanks for asking."

"Well, hey, it's good to see you again."

"Good to see you, too."

Shelby continued toward the store entrance, his steps uncertain, as if he was trying to decide what to do. Before going in, he peeked back at me one last time, smiled, and waved.

The glare was bright on Wal-Mart's glass front doors. However, when the next customer emerged, I glimpsed Shelby standing by the pay phone, the receiver at his ear, speaking excitedly. So after twenty-seven years, our grudge-match continued.

I glanced at my watch. Ten seconds later, I glanced at it again. What was keeping the kids? I opened the door, prepared to charge inside, pink sweats or no pink sweats. Finally, Steffanie appeared. Harry was right behind her, pushing a shopping cart full of supplies.

"Let's go! Let's go! Let's go!" I cried.

The supplies were tossed haphazardly into the back seat. I turned the ignition and reversed out of the parking stall. Shelby stepped out onto the sidewalk as we sped away.

"What did we get?" I asked, driving over the speed limit for the first time since we had left Salt Lake.

"Everything on the list," said Steff. "Only one dollar and twenty-two cents left."

"Did you get the rope?" I asked.

"We weren't sure what kind of rope you meant," said Harry. "Is clothesline okay?"

"It'll work. Dig it out and tie knots every ten or so inches for at least five yards."

"Don't you think it's time to tell us where we're going?" asked Steffanie.

I pointed up at Cedar Mountain. "See that road that switchbacks all the way to the top?"

Steffanie's eyes bugged. "We're going up *there?*"

"Yup. Provided, of course, that we don't meet any cops."

We *did* see a patrol car, sirens blasting, lights blazing, coming from the other direction, but it whizzed by without slowing down. The Winnebago driving ahead of us shielded our car from view.

Three minutes later, we turned off the highway and began our ascent up the slope of Cedar Mountain. The dirt road was in better shape than I remembered. Back when I was a kid, it took no less than a four-wheel drive with extra-high clearance to traverse it. On a few corners we met some muddy stretches from spring runoff, but the Subaru navigated them splendidly. I noticed fresh tire tracks in patches of mud. Several other vehicles had recently made this same climb. I felt closer to Melody now than I'd felt for the last ten hours.

Near the top, the road forked. We took the lower fork. After driving another twenty yards, I noticed a thick bank of saplings below the road. I stopped the car.

"Let's unload," I said.

We organized all the gear, stuffing everything into the two backpacks. I took a portion of the nylon clothesline and bundled up the two Indian blankets. I was glad Harry had brought his Boy Scout knife, as it hadn't occurred to me to add a knife to the list. I told the kids not to pack the rope and flashlights; we'd need them right away.

"Are we going in a cave?" asked Harry.

"You guessed it," I confirmed.

I climbed back into the car and maneuvered the hood to aim downhill. Then I stuck it in neutral and asked the kids to help me push.

Steffanie struggled to comprehend all this. "We're sending the car down there? But what if we need it later?"

"We won't," I replied.

Harry got a kick out of watching the Subaru bounce into the thicket of saplings. Some trees were uprooted; most sprang right back. It crashed into some larger cottonwoods beyond and stopped.

"Darn," said Harry. "I was hoping it would blow up, like in the movies."

Thank goodness it hadn't.

The trees hid most of the car from direct view. If anyone was looking for it, the trail of debris was obvious. But if they weren't, it might not be discovered for a long time, especially after the spring leaves filled in. It was the least I could do to try and keep Sabrina's name out of all this mess.

The scenery as we walked toward the cliff line was exactly as I remembered it from twenty-seven years before. The ruined walkway looked only slightly more ruined than before. The mossy steps still cut into the rock; the stone platform still lay at the mouth of the cavern; and a rusty gate continued to bar the entrance to Frost Cave. I stood there for several seconds, reminiscing in nostalgia.

"We're going in there? Kool!" said Harry.

"But why?" moaned Steff.

"Because that's where we'll find Melody," I said.

"In a *cave?*" Steff cried. "How do you *know* this?"

"Because the men who kidnapped her came from in there."

"What are they? Neanderthals?"

I almost answered her in the affirmative.

"How do we get inside?" asked Harry.

"We just climb." I noticed something disturbing. The space at the top of the gate—the space I had slipped through as a child—had been blocked with a metal grating.

"Uh-oh," I whispered.

In high school, I had learned that getting a key to that gate was simply a matter of asking for it from the Bureau of Land Management, then signing a statement which indemnified them from responsibility. But because I remembered the space, I hadn't felt it would be necessary.

Harry examined the gate. He turned back gleefully. "It's not locked, Dad!"

He was right. Whoever had been here last forgot to pinch the padlock. If Jacob had left Salt Lake right after Melody was kidnapped, the last spelunkers had passed through here no more than two or three hours ago.

"All right, let's get going."

I turned back and noticed that Steffanie was crouched on the platform, picking something small and shiny out of the dirt.

"What is it?" I asked.

For several seconds, Steffanie could not reply. She said with difficulty, "An earring . . . with a little dolphin and a cubic zirconium. It's been broken." She looked up at me with hope in her eyes. "It's Melody's."

I examined it closely. There appeared to be a drop of dried blood on the stem. I glared into the mouth of the cavern, my veins boiling. They had hurt my baby daughter.

So here the wondrous journey would begin—the grand quest for my daughter's life. A journey into the tender memories of my childhood and toward an unknowable future that could only be brighter than the one I had left. I was abandoning a world that had gone totally wrong for us. But could the prospects be so much better in the mysterious and ancient world of the Nephites?

We entered the cavern. The last light of the modern century dwindled and then extinguished behind us. At that moment, I wondered if I would ever return here. A lump came into my throat; I swallowed it hard and went on. Before us now loomed endless tunnels through solid rock and darkness. At the end, we would find the light and spectacle of another age.

It was time to tell my children everything.

Part Two:

THE EXODUS OF ZARAHEMLA

CHAPTER 13

Only one candle burned now. The little flame flickered in a breeze that swept up from some indeterminable cavern depth, perhaps the same place where phantoms and the other laughing incarnations of Halloween originated. Shadows of stalactites and crystal formations contended for space on the surrounding walls.

My children watched the little flame in silence for a long time. They had listened to my tale with patient fascination. In unrestrained detail I recounted both times in my life when I had encountered the inhabitants of an ancient civilization. I admitted that Uncle Garth and Aunt Jenny had played an equal part in these encounters; and, for the first time, I also revealed the true reasons for Garth and Jenny's disappearance. Their aunt and uncle, I told them, had made this same journey through these caverns two years before.

Only Harrison interrupted to ask questions.

"Did you ever write down any of this stuff about Nephites and Lamanites and cursed swords?"

"Yes. I kept journals. They're in the attic."

"How come you never told us before?" he wondered.

"I did, in a roundabout way. Remember all those adventure stories at bedtime? The ones about Captain Teancum and the Hill Cumorah?"

"Those stories were *true?*" said Harry.

"More or less. I may have embellished some of my own heroics—for the story's sake, of course."

The little candle made Harry's eyes flicker with wonder. "This is *so kool!*" Then he glanced at me warily, one eye half shut. "This isn't gonna turn out like the tooth fairy, is it? Because I know you and Mom used to stuff those bills under my pillow."

"I assure you," I told him, "everything I've said is perfectly true."

Shortly after I had finished, Steffanie moved away from our tiny circle and curled herself up in the Indian blanket at the base of a gigantic stalagmite. I couldn't read her. She acted as if I'd just recited a chemistry lecture: interesting, but seemingly inapplicable to her life. And then I heard a sniffle. I could see that her cheeks were moist. Did she weep out of fright, dreading what might lie ahead? Or because she was convinced that her father had lost his mind?

Maybe she was just tired. We were all so miserably tired. It had been a long day of scaling steep descents and crawling through dusty passages. At least the hardest part was over—the part where we utilized the rope. We'd used it shortly after entering the cave. About fifty yards inside the entrance, the tunnel gave way to a gaping pit. Inside this pit, behind a narrow shelf in the cliff wall, unfolded the secret route that we had discovered when I was thirteen years old. Ten hours had elapsed since my children and I had scaled the walls of that pit and begun our long journey into pristine passages that beckoned forever downward. Now, every muscle in our bodies ached. Our kneecaps throbbed from multiple bruises.

Harry dropped off to sleep quickly, his mind swimming with visions of Lamanites and Nephites. I slid over next to my daughter at the base of the stalactite and began stroking her hair.

She wiped away a tear. "Dad," she whispered, "how much further are we going?"

"All the way," I replied.

Steffanie was silent. I could tell that things hadn't quite sunk in for her yet. It reminded me of the first time Renae and I had gathered the children in the living room to tell them about the cancer. Our words were plain enough, but it just wasn't real. The concept that one day Mom might not be there to cook their breakfast or tuck them in at night was incomprehensible. My stories about the Nephites were equally difficult for her to digest.

"We're getting closer," I added encouragingly. "We'll sleep for a couple of hours. After that, five or six more hours—tops."

"We're so deep already," she said weakly.

"Don't worry," I assured. "I know exactly where we are. Now and then I see something familiar, like that crystal pillar over there. It all comes back."

She approached her next question with caution. "Did Mom ever . . . know all this stuff about Nephites and . . . ?" She stopped there.

"Your mother knew everything," I replied. "She was at my side almost every step of the way when I carried the Sword of Coriantumr to the Hill Cumorah."

Steffanie shook her head. "It's all just so . . . weird, Dad. Three times today I almost turned around and went back. If we hadn't found Melody's earring . . . I just don't know what I should do."

"What you should do is stay here with us," I said adamantly. "Don't you think you're safer here? There may be people still in Salt Lake looking for you and Harry. As long as you're with me, I won't let anything happen to you."

"You can't promise that," she contended. "Nobody could. You don't know what's going to happen. What if they're waiting to ambush us somewhere in the cave? What if they're listening to us right now? Even our whispers echo in this place."

I leaned back against the stalactite and sighed. "I'm doing the best I can, honey. We have to have a little faith. We have to believe that God is watching over us, helping us."

Steffanie huffed. "He hasn't helped us much before now."

"Of course He has," I insisted. "Why would you say such a thing?"

She shrugged. "I dunno, Dad. Sometimes I wonder if there is a god."

I almost choked. "How long have you wondered this?"

"All along, I guess."

I arose and began pacing anxiously. Had I really just heard what I thought I'd heard? How can a kid go to church for fourteen years—how can they join in family prayers ever since they were old enough to speak—and not believe in God?

Steffanie placated me. "Don't have a cow, Dad. I believe in God, okay? I was just kidding."

"What about everything I've been saying? If we really end up back in Book of Mormon times, that proves that the Book of Mormon is true, right? Doesn't it also prove that there's a God?"

She turned away. "If you say so, Dad."

I was nearly beside myself. How could any daughter of mine be an atheist? To me, the very sun in the sky was evidence enough of God's existence. I never understood why this wasn't obvious to everyone.

I sat beside her again, trying to be calm. "Talk to me, Steffanie. What caused you to feel this way?"

"Nothing *caused* me to feel this way. It's just how I feel. If there really is a passageway to another world through this cave, I'm sure there's a logical explanation. It might even be one of the greatest scientific discoveries of our age."

"But it wouldn't prove there's a God?"

"I don't know. Not necessarily."

I began mumbling to myself. "How can I be hearing this? It's too incredible . . ."

"I knew you'd freak out if I told you how I really felt," Steffanie snapped. "Remind me not to tell you my true feelings anymore. If you don't mind, I'd like to go to sleep now, Dad. Just let me get some sleep."

"All right," I said. "All right. Get some sleep. We'll talk about this later."

"I'm sure we will."

She closed her eyes and her body went perfectly still, as if sleep had overcome her instantly. I climbed under the Indian blanket with Harry, wondering what I could say to my daughter tomorrow. Wondering if I could say anything at all. Wondering where I had gone wrong as a parent.

Finally, my thoughts turned back to Melody. I drifted off to sleep wondering what fate might lie ahead for my little family.

* * *

Once I stayed up late and watched an old movie called The Mole People *about a secret civilization living underground. The movie was pretty bad, but I was still impressionable enough that mole people visited me in my nightmares. As Marcos and the others guided me deeper and deeper into the mountain, I kept imagining a city of mole people greeting us around the very next bend.*

Marcos removed the handcuffs shortly after we entered the cave. I needed my hands to climb. Besides, most of the tunnels were too thin for me to try and slip past him and escape.

We continued our downward spiral into the heart of the mountain for hours. I felt certain someone would mercifully allow us to stop and rest at any moment. But we just kept on going—another passage, another slope, another bend. After a while, my mind began to wander; my movements became automated. And still Marcos prodded me on. When Marcos let up, Jacob or Balam prodded him. *My internal clock for estimating the passage of time went on the fritz. Had it been twelve hours? Thirteen? Fourteen? Twenty?*

Finally, I collapsed.

When I awoke, the sun was beating down. Yellow butterflies swirled about my head, and I smelled pine. Marcos stood nearby. He noticed that I'd opened my eyes.

"She's awake," he informed the others.

Jacob's voice boomed from somewhere above my head. "Good. Put the collar around her neck and bring her to the head of the company. And have her change into more dignified clothing. You would do well to follow this advice yourself, Marcos. From this time henceforth, we will see to her every comfort."

"Yes, my Lord."

Comfort? I was supposed to feel comfort as I was paraded about with a collar around my neck?

My thoughts came into better focus. I was surrounded by many men—hundreds of them!—wearing only a single cloth around their waists, one end falling in front and one behind. Most of them were perfectly bald, except for a lone braid at the back of the head. Their arms, legs, and cheekbones were painted red, as was a circle around their navel.

I saw Balam. He'd shed his shirt and jeans. He now wore a red pullover with black designs on the trim. The holes in his face bore the weight of various ornaments. From his lower lip hung crystals with blue feathers. From his cheek dangled a chain and a pair of golden half-moons. From his ears hung what looked like the skulls of small animals, rodents or birds. The teeth and crowns of these little skulls were plated with gold, and the eyes were plugged with polished green gems. I was surprised that the weight of it didn't tear the skin. He grinned as he saw my eyes widen in astonishment.

Everyone in the crowd stared at me as if I were a circus freak. I started to rise and they backed away.

"Do not fear!" Marcos called out to them. He said to me privately, "They have never seen a girl with such pale skin. They think you are supernatural, like Shabba, the demon seductress who leads men into the forest and causes them to lose their way."

I was hardly hearing him. My heart was racing, my eyes darting this way and that. The land was tropical! The birds, the humidity, the leafy hillside—tropical! There were pine trees—a kind I'd never seen before—sprawling up the side of the mountain. Did I say mountain? Smoke billowed out of the top. It was a volcano!

A kind of terror gripped me that I'd never experienced before, as if I'd been abducted by aliens and taken to a world a million light years from Earth, with no hope of ever returning.

"What's going on?" my voice screeched. "Where are we?"

I noticed a cave entrance along the jagged hillside, partially hidden by hanging vines. A troop of twenty or thirty men were rolling an enormous boulder across the entrance. But it couldn't be the same cavern—could it?

"Welcome to Melek," said Marcos.

"Melek?" My knees felt weak; my hands were trembling. Marcos saw that I was about to faint again. He took my arm.

"You're a long way from home, Miss Hawkins."

My teeth began chattering. "W-what c-country is this?"

"I already told you. Melek. But we won't be here long. Our journey's just begun."

"Are we still . . . is it still . . . America?" I almost said "Earth," but in my mind the question just sounded too absurd. Either way, I was totally uncertain of the answer.

Marcos laughed wryly. "I'm afraid not. At least not any America you know."

I wondered if I'd fallen into some sort of coma. "H-how l-long was I unconscious?"

"Twenty-five minutes or so."

"But that can't—"

Marcos grew impatient. He came out with it all at once. "We're not even in your century anymore, Melody Hawkins. The Omnipotent One—ruler of death and night—carried us through the tunnels of Akmul to another realm. We've gone back. Two thousand years back. Don't worry. You'll get used to it."

Get used to it? Did he think it was like moving to a new neighborhood, or setting back the clock for daylight savings?

My hands felt deathly cold, yet perspiration dripped down my back. All the blood rushed into my legs. It felt like the end of a cartoon where reality fades to a small circle of light in the middle of the screen. And then only a pinpoint. And then nothing.

My body was slipping into shock.

CHAPTER 14

Cocooned in our Indian blankets, we slept about four hours. It was nearly as cold here in the cave as it had been on the Wyoming plains with Sabrina's broken car window. I promised the children we'd find warmth again very soon. Our journey then continued as we descended the tunnels in silence. Toward the end, even Harrison's eager eyes began to lose their sparkle. Once I caught Steffanie glance covertly back up the passageway, tempted again to abandon us and return to the modern world.

I took her hand reassuringly. "I guarantee you, Steff, we'll get out of here much sooner by going forward than backward."

"Promise me," she said, "if we don't reach the end soon, we'll turn around."

I frowned. "Please, honey. We can't give up now. We're so close."

Actually, I had no idea how close we were. After all, it had been twenty-seven years. Now and then, something would look vaguely familiar—a dripping stalactite, a bed of crystals—but I couldn't be certain.

Finally we dropped down into a triangular room that thinned into a tiny crawl space. Suddenly, I knew *exactly* where we were.

"Hey, it's nice in here!" Harry observed.

A current of thermal air slapped our faces. The source of warmth was a narrow tunnel leading upward, barely large enough for me to squeeze through. I'd stood here before when I was a much shorter person and didn't have to bend my knees. Garth and Jenny were at my side.

"We made it," I said.

The beams of our flashlights blazed the way as we climbed into the tight passageway. Within moments, we were able to stand erect again. Our flashlight beams lost all definition, smothered by a source of natural light.

"Turn off your flashlights," I told the children.

We stood on the brink of a great expanse. The surface of my children's faces swarmed with a thousand sparkles of iridescent light. As far as the eye could see, the walls were alive with cascades of pure, foaming water, all of which gathered into a wide and icy rush fifty feet below. The river was finally sucked into a narrow underground conduit, re-emerging, as I remembered, in the middle of a blue-green lake surrounded by a black-green jungle.

"Kids," I said, my voice like a ringmaster, "may I present to you, the Rainbow Room." The words "Rainbow Room" echoed twice, thrice, four times.

"I've never seen anything so beautiful . . ." Steffanie mumbled.

"It's like Christmas lights," added Harry. "What makes it glow like that?"

"I'm not sure," I said. "Some kind of phosphorescence."

Such was my best guess. I'd only seen phosphorescent minerals once, in a black light display at the natural history museum in Vernal, Utah. Compared to this, the display in Vernal was like a candle in the midst of a thousand search lights.

Harry started forward onto the chalky, crystalline ledge to peer over the cliff into the swirling river. I nabbed him by the collar and yanked him back.

"That shelf out there is about two inches thick," I scolded. "You'd fall right through. Believe me, I know."

"So where are the jungles, and the pyramids, and the Nephites?" asked Harry.

I mussed his hair. "Just wait, kid. Soon you'll see enough Nephites to last you a lifetime."

I led the children into a honeycomb of tunnels to our right. I had no intention of having my family cannonball into the river and enter the Nephite world in the same manner as I had when I was thirteen years old. Garth, Jenny, and I had nearly drowned. And yet I wasn't quite certain how to proceed from here to find the exit. Years ago, when we had journeyed back to the twentieth century, we had climbed up through a muggy cavern at the base of a volcano. But as I recalled, that old return route hadn't taken us directly through the Rainbow Room. And yet a passage connecting the two tunnels couldn't be very far. When I was a kid, I remembered hearing the rush of the underground river through the walls.

We poked in and out of various passages for another hour before I realized we were traveling in circles. I could now freely admit to myself that we were seriously lost. I'd even lost my bearings with respect to relocating the Rainbow Room. That's when we found the arrow.

At a certain fork in the tunnel, we noticed that someone had broken off a dozen tiny stalactites from the low ceiling and arranged them on the floor in the shape of an arrow. The arrangement might have lain there undisturbed for a thousand years. I suspected, however, that it had been arranged by Garth and Jenny two years before, or perhaps by Muleki, the son of Teancum, on his homeward journey eighteen years ago.

We set out in the direction indicated by the arrow and soon found ourselves shin-deep in black, greasy water. The air became stale and muggy, pungent with the odor of dead and rotting things. It was hard to breathe. But we pushed on, and within a couple hundred yards we stepped out onto dry ground.

All at once, my senses awakened. I was engulfed by a sense of familiarity; I'd been here before. As we walked on, the tunnel started to open up wider and wider. And then—

And then it came to a solid dead end.

"Well that's weird," observed Harry.

"We're trapped!" whimpered Steffanie.

I felt along the wall. "I don't understand. This is *it.* The cave opened up *right here.* I'm certain of it." For the first time, my voice betrayed a hint of panic.

"Dad!" Harry cried. "Come over here!"

My son lay down on his back, pointing upward toward a fissure in the ceiling. I knelt down and gazed up into the narrow slit.

"Do you see them, Dad?"

"Yes," I replied. "I see them."

"See what?" asked Steff.

Harry and I answered in unison: "Stars!"

Three specks of yellowish light were visible through the breach.

Steffanie joined us, lying next to Harry on the cavern floor. "I don't see any stars."

Curiously, the stars had disappeared. Where had they gone?

"A cloud moved over them," said Harry. "That is, *under* them. There! See?"

One speck revealed itself.

"Then we really *are* trapped," concluded my ever-positive daughter.

I realized this was Jacob's doing. Melody's kidnappers had blocked the entrance with a large boulder. They'd likely been obstructing it in this fashion for decades. No wonder Gadiantons had been the only ones to use the time bridge for the last twenty-seven years. But the fact that Jacob had rolled such a massive boulder over the entrance made it obvious that he was traveling with considerably more men than I'd previously thought. An entire army of loyal Gadiantons must have greeted him as he emerged.

I boosted Harry toward the ceiling. He found some footholds, removed the pocketknife from his pocket, and began to chop at the rocks and vines that had been pinched at the place where the gap was sealed. Steff and I shielded our faces from the falling debris.

"I think I can dig our way out!" Harry announced.

So we set the mole to work. After twenty minutes, the first knife blade broke. There were two smaller blades remaining. I climbed up and took Harry's place. I clawed with my fingers almost as much as I used the knife, and dirt grimed up my fingernails. At last, several large stones began pulling loose. Two hours later, just as claustrophobia was starting to get the better of me, I broke through. The stars became visible again—as well as a blazing white moon, low on the horizon. It was nearly morning.

"I'm through!" I called down.

The children sent up a cheer.

I pushed my head out of the hole and sucked in a breath of pure, refreshing air. It took a moment for my senses to regain their grasp of distance and proximity. And then it rushed in all at once.

The world seemed impossibly rich and clear, almost incomprehensible. So many shapes, hues, and sensations. For a moment it was as if the scales had fallen from my eyes, and I viewed the world with the clarity God took back from the first human beings. Toward the eastern sky, a warm band of magenta light rested against a silhouette of tall volcanic cones. To the north spread a horizon of older, softer mountains. In the middle distance rested an immense basin rippled with lesser hills and pillows of motionless, pink clouds in their pockets. My first view of the Nephite world in nearly three decades was breathtaking.

I dropped back inside, so saturated with excitement that I was actually trembling. I lifted Harry up into the gap. Then I boosted Steffanie, and then the gear. The gap was tight and slick. The three of us squirming out of that hole, our bodies encrusted in mud, must have looked like zombies rising from the grave.

When I popped through the second time, the children already stood down on level ground, their faces aglow with enchantment. Steffanie spun in a circle like Julie Andrews in the opening scene of *The Sound of Music,* while Harry laughed delightedly at her mud-smeared face and hair. I climbed down and joined them. The three of us embraced.

"It really *is* a new world," Steffanie declared.

I presented to her the glorious morning panorama with a sweep of my arm. "Can you see God out there now?"

She tilted her head and smiled coyly. "I love you, Dad." Best, she decided, not to spoil the moment with an argument.

The moon fell off the edge of the world, and was replaced by a radiant sun. Bird sounds, timid at first, began rising in volume like a warming orchestra.

I examined the immediate area. The ground around the cavern had been used as an encampment for a large number of men: half-buried pit fires, animal bones, and other assorted rubbish lay everywhere. The ashes in the pit fires were still warm; King Jacob's army had probably departed last night. It shouldn't have surprised me that Gadiantons would travel under cover of darkness.

We gathered up the gear and began our hike into the valley. Soon we came upon a clear-water spring surrounded by high ferns and sprays of small white flowers, like daisies. We washed ourselves as best we could in the gurgling water and refilled our canteens. The kids pulled the Wal-Mart tags off our brand new clothes. I was more than glad to get out of Sabrina's pink sweats.

"So where are we going first?" Harry asked.

I pointed into the valley. "Somewhere under that pocket of clouds is a small city. A Lamanite settlement."

"Lamanites?" said Harry with alarm.

"Good Lamanites," I clarified. "They call themselves Ammonites. They were converted to Christ by the sons of Mosiah. The name of the settlement is Lamoni."

"Why are we going there?" Steffanie wondered.

"For one thing," I said, shaking the near-empty bag of trail mix, "we need food. We've gone through this like a pack of chipmunks. For another, we might find your Aunt Jenny."

"What about Uncle Garth?" asked Steffanie.

"Maybe Garth, too," I said with less confidence. "And we might find out if someone in Lamoni knew about the Gadiantons who camped at the base of the volcano. They may know where these Gadiantons came from. Then we'll know where they took Melody."

Despite their exhaustion, the children were invigorated by my promise that Lamoni was only a short jaunt into the valley. When I'd made this hike with the Prophet Helaman twenty-seven years before, it had taken us only two hours. But that was uphill. I anticipated introducing my children to their first true-blue Lamanites within the hour.

Would they remember me? I wondered if the story of Garth and me serving as interpreters for Captain Teancum had become a minor legend. Maybe not important enough to have been included in the Book of Mormon or anything, but still a tale handed down for a generation or two. Garth and Jenny may have already reaped a hero's honors. The mere mention of my name might stir up feelings of deepest reverence in the hearts of the first people we met. It might be fun to watch my children swell with pride—especially Harry, who sometimes felt I was so dull that he had to invent stories to impress his friends. Soon he would learn that dear ol' Dad was a living legend.

My estimate for reaching Lamoni was right on. In thirty minutes we could see a web of human settlement in the valley below, partially hidden by morning mist. It appeared to radiate out from a central plaza—the same plaza where I remembered a large synagogue had stood. The size of the tiny village appeared to have doubled.

We discovered a footpath between a pair of twin hills. The hill on our right hid any further view of Lamoni for the next twenty minutes. I recognized this part of the trail now. Shortly beyond this ridge the foliage would thin, then we would come upon our first Lamanite hut. This would be the home wherein I'd once met one of the greatest missionaries the world has ever known. Ammon had been very old and feeble at the time; by now he'd surely passed away. Maybe his hut had been turned into some kind of shrine, like George Washington's home at Mount Vernon, or the Beehive House of Brigham Young.

As the foliage started to clear, my lungs filled with anticipation. I broke into a run. I was thirteen years old again.

"Come on!" I called to my children. We scampered along the footpath.

"How come all the corn is burned?" Harry asked, but I didn't pay him any attention. My focus continued straight ahead, awaiting the appearance of Ammon's hut.

Then I saw it, and my spine went rigid.

Only a charred center pole of the entire edifice was left standing. The adobe walls lay in a crumbled, blackened heap. Lizards scurried over the cold remains. The path to the front door, once boasting a dozen varieties of colorful flowers, was now choked with weeds.

"What happened, Dad?" asked Harry.

I shook my head in consternation.

All along the road leading into the settlement, the vision was the same. House after house, building after building, was transformed into a graveyard of burned-out debris. Animal pens had been torn down. Pottery shards and broken tools lay scattered about the streets. Harry found a child's leather sandal in the dust. He lifted it up and rolled it in his hands.

The city of Lamoni was dead.

The destruction looked recent—maybe within the last couple of weeks. Even the crops had been torched. A hundred acres of scorched and trampled corn stretched out from the city. An occasional blackbird fluttered up from the mangled stalks, its hunt for edible kernels on the roasted husks exhausted. My children didn't know what to think. They searched my eyes for answers. I had none to give them.

I noted that a haunting red symbol had been painted on every stone wall left standing—an abstract image of a fearsome beast with wide eyes and four snarling fangs. A jaguar.

An eerieness settled over me, a foreboding of what we might find next. The place was swarming with flies. Would we discover blackened corpses inside the buildings? We walked closely together for security. To my relief, there were no charred, unburied victims. If anyone had been killed, the bodies had long since been removed.

I experienced the keenest sensations of déjà vu. The first time I had entered an ancient village, when I was thirteen, it had also been abandoned, and its only occupant was a lone blind man. But the abandonment of that village had been voluntary; Lamoni had been the site of a merciless raid.

The city whose population had doubled looked as though it had disappeared in one fell swoop. Shortly we found ourselves in the central plaza, or what was left of it. The synagogue stood as a hollowed-out ghost. Jaguar symbols, like teenage gang graffiti, plastered the exterior of the soot-darkened walls, the red paint running in many places before it dried. Burning Lamoni had been a hit-and-run campaign. The attackers had been anxious to leave. The tactic of cowards, I decided.

"It's so terrible," said Steffanie. "Who would have done such a thing?"

I had a pretty good idea.

Steffanie and I entered the remains of the synagogue. Chunks of charcoal from the collapsed wooden roof crunched beneath our feet. Detailed stonework inside and around the doorway had been smashed and defaced, as if someone had been determined to erase all memory of this building's significance. In the middle of the synagogue sat a wide stone basin filled with ashes. It occurred to me that this structure may have been converted into a temple. The basin looked like an altar for performing the rites of the Law of Moses.

It was several minutes before Steff and I noticed that Harry had wandered off. My daughter groaned. "Leave it to Harry to goof around at a time like this."

We exited the ruined building and called Harry's name. There was no response. I began to worry. Suddenly my son dashed out from between two skeletal structures on the east end of the plaza, his legs pumping at full speed.

"Daaad!" he cried, his eyes wide with terror. He glanced back over his shoulder, as if something were pursuing him.

I opened my arms to receive him. "What is it?"

I heard the voices of his pursuers before I saw their faces. Within seconds, the east end of the plaza boiled with dozens of angry people. At first I thought the raiders had returned—the Gadiantons who had destroyed this village were back! But these natives were not men of Jacob. They were Lamanites, but they were no less inflamed with hatred and vengeance.

"There's two more of them!" someone shouted.

"Don't let them escape!" cried another.

"Kill them!" shouted a third. "Stone them!"

The men began to charge. We stood frozen with dread, my children clinging to my sides. My childhood memories of a peaceful fantasy land vanished in an instant.

The world of the Nephites had been turned upside down.

CHAPTER 15

We survived the moment only because someone suggested that we should rightly receive public humiliation before our execution.

"What is our crime?" I demanded. "What are we accused of doing?"

"You're robbers!" they spat. "And murderers!"

They were blaming us for the destruction of Lamoni. They thought we were *them*—Gadiantons! But how could they think this? Even if they blamed *me,* how could they blame a fourteen-year-old girl and a ten-year-old boy? What evidence made them so sure? To a mob foaming with hate, little evidence was necessary. We were strangers. Our nationality was strange. We wore strange clothing. This was all the evidence they needed.

My children were severely warned to keep silent. Steffanie looked up at me pleadingly, almost accusingly. How could I have brought them here? What delusion had convinced me that this place was some kind of paradise? How much time had passed? What year was it now? 20 B.C.? 10 B.C.? Had the Christ already been born? I suddenly wondered if I had been better off in my cell at the Salt Lake County Jail. At least my children were safer—well, two of them anyhow.

We were marched to the next city, two or three miles deeper into the valley. As it turned out, this was a much larger settlement than Lamoni, which in contrast seemed like a mere suburb. If the city had been here during my first sojourn in this land, I didn't remember it. They called it Laman, and it was the filthiest city I'd ever seen among Nephites or Lamanites. This surprised me. Thinking back, it had seemed to me that the Lamanite converts of Christ were among the cleanest, most industrious people I had ever known. Maybe the city's appearance had been affected by the influx of all the refugees from Lamoni. No; the buildings couldn't have dilapidated so quickly. But it was more than just the buildings and streets. The people themselves looked worn and coarse. There wasn't much life behind their eyes.

Hundreds of citizens turned out to watch as we were paraded down the main avenue of the city. I noted two classes of people in Laman: the filthy rich in their colorful garb who leered down from the windows and parapets of their two-story houses, occasionally shouting obscenities and insults; and the miserably poor, draped in shabby, moth-eaten pullovers, who had no shoes and stood at the edge of street, spitting and tossing garbage. When I was here before, I hadn't noticed any class distinction whatsoever among the converts of Ammon. There had been no poor at all.

There was something else I found strange. Many of the Lamanites looked physically different. The wealthy, as well as most of the poor under the age of thirty, had flattened foreheads and squinting eyes—almost cross-eyed!—as if the Lamanites of the last generation had interbred with an entirely different race of people.

Never in their lives had my children been subjected to such a gauntlet of abuse and humiliation. Their minds had barely started to adjust to the new and strange reality of where we were—and now this. They were frantic with fright; it must have seemed to them that our journey through the cavern had taken us into the very nucleus of hell. Harry managed to project some anger; when a boy his age stepped forward and pelted his shirt with a rotten wad of fruit, he scraped it off and flung it back into the youth's face. But this only inflamed the crowd further. I pulled Harry around to my other side to shield him from the shower of garbage that followed.

The procession stopped in the center of the marketplace. They forced us into one of several open-air cages. Jail in this town meant both incarceration and public display. The market itself was closed today. The stalls were empty; no merchants hawked their wares. Prisoners, it seemed, were the only attraction.

At present there was only one other captive besides ourselves. I thought perhaps I knew this man's nationality by the roundness of his features. He was a either a Nephite or a Mulekite, about thirty years old. A thick black crop of hair ran down to his shoulders. He watched us with a wary, examining eye as the Lamanites tied strong cords through the posts on the door of our wooden cage.

One of the ringleaders who had escorted us from Lamoni shouted to the crowd, "Get the chief! He will condemn them. Send round the proclamation! The robbers and the demon-prophet will be stoned together!"

A general cheer rose up and the people dispersed, but not before pelting us with a few more handfuls of garbage and dung. As the assailants emptied their hands, they would generally remind us how we had murdered a son or a brother or a friend. We gathered in the center of the cage. I put my arms around my children to protect them as best I could. In this position I could feel their trembling shoulders and rapidly pounding hearts.

"Why do they think we've done these things?" cried Steffanie. "Why don't they believe us?"

I shook my head. Could anyone comprehend the reasoning of a mob?

The last of the jeering crowd ebbed away. Guards were posted nearby, armed with clubs whose shafts were inset with obsidian blades, sharp as razors. I'd handled one of these weapons when I was a kid. They could cut a man in half.

I found it curious that the ringleader had used the word "chief." Among the Nephites and Lamanites, I'd heard leaders referred to as "kings" or "judges," even "chief judges." But the singular title of "chief" seemed unique—rather like an American Indian.

"What are they going to do to us, Dad?" Steffanie asked.

I pulled her head inside my arms. "I don't know."

Harry's spirits seemed surprisingly high. He, too, tried his hand at comforting his sister. "Everything'll be okay, Steff," he said. "Dad knows people here who can help us. Right, Dad?"

My face drooped. How was I supposed to answer? It was as if Harry had decided this whole thing was some kind of virtual reality game where you couldn't *really* get hurt. To convince him otherwise, all I would have had to show him was the welt on my back where I'd been pummeled by a corn husk.

"I don't know anyone anymore, son," I confessed.

Harry tried hard not to sound discouraged. "Well, it doesn't matter anyway. We'll be okay. I *know* we will." And with that sentiment, he plopped down in the corner of the cage just opposite the other prisoner. I hung my head, wondering if it would have been better if I had lied. Steffanie's sobbing abated a little. She settled into the other corner and began scraping the garbage off her clothes and shaking it out of her hair.

Harry gaped through the wooden bars at the man the Lamanites had declared a demon-prophet. The man sipped water from an earthenware bowl, and Harry licked his lips. We hadn't drunk anything since we left the fresh-water spring below the cavern, several hours back. Our canteens and the rest of our gear, including Harry's knife, had been confiscated.

The prisoner noticed Harry and leaned forward, wiping his mouth. "Are you thirsty, boy?"

Harry nodded.

The man maneuvered the bowl through the bars of his cage, careful not to spill, and extended his arm as far as he could. Harry stretched out to take it, but his reach was too short. My own arm made up the distance. There wasn't much water left. I urged Harry to share it with his sister. But the bowl wouldn't fit into our cage; the gaps between our bars were more tightly woven. Harry and Steff drank by holding the bowl outside the cage and pressing their faces into the gap, lips protruded.

I nodded to the Nephite. "Thank you."

He squinted one eye, as if taking aim at me down the barrel of a rifle. "Are you truly robbers?"

I shook my head. "No."

He sat back. "Neither am I a demon. But the people here can no longer discern the difference."

"Why do they say you're a demon?"

The Nephite reflected on the question a moment, surveying the vacant marketplace. "Because," he began, "I know their thoughts. I know their hearts. And I testified of these things." His face grew stern again. "If you're not a robber, what are you?"

I was a bit confused by the question. "An honest man," I replied. "A law-abiding citizen."

I was afraid his next question would be, "A law-abiding citizen of where?" I wasn't sure I was ready to discuss Frost Cave and time-tunnels. I might estrange my only potential ally.

The Nephite leaned forward. "Are you a Christian? Has the joy of our Lord, Jesus Christ, the Anointed One of Israel, entered your heart?"

His tone was almost chastising, as if he half expected me to wither in shame. This was likely the usual response he received at such a question. My children perked up. I could hardly contain my excitement.

"Yes!" I replied. "Who are you? What is your name?"

I fully expected to hear a name as familiar as Moroni or Helaman.

"I am Shemnon," said the Nephite.

"Shemnon?" I thought hard. "I'm afraid I . . . haven't heard of you."

It was a stupid thing to say, but Shemnon didn't appear offended.

"What is *your* name?" asked Shemnon.

Now was the moment of truth. Had my legend been handed down from generation to generation? "Jim Hawkins."

"I'm afraid I've never heard of you, either."

We were even.

"But I'm glad to know you now, Jimhawkins," he added. "Although I wish the circumstances had been better."

"This is my daughter, Steffanie. And my son, Harrison."

Harry whispered to me, "How come we can understand him? Don't Nephites and Lamanites speak a different language?"

"I'll explain later," I whispered back. It didn't seem timely to stop and explain to my son that the one certain phenomenon attending a time-traveler between our two centuries was a kind of natural "gift of tongues" (for lack of a better phrase). This ability seemed to attend anyone who came through the cavern, whether the individual was righteous or evil.

"Unusual names," Shemnon remarked. "Where are you from, Jimhawkins?"

"Utah," said Harry.

"Where?"

"Far away," I translated. I added one more footnote to make my answer at least geographically correct: "Beyond even the land northward."

Shemnon became animated. "Beyond the land northward? Since I was a child I have heard about the ships—the *sailing* ships that went north. Many say they were destroyed. Others say the Lord carried them to a new promised land. Is this Utah the land of Hagoth?"

Until he said Hagoth, I couldn't figure out what he was talking about. Now I got it. Shemnon thought we were somehow descendants of the Nephite peoples who had sailed north after the great war with Amaliakiah and Ammoron.

"No," I said. "We are not the descendants of Hagoth."

Shemnon sighed in disappointment. "The people of my land have waited for two generations to learn what became of Hagoth. Perhaps we will never know. Hagoth was a countryman of mine. I am from Bountiful. My mother is there, although my wife and son are currently in Zerahemla."

His eyes saddened. Thinking of his wife and son brought him no pleasure, under the circumstances.

Steffanie braved a question. "Why did you come here?" She glanced up at me, as if part of her question were aimed at me in reproach.

"To continue what I started," Shemnon answered. "Five years ago, I preached in this very marketplace. There was not a man, woman, or child among them who did not embrace the holy prophets and look forward with joy to the resurrection of our Lord. Now they are a ferocious people—like their ancestors. Most have dabbled in the secret works. They are lost and no longer wish to be found."

"Will they kill us?" asked Harry timidly. At last he seemed to have embraced the reality of our situation. It saddened me deeply.

Shemnon looked at my son with empathy. I suspected he saw in Harry something of his own son. "We are in the Lord's hands, young one." He looked back at me. "But they will not execute us without the approval of the chief. It is their law."

"Who is the chief?" I asked.

"I'm not sure," said Shemnon. "The means of selecting a leader varies from tribe to tribe. It has been this way since our chief judge was murdered in the thirtieth year of the sign. I know who *should be* chief in Laman, according to tradition and seniority, but few here would tolerate leadership from a man of righteousness. I'm not even certain if this man is still alive. When I was here last, he was gravely ill."

"Who?" I asked.

"Samuel. The prophet of the sign."

Harry guessed it first. "You mean Samuel . . . the Lamanite?"

"That is how he is called in Zarahemla," said Shemnon. "Long ago, he prophesied among the Nephites. But he has served his own people far longer. In the land southward, he is known as Samuel the Stargazer. Here in Melek, he is Samuel the Healer."

"He's a doctor?" I inquired.

"There is no greater healer among all the tribes—Nephite or Lamanite. They would have stoned him years ago, if not for his arts. But his age is great. I suspect the Lord has already taken him home."

From Shemnon's words, I tried to decide what year it was. Two generations since Hagoth. Samuel's mission to the Nephites was over. The sign of Christ's birth had come and gone, but the sign of his death and resurrection had not occurred. A tingle rushed up my spine. At this very moment, in a land beyond the oceans, a mortal man named Jesus Christ lived and breathed, ate and slept, his veins pumping rich red blood, like mine. The thought stirred my soul with the most exhilarating sensations.

I contemplated further. According to Shemnon, in the thirtieth year of the sign, the chief judge of the land had been murdered. The government had collapsed. The people had formed into tribes. I wished I still had Sabrina's Book of Mormon to confirm all this. For all I knew, the Lamanites had already burned it.

I decided to ask Shemnon directly. "According to your reckoning, what year is it?"

He puzzled a bit over the expression "according to your reckoning," and then replied, "It is the thirty-third year since the sign was given: the day, the night, and the day without darkness, and the appearance of the new star. But the year is nearly at an end. The thirty-fourth year will soon commence."

My heartbeat echoed in my chest. A surge of blood rushed through my ears. "Then it's here," I said almost absently. I turned to my children and declared it with greater resolution. "It's here!"

"What's here, Dad?" asked Harry.

I glanced back at Shemnon. Was it right to reveal it to a Nephite? I still remembered my frustration of so many years ago, when the memory of my first experience among the Nephites was taken away—and all because of my big mouth. Yet I had a strong feeling, a firm suspicion, that Shemnon already knew. In fact, his face was beaming.

"Yes," Shemnon confirmed. "The time is very soon. I have awaited the day all of my life."

"What's everybody talking about?" cried Steffanie in frustration.

I embraced my daughter and pulled my son into the circle. Then I leaned back to see their faces. "He's coming. The Savior is coming."

Steffanie searched my eyes. The atheist appeared to have at least converted to agnosticism.

"Will he save us?" asked Harry.

I smiled ruefully. My son's statement had a double meaning. He meant to know if Jesus would arrive soon enough to save us from the mob. At this particular moment, the deeper significance of his question had very little practical meaning.

"He'll save everyone," I answered. "Everyone who believes."

I embraced my son more firmly. After a moment, he whispered, "Then . . . I believe."

* * *

As the day progressed, I was amazed at how swiftly my joy at the Lord's coming eroded into nail-biting apprehension. I pondered the full account as I remembered it from the Book of Mormon. In a matter of months, maybe weeks (maybe days!), this land would become enveloped in a storm of destruction unrivaled in the annals of history. All I could think about was my daughter, Melody, caught out there alone in the maelstrom. I doubted seriously if Jacob's destination was a safe haven. Quite likely, wherever they were going would be a primary target of God's wrath.

I also thought of Jennifer and Garth. They would be caught in it, too. We would all be caught in it. I recalled from the scriptures that only the more righteous part of the population was spared, and I was entirely uncertain which of us—if any—fell into this category. Considering that we were strangers here—intruders out of time—it was conceivable that we were *all* expendable.

The afternoon heated up. Our cage offered very little shade from the sun. Once I asked a guard if he would bring us more water. He refused, claiming that to do so would incur upon him the harshest punishment.

"It is up to the people to bring food and water," he said. "They decide who is worthy of refreshment and who is not."

This, I decided, explained why earlier Shemnon had received water while we had been ignored. There was at least one Christian in this town who took pity on a fellow Christian. But for us—a suspected robber and his children—there was no pity.

Harry and Steffanie tried to rest, but each time they were about to fall asleep, someone disturbed them by spitting into the cage or screaming an insult. As time wore on, my children became less and less submissive about the abuse.

"You murdered my only son!" one lady clamored.

"We didn't murder anyone!" Steffanie shouted back. "Did you see us do it? I don't think so!"

"Get some eyeglasses, you blind bat!" added Harry.

The lady held up a stone. "Mine will be the first."

"You probably can't even throw it, you old coot!"

The woman retreated, more set on vengeance than ever.

I yanked the children back, scolding them harshly. "What do you think you're accomplishing?"

"But Dad—"

"But nothing! You're only aggravating them worse. That old woman's pain is real. She lost a son."

"But *we* didn't do it!" said Harry.

"She wants to kill us!" reminded Steffanie.

"Don't give them any more reason! Now I mean it!" I sighed and softened my tone. "Show some dignity. In the same situation, our Savior felt it was best to say nothing."

"But they're going to *kill* us!" said Harry with emphasis, and his eyes filled with tears.

It tore at my heart. My children had never faced a threat of death before. No one at such a tender age ever should. I tried to comfort them, but my words sounded hollow. Nevertheless, the proper spirit took over, and after a few minutes Harry and Steffanie mustered the dignity I'd proposed. For the rest of the day they were content to reply calmly, "I'm sorry about what happened, but we didn't do it. We're innocent."

A little later, from the neighboring cage, I heard Shemnon remark, "It's your clothes, you know."

"Our clothes?" I considered him carefully. "I don't understand."

He explained. "The people of Melek have seen clothes like yours before. They associate such apparel with sorcerers—the men of King Jacob. They blame King Jacob of the Moon for the raid on Lamoni. A portion of his secret band was sighted in these mountains a few weeks ago, just before Lamoni was burned. It is rumored that they were seen again only yesterday. No one knows why they are here, or what would make them leave their secret city in the north. So you see, your family was simply in the wrong place at the wrong moment."

This made sense. Over the last generation, only Gadiantons had used the time-tunnels. Anyone dressed in modern apparel like ours would have been associated with secret combinations. People like Marcos Alberto Sanchez. There may have been dozens of men and women whom Jacob had commissioned to move freely between both centuries.

But unlike the people in this city, I knew precisely why King Jacob had come to these hills. He'd come for my daughter. He needed her for some purpose I did not fully understand. I also knew why the village of Lamoni had been raided and burned. Jacob's army would have needed provisions to survive, and Lamoni was easy pickings.

"Did any part of this rumor," I asked Shemnon, "state that these men carried a prisoner with them? A young girl, about sixteen, with white skin like ours and dark hair?"

Shemnon looked at me quizzically. "I have heard no such rumor. Who is this girl?"

"My daughter."

"And she was captured by Jacob's band?"

"Yes. We were searching for her."

"I'm truly sorry," said Shemnon. In a surprising display of anger, he clenched his fists and declared, "Viler creatures have never walked the earth than those men of Jacob. Is there any indignity they will not commit?"

His question was rhetorical; nevertheless, its inference made my flesh crawl. I felt a sense of helplessness more pervasive than ever before. And yet compared to Melody, my own plight at this moment was no less severe. But if I were to die this day, or if my two younger children were to die, at least we would stand together. At least I could tell Harry and Steffanie one last time that I loved them. With Melody, I would have no such opportunity.

"Where will they take her?" I inquired.

"For what reason was she kidnapped?" Shemnon wondered.

I hesitated answering, first because I wasn't sure if it was wise to go into details, and secondly because I didn't want to wrack my brain thinking about it anymore. Shemnon looked into my eyes. Suddenly he felt ashamed to have asked; he knew the answer to that question might be too horrible to contemplate.

At last he said, "They will probably take her to their secret city. That is . . . if she is allowed to live."

"Secret city? Where is it?"

"No one quite knows."

"Why do they keep it a secret?"

"With Gadiantons, everything is secret. There may be people in Zarahemla who know its location, but even those who claim such knowledge have pledged to sacrifice their own lives before revealing it. They say it is in the far north, but that is *all* that is said. And if anyone hints to show you the way, beware. You would be killed the moment you are alone in the wilderness."

Shemnon restated that I could never have found this place on my own. I wondered if he was trying to comfort me, since it now seemed unlikely that I would ever have a chance to try. Nevertheless, his statement that people in Zarahemla might know its location stuck in my mind.

I reconsidered what he had said about our clothes. "Surely not everybody dressed like us has proven to be sorcerers. There should have been two others who arrived in this land in these kinds of clothes. Two other Christians, like us. A man and a woman. The man would have been called Garth Plimpton. The woman would have been his wife, Jennifer."

Shemnon's eyebrows shot up. "You know the pale prophet? You know Garplimpton?"

I wasn't surprised to hear him slur Garth's name, as they usually slurred mine. But "pale prophet"? This title threw me for a loop.

"Garth is a *prophet?*"

My children drew nearer to listen.

"He is called the pale prophet," Shemnon explained. "He is a missionary, like me."

"Where is he?" I asked frantically.

"Where is his wife, Jenny?" asked Steffanie.

"I'm afraid I don't know," said Shemnon. "I saw Garplimpton three years ago, at the council—the last great council before the breakup of the government. I have not seen him since."

Three years? But only a little over *two* years had elapsed since he and Jenny had left our time. And yet Shemnon said that three years only accounted for the time since this council had taken place. Just how many years had Garth and Jenny been living among the Nephites?

Shemnon continued. "Garplimpton was surely called as I was called—to preach repentance and the remission of sins through faith on the Lord Jesus Christ in some far corner of the land. But only Nephi would know where the Lord has sent him. Nephi is the keeper of the holy records. He is chief prophet in all the lands northward and southward."

"Garth the prophet," I mumbled again. It sounded so absurd. But the more I thought about it, the less absurd it became.

An hour later, we heard the murmur of a large crowd. They approached down the long avenue that emptied into the market square. Many were chanting. The words became clearer as they got closer. "Remember Lamoni!" they shouted. "Avenge our dead! Remember Lamoni! Avenge our dead!"

The chief of the tribe had arrived. Four attendants, as well as the entire citizenry of Laman, followed on his heels. The crowd's chants were not meant for us; the intent was apparently to persuade their chief. They were determined that he would submit to the will of the mob. Nothing less would be tolerated. Receiving his official condemnation was strictly a formality. Our hopes of seeing the sun set this day were dimming.

I half expected the chief to be wearing a headdress of eagle feathers, like a Cherokee or a Sioux. I wasn't so far off. On either side of his head were tassels of rich blue and green feathers. More feathers hung down his back. Chains of precious stones dangled around his neck, and gold bracelets jingled on his wrists and ankles. Each index finger boasted a large ring—one of turquoise, the other of jade. A black fur cape was draped over his shoulders. The fur was coarse, like a wolf or a panther. As I watched him draw near, I sensed that he felt awkward in such garb. But what he lacked in grace, he made up for in malevolence.

The crowd silenced as he stepped up to the cage. My children and I stood in the center, looking helpless and pitiful. The man who would decide our fate examined us with contempt. He was a young chief, early thirties maybe. I noted that his forehead was round, not flat like so many others of his generation. His eyes were not squinted.

He stepped over to Shemnon's cage and gave him the same disapproving glance. The crowd watched the chief's every move, as if in judgment not of us, but of him.

Shemnon seemed to recognize their leader. He spoke the chief's name as if it were a question—as if it surprised Shemnon to see him arrayed like this.

"Mathoni?"

The chief recoiled and spit full force into Shemnon's face. The crowd roared with approval. Shemnon did not wipe his face. He stood stock still, his eyes never wavering from those of the chief.

Mathoni spat at us with somewhat less concentration, and missed. It splattered against a bar of our cage, but the mob roared approval just the same. He then faced the citizens and pointed back at us. The crowd quieted.

"These prisoners have been accused of the grossest crimes imaginable!" Mathoni declared. And then he enumerated them: "Murder!"

The mob shrieked in unison, "Yes!"

"Robbery!"

"Yes!"

"Priestcraft!"

"Yes!"

"Performing miracles by the power of the devil!"

"Yes!"

"And for these crimes, they must be brought to justice! They must face the wrath of us all! They must die by stoning!"

The marketplace became a maelstrom of insanity. In the midst of such delirium, I felt a billion miles from home. Could anything in our century compare with such a scene? The conflagrations of Nazi Germany or racial South Africa? Certainly nothing in my sheltered experience compared to this. Several men approached our cages to untie the door before dragging us into the street.

But Mathoni wasn't finished. He raised his hands. "Listen to me! Are we not a tribe of law? Are we not a tribe of justice?"

Again the mob cheered, but with less enthusiasm. They looked somewhat bewildered.

"We *will* execute them," he continued, "but first they will be tried and sentenced according to our laws! At dusk, they will be stoned. At dusk, we will have our revenge!"

Only about half the crowd cheered now. The other half clamored, "No! Sentence them now! Stone them now! Why wait for dusk?"

"Let it not be said that we are a tribe without law!" the chief contended. "In the city of Laman, there is fairness! In the city of Laman, there is justice!"

"What about Lamoni?" someone shouted back. "Was there justice in Lamoni?" Several voices approved the man's words.

"You will have your justice," Mathoni replied sternly, *"at dusk!"*

The wailing of the crowd faded into muttering. Chief Mathoni had stayed the people's wrath, but they didn't like it. They didn't like it at all. They weren't sure if they trusted their chief. It was a miracle that they restrained themselves from rushing us in one body and tearing our cages apart. In many faces I saw exactly that desire. They faltered only because they were uncertain whether everyone around them shared the same urge. In a matter of minutes, they would realize their unity. Mathoni had to act fast.

"They will be tried on the temple steps under the watchful eye and judging ear of all the city!" promised Mathoni.

"And on the steps they will be stoned!" someone added. This idea was heartily sanctioned by the citizenry.

"So be it!" shouted the chief and spat at us again, this time hitting my shirt.

Knives of flint cut the ropes on our cages. My children clung to me; again I could feel their hearts racing.

After we had exited the cages, Mathoni forced us all to stand together. He stepped toward Shemnon again, glowering down on the demon-prophet. He struck Shemnon across the cheek; the Nephite staggered. The frenzy of cheering was louder than ever before, almost deafening. Shemnon and I stood exactly side by side. When the fury was at its loudest pitch, Mathoni leaned in between us. He mouthed his words carefully to be certain we would not misunderstand.

"Do not fear," he said. "If any of you die this day, I will die with you."

Then he clenched his teeth and struck me hard across the cheek.

CHAPTER 16

The temple in Laman was somewhat larger than the one in Lamoni. It had been constructed upon a stone foundation that rose eight steps higher than the earth surrounding it. The structure looked every bit as dilapidated as the other buildings in the city—even more so. There was evidence of vandalism. Stonework had been shattered with mallets. Rubble was strewn about the grounds. Anything of obvious value, such as gold vessels, trim, fine awnings or curtains, had long since been stripped and plundered. I doubted if it had functioned as a temple for several years. The synagogue facing it on the north appeared to have suffered the same fate. If there were any Christians left in Laman, it was doubtful that they had worshipped in either place for some time.

The four attendants who had accompanied Chief Mathoni into the square personally frog-marched Shemnon and me up the temple steps with our arms pinioned. The children walked between us, both at wit's end with fright. The mob filled the entire temple courtyard, and hundreds more pressed in around all four sides of the building.

Earlier, when the chief had secretly communicated his intention to spare our lives, I felt a warm surge of optimism. I realized his slap in the face was all for show, no matter how real it may have felt. But in light of the crowd's rabid lust for bloodshed, my hopes for rescue had cooled. Our only possibility for survival might be if a providential tornado swept in and whisked us off to safety. Despite his good intentions, Chief Mathoni was powerless against the masses. The only question was whether he would be true to his oath and die with us.

My first hint that an escape plan of some sort was in the works came from one of the attendants who held my arms. As he stood us between the pillars in front of the temple doors, he whispered some very peculiar instructions in my ear: "Disagree with everything. Interrupt frequently. Be as obnoxious as you can possibly be."

I looked at the attendant questioningly. He confirmed his instructions with a cryptic nod. I glanced at Shemnon; the attendant holding his arms appeared to have communicated the same instructions. For a moment, I wondered if the attendants were on the side of the mob. To act in the way they were suggesting might get us killed sooner than necessary. But Shemnon looked at me reassuringly.

A moment later, a man dressed more elaborately than the chief (if such a thing was possible) emerged from the crowd. Strings of tear-shaped pearls dangled all the way to his navel. The soft fur of his cloak had been dyed purple, black, and yellow. His mouth had been painted bright red—not just his lips, but his *teeth!*

"I am Zeragosh," he said. "I will represent you in these proceedings. Keep silent and we will conclude this matter as quickly as possible."

Our lawyer then took his place near the base of the steps. I soon realized that Zeragosh also represented the voice of the people. So much for a democratic trial.

Mathoni and his attendants stood to our right, in front of one of the pillars. The mob was anxious to get these proceedings over with. Many had already filled their hands with stones.

The chief called the trial to order. "If there are any witnesses, let them step forward!" At least a hundred men and women pushed their way through to the base of the temple, all anxious to play a part in this charade and earn the praise and envy of their fellow citizens.

Zeragosh stuck out his jaw and scanned the faces. It was entirely at his discretion who would testify, much like choosing a member of the studio audience for *The Price is Right.* But at least selection in a game show was random. Zeragosh showed a definite preference to those wearing nicer apparel.

"Are there any witnesses for the accused?" asked Mathoni.

No one stepped forward. Who would have dared?

"Then we shall first hear from my brother, Amgiddonah," said Zeragosh.

An excited Amgiddonah started forward. He was dressed almost exactly like his brother, except that the fur of his cloak was died pink and brown.

"No!" I cried. "Not Amgiddonah! Anyone but Amgiddonah!"

Amgiddonah hesitated.

"The accused must remain silent," said Chief Mathoni, "until the end of these proceedings!"

"At least find a witness who isn't quite so ugly!" I clamored.

The crowd roared with laughter. Amgiddonah reddened. Apparently he wasn't all that popular anyway, particularly among the poor majority. My children gaped at me. Hadn't I lectured them earlier about dignity?

"Silence!" blustered the chief.

Amgiddonah paid me a poisonous glance and took his place in the center of the steps.

"What have you against the accused?" asked Zeragosh.

"I was present when Shemnon, the demon-prophet, condemned us all to a fiery destruction if we would not repent. When we asked him what were our sins, he told us selfishness and greed. Then he promised to save only those who would pay him generously for his preaching!"

At the top of his lungs, Shemnon declared, "Oh child of hell! When did you turn your back on the Lord your God?! When did you give your heart over to the father of lies?!"

"And when did you start wearing pink fur and pearls like a girlie-man?" I added.

The crowd was rolling. Mathoni became frantic. "Silence! Silence! One more outburst from either of you, and I will see that you are flogged before you are stoned! As well, you shall be prevented from further witnessing these proceedings!"

Flogged before we were stoned? I was beginning to doubt the wisdom of the chief's plan. Had I understood the attendant's instructions correctly?

"Be quiet, Dad," whispered Steffanie. "What are you trying to do to us?"

My daughter hadn't heard my instructions. I glanced over at the attendant again. His expression seemed to say, *You're doing just fine.*

"We shall now hear from Israel, the hunter," Zeragosh announced.

The ringleader who had first apprehended us in the ruins of Lamoni stepped forward. In his arms were the two backpacks we'd purchased at Wal-Mart. He placed the backpacks on the bottom step and began digging through the contents. He held up the flashlight and matches.

"These were with the robbers when we captured them," declared the hunter. "They are the implements of their sorceries and spellcasting!" A murmur rumbled through the crowd.

"We need no further evidence!" someone shouted. "Step away! We will stone them all!"

"We will hear *all* the evidence!" Mathoni thundered.

And then the chief looked at me. I read his eyes: *It's now or never.*

I scrambled for something to say. "Don't touch those!" I shouted. "Anyone who touches them will turn into a babbling idiot! Oops . . . too late."

My children thought I was nuts. They stared at me with cringing expressions.

"Dad, have you completely lost it?" asked Steffanie. I wished I could have admitted that I felt as ridiculous as I sounded.

"And now I'd like to sing you a song!" I continued. *"Val-garee! Val-garah! Val-garee! Val-garah-ha-ha-ha-ha-ha!"*

The chief stomped his foot and pointed a sharp finger. "I warned you, robber!"

"And I have warned all the people of this land!" cried Shemnon. "If you do not repent, fire shall rain down from heaven and your city shall be consumed as a dry reed!"

"Remove them!" Mathoni ordered his attendants. "Seal them inside the temple until we have finished! Fetch scourges, that they may be flogged!"

Just how far did the chief intend to carry this bluff? The attendants seized us roughly. The large wooden doors of the temple were opened, and the four of us were forced inside. The inner room was dark, its only light source a hole in the roof above the temple altar. Birds flew in and out of the wooden beams that sagged like the rib cage of a cow, and rainwater had formed puddles in various places.

The temple doors were closed. The attendants remained inside. I wondered why; there seemed no reason for them to stay. The room wasn't very large, and there were no possible escape routes.

One of the attendants approached Shemnon and embraced him. "Shemnon," he said, "it's good to see you."

"Mathonihah," said Shemnon, "you look well."

"You shouldn't have come back," said Mathonihah.

"It was not my decision," Shemnon insisted. "It was the Lord's. He commanded me to return here, much as He commanded your father to return and preach to the Nephites so many years ago."

"My father will be glad to see you," said Mathonihah.

Shemnon gasped excitedly. "Samuel lives?"

"He resides at the confluence of the rivers. Do you know how to get there?"

"Yes, but—" Shemnon looked around to confirm that there was no escape. "How are we—?"

Mathonihah smiled. "The Lord has provided a way."

Mathonihah led Shemnon over to the limestone basin in the center of the floor. The altar was filled with leaves, its rim soiled with bird droppings. He bent down, stretched his arms, and grasped its edges; his face muscles strained as he tried to move it. The stone wouldn't budge.

"I will need help," he confessed. He looked at Shemnon, then at me. Standing erect again, he said to me, "I do not know who you are or why you have come among my people. You and your children are spared only because my brother, the chief, desires it."

"It's all right," said Shemnon. "They are Christians."

Mathonihah remained suspicious. "Then why are they dressed like sorcerers?"

"Don't judge their clothing," said Shemnon. "Judge their hearts. Jimhawkins is a friend to the pale prophet."

The origins of the pale prophet could only have been a mystery. Even so, a connection with the pale prophet made our presence a little easier for Mathonihah to swallow. He sighed. "I apologize. There are so many enemies—so many spies."

"I understand," I said.

"These are perilous times," Mathonihah continued. "The people want to depose my brother and then kill him. By calling on him to condemn Shemnon and your family, they had hoped he would finally reveal himself as a Christian and a traitor. It appears that his struggle to lead this tribe in righteousness is at an end."

All of us, including Harry, gathered around the altar and pushed until the stone began to move. Its obnoxious grinding against the floor caused us some alarm, and we looked to the door to see if anyone would investigate the sound. The crowd was still caught up in the trial.

Beneath the altar, cut through the mortar of the temple floor, loomed a tunnel. It went down about eight feet and then veered to the north.

"My father had it dug," Mathonihah explained, "shortly before this temple was dedicated to the Lord. He told me at the time that he did not know the reason the Lord wanted it here. It comes out inside the synagogue to the north. Before this day, I don't believe it has ever been used."

Except by spiders, I noted. Several of the little brown and red rascals scurried out of the hole, grateful to have escaped at last. Steffanie winced. Webs crisscrossed the hole like a fish net.

"Now hurry," Mathonihah directed. "My brother will prolong the trial as long as he can. After today, none of us can remain in Laman. When it is learned that you have escaped, we will try to flee in the confusion. If we make it, we will meet you at the house of my father after dark."

"You will make it," said Shemnon encouragingly. "We will see you tonight."

I was lowered into the tunnel first and broke all the webs. After everyone had touched bottom, Mathonihah and the other attendants slid the altar back onto its foundation.

As the light pinched off, the tunnel took on a haunting blackness. We couldn't even see our hands in front of our faces. Suddenly my skin felt itchy; I'm sure it was psychological. I imagined that we were about to walk into a gauntlet of spider webs. The walls could have been covered with black widows, and we wouldn't have known it.

Shemnon and I led the way. The ceiling was low; I raised my arms to avoid bumping my head. I recalled that a similar tunnel for a similar purpose had been excavated beneath the Salt Lake Temple.

The tunnel ended abruptly. For a moment, we thought it was a fruitless dead end. But the ceiling was flat. Shemnon and I got in position and arched our backs upward. A thin stone slab gave way, and dusty light filled the passage.

The synagogue above us was not fully enclosed. Its thatched roof was supported by skinny wooden pillars, its perimeter encased by a low stone barrier. This barrier was the only thing that prevented the crowd, still gathered in the temple courtyard, from observing us as we emerged from the pit. We helped each other out and crawled to the edge to peek over the barrier.

The trial was still in progress. Another witness testified that he had personally seen me and my children in the presence of known robbers. Shemnon, said the man, had threatened to destroy the city with evil spells if they didn't give him all their gold and silver. Chief Mathoni listened without expression. His brother, Mathonihah, and the other attendants had joined him beside the temple pillars, no doubt so they could show as much surprise as everyone else when it was discovered that we had escaped. My heart went out to the chief and his brother. In a few short minutes, their plight would become as desperate as ours. Perhaps more so.

Thick woods and shrubs pressed against the synagogue's northern flank, overgrown from years of neglect. We slipped over the barrier and disappeared into the foliage. Our destination was now the confluence of the rivers—the encampment of Samuel the Lamanite.

CHAPTER 17

My primary fear when I had first embarked on this escapade was that my children would seriously impair my progress. These fears dissolved about the tenth time they called back to me, "Hurry up, Dad!" If climbing through the cavern had not been enough to show how nine years behind a desk had shot my stamina, galloping through a tropical forest cinched it. We dodged trees, forded creeks, hurdled stones, and scaled briery hillsides, seeking to put as much distance between ourselves and the mob at Laman as possible before they learned of our escape. Every quarter mile, however, I found it necessary to lean against a tree and pant for several minutes before we could continue.

Shemnon remained confident that we would reach the confluence of the rivers before dark. One fork of these rivers could be heard roiling in the ravine to our right. All of us were dying of thirst, and none of us could continue without a drink. We parted the foliage until we found the riverbank. The rapids sent up a cooling mist that created the illusion of clean water. Only as it swirled behind a rock could we see how mucky it was. This didn't faze Shemnon, however. Following his example, each of us knelt for a long draught. I couldn't help wondering how many microorganisms I swallowed in each mouthful. Thinking back, I hadn't gotten sick the first time I'd been among the Nephites. Maybe time-travel made us immune to such things. Still, I wouldn't push it. I determined to boil our drinking water whenever possible.

We followed along the river now. The ground leveled out and the rapids melted into a lazy current. We began to feel safer, and our pace slackened. The evening sky went golden. Flocks of blackbirds dilated and shattered like shoals of fish. The humidity thickened and made our clothing stick to our skin. Exhaustion and stress began to overtake my children. Harry's feet started to drag, and Steffanie looked as if she was sleepwalking. She focused on Shemnon's ankles, believing that if she could just follow those ankles, she wouldn't lose her way.

Before long, I smelled woodsmoke and roasting corn. The river emptied into another channel nearly twenty-five yards wide; we had reached the confluence. Near the precise juncture of the two rivers, ten feet in from the bank, a wooden platform had been erected about five feet off the ground. Resting on this platform was an oval-shaped hovel of woven branches. Like the synagogue in Laman, it was not completely enclosed. The walls reached halfway toward the roof, like the railing on a deck. The palm-thatched roof was suspended by poles at all four corners, and on the west hung draperies of softly tanned animal hides to shade the interior from the sinking sun.

Several rough canvas tents had been erected at the base of this platform. These belonged to visitors—families who had traveled far distances to seek a cure and blessing from the great healer. They had arrived in sleek canoes carved from the trunks of the tall red mahogany that grew near the riverbanks. Almost everyone in this neck of the woods used the river to travel. It was not as common for visitors to suddenly materialize out of the dense woods, so they watched us warily.

"It's all right," said Shemnon. "We have traveled far to see the healer."

The people nodded and turned back to their chores of cooking and caring for the ill, usually children. Only the sickest of them camped overnight or longer; most received Samuel's services and promptly paddled home to tiny settlements up or down the widest river branch. Samuel, the Lamanite prophet who had once boldly foretold the signs of the Savior's birth and death in the capital city of the Nephites, had contented himself in his final years to serve as a healer in the remote forests of Melek.

From within the house on the platform rose the steady squall of a child in pain. As we approached the ramp, I could see a family gathered inside. They hovered around a boy, about seven, who lay on a reed mat. Kneeling over the boy was a slender, frail old man. I guessed he was in his mid-seventies, which for a Lamanite, was considerably old. The boy on the mat had cut open his shoulder somehow; the injury was deep. The old man had pressed a poultice against the wound, and his shaky hands were wrapping it in place. The family—a mother, father, and a young daughter of twelve or so—looked on nervously.

Shemnon paused in the entranceway. We stopped behind him. The parents glanced at us, but the healer remained focused on his work.

"Elder Samuel," said Shemnon. "It's good to see you." Samuel did not respond.

The father shook his head at Shemnon. "The healer is touched. His ears no longer hear—"

Samuel the Lamanite, oblivious to this ongoing conversation, interrupted. He'd finished wrapping the wound. "Now you must change the wrapping morning, noon, and again at night. Do you remember how to make the poultice?" His voice trembled. It appeared that he was no longer the powerful orator who had shouted the prophecies of God from Zarahemla's walls.

"Yes," said the father slowly, nodding his head to be certain that Samuel understood. "I remember."

"Good," said Samuel. "If it festers, you must bring him back. And you must pray for him. Do you pray?"

"We pray, Healer."

"Do you pray to the one true God of Israel?"

"Yes, we pray to Him. And to the other gods, too."

"Very good," said Samuel. He had not understood the man's second statement. "Do you remember how to make the poultice?"

The girl giggled at Samuel's repetition. The mother scolded her. The father nodded again and lifted the boy in his arms.

"Very good," said Samuel. "May the joy of Jesus Christ go with you."

The family had squeezed past us down the ramp when Samuel finally noticed us.

"Come in, come in," he said. "Sit."

"Samuel," said Shemnon, "do you remember me?"

"Yes, of course. What is your affliction, my friend?"

Shemnon gently took Samuel by the shoulders. "It's me—Shemnon. Five years ago, I came here to preach the word of God."

"What's that?" said Samuel. "A preacher, you say?" Samuel obviously did not remember him.

Steffanie leaned toward me. "What's the matter with him, Dad?"

"He's old, honey," I replied. "Just old."

I knew that the mantle of a prophet did not exempt an old man from the infirmities of body and mind, but it was still very disheartening to see. And then I felt ashamed. This was Samuel the Lamanite! Did it matter that he was "touched"? Frankly, it was remarkable that he still served in his capacity as a healer. Over the years, such services must have become second nature to him.

"I, too, am a preacher," added Samuel. "There is no greater joy in this life. The sign is at hand. Do you preach of the Christ?"

"I do," Shemnon replied.

"A preacher must preach of the Christ. There is no greater joy in this life."

"Yes," said Shemnon. "No greater joy."

I turned to my children. "Do you want to meet him?"

They shook their heads.

"Of course you do," I said. "Do you know who this is?"

"It's not how I pictured him," said Harry.

"What did you expect?"

"Someone, well . . . taller. Less confused."

Samuel stepped toward Steffanie. "Do you need a healer?"

"No, thank you," she replied.

He reached out to touch my daughter's face. "You are very pale."

Steffanie drew back. "Dad—"

"It's all right," said Shemnon. "He won't hurt you."

I was growing perturbed. My children were acting awfully rude.

"You must eat more flesh, young lady," Samuel advised. Steffanie backed away even farther.

Shemnon had accepted the fact that Samuel did not remember him. He sat Samuel down on the floor mat and said, "Your sons are coming." He mouthed the words carefully to help Samuel read his lips.

"My sons? Very good. They play in the forest from dawn until dusk. They must come in now. It's time for supper. Did you meet Bethel, my wife?"

"Not yet, Elder Samuel," said Shemnon sympathetically.

A woman with a tray of food made her way up the ramp. She was very young—young enough to be his granddaughter.

"Is that her?" I asked.

Shemnon turned away from Samuel. "No. His wife Bethel has been dead for more than ten years." I felt a little foolish.

The food was corn tortillas filled with meat, red vegetables, and sage. My children gawked at Samuel's tray. They'd eaten nothing since we'd finished up the last of the trail mix at breakfast.

The woman looked us over, noting that no one looked ill. "Are you here to see the healer?"

"We are here to see the prophet," Shemnon replied.

The woman smiled. "I am Manoah. We care for him. There are many Christians along the river. We all care for him."

Shemnon nodded. "So this is where everyone has gathered."

Manoah studied Shemnon's face. She spoke uncertainly. "Are you . . . ? Are you the Nephite who preached in Laman? The one who was taken? The one who was to be stoned?"

"Yes," he replied. "But the Lord has delivered us."

Manoah looked astonished. "Welcome!" she cried enthusiastically.

For the rest of the evening we were treated very well, almost like kings. Once again, Shemnon apologized for the clothing worn by myself and my children, assuring them that we were not sorcerers. They prepared more food for us. When our plates arrived, the children gobbled up their tortillas greedily.

"This is great!" said Harry. "Tastes like chicken."

Steffanie stopped in mid-bite. She'd heard people describe some very bizarre meats as tasting like chicken. "*Is* it chicken?" she asked reticently.

"Duck," said Manoah.

She looked relieved. "As long as it's not alligator or salamander or something."

"Those meats are unclean." Menoah looked mildly insulted at the suggestion that she might disobey the Law of Moses.

As Menoah returned to the fire to see that a plate was being prepared for me, I wandered down by the riverbank and made a bench of a gnarled log that lay half submerged in the sand. The sun was gone now; only a hint of purple light crept up from behind the distant hills. I looked off longingly toward those hills. My daughter was out there somewhere. Every moment took her farther and farther away.

After a minute, Shemnon approached me. "How are my children?" I inquired.

"The prophet is telling them tales from his boyhood."

"Are they listening? Are they being polite?"

"Actually, they looked quite enthralled. He is recounting the great jaguar hunts that he enjoyed in these woods as a boy."

"I see," I said. "I'm glad."

I focused again on the silhouetted hills. Shemnon planted himself at the other end of the log.

"Where will you go now, Jimhawkins of Utah?"

I hesitated, then said, "This secret city in the north . . . does it have a name?"

"Jacobugath," Shemnon replied uneasily, as if the sound itself carried a sort of curse. I thought I recalled such a place having been mentioned in the Book of Mormon, but I'd forgotten any details. If only I still had Sabrina's copy.

Shemnon looked at me searchingly. I could tell he had many questions he wanted to ask me. Questions about our mysterious origin. Questions about how I came to know Garth Plimpton. But for now he restrained himself. Instead, he tried to talk some sense into me.

"You would die if you attempted to reach the secret city alone with your children. If wild beasts did not destroy you, the assassins of Jacob would."

"She's my daughter," I replied. "What else can I do?"

Shemnon sighed. He realized that any argument he might present paled in comparison with mine.

"At least come with me to Zarahemla," he urged. "You should consult the Prophet Nephi."

"Is Zarahemla to the north?" It didn't make sense to me to travel in a direction that would take me farther from Melody.

"Zarahemla is to the west," he answered.

I started to decline. Shemnon stopped me. "Jacob's band will keep to the mountains and wilderness to avoid being seen. If you come to Zarahemla, you can travel north along the rivers, through the most capital parts of the land. You may even overtake him."

I considered his words thoughtfully. I wondered if Shemnon was misleading me for my own good. If he could persuade me to follow him, I might lose Melody, but at least the rest of us would live. "I don't know," I sighed.

"There is wisdom in my advice," he assured. "Please consider it carefully, prayerfully."

He left me alone with my thoughts. I watched the dancing reflections of the campfire on the surface of the river for a few more minutes, until the mosquitoes began to eat me alive. Then I rejoined my family in Samuel's hut.

The prophet of the Lamanites rambled away the evening. He spoke most often of his wife, sometimes in the present tense and sometimes in the past. He recited his jaguar stories a second time, either for my benefit or because he didn't realize he'd told them once already. Several times he stopped to report the prophecies of Christ. It was at these moments that he seemed most lucid.

"The sign is at hand," he told us. "Three days of darkness. And then He will rise, spirit and body reunited, never to be separated again. Everywhere, the people must hear the good news of Christ."

One more patient came to visit Samuel after dark—a young Lamanite mother, not much older than Steffanie, with her husband and an infant child, only two or three weeks old. They had journeyed from upriver a considerable distance. The child was barely alive. For some reason, the woman had stopped producing breast milk. The father explained that no other women in their village would nurse the child because he and his wife were Christians.

I tried to observe quietly from the other side of the room, where my children had settled down to sleep, but Samuel wouldn't let me. He did something quite remarkable. He looked at me and said, "Will you assist me in the blessings?"

I don't know how he knew I held the holy priesthood. In my more skeptical moments, I've wondered if he simply chose the closest adult.

I'd forgotten that the Nephites even *had* the Melchizedek priesthood before Christ, but Samuel proceeded with the blessing in the same manner as I had performed it so often upon the heads of my children. I did the anointings. I'm not certain what kind of oil it was. Olives, of course, didn't grow in this part of the world. Samuel pronounced the blessing on both mother and infant. I half expected his voice to suddenly strengthen and resound, like the typical stereotype of an ancient prophet. But it was the same tremulous, squeaky voice as ever.

The child would live, Samuel declared, and the mother would receive the wisdom to care for it. The promises were made in the name of Jesus Christ.

Samuel found a jar among his various medicines and supplies. It was filled with a kind of thin, milky syrup. He also found a nipple-shaped object composed of a material that resembled rubber. (Come to think of it, rubber *did* come from this area of the world.) The nipple looked as if it had been molded over a human finger and then pierced with a small, sharp instrument. Attaching this nipple to a leather water pouch, he constructed a makeshift baby bottle. The syrup, Samuel explained, was sap from a certain tree. In the absence of milk, he told the father how the sap could best be harvested.

I would have never believed it would work. Sap from a tree? The baby would never drink it. But that same baby, so weak when it arrived that it couldn't open its eyes, sucked contentedly the instant Samuel put the nipple to her mouth. It was one of the most extraordinary things I've ever seen. If I had ever doubted that the Lord could work miracles through an aged prophet whose mental powers were fading, such feelings were put to rest forever.

Harry and Steffanie had fallen asleep on each other's shoulders, their mouths hanging open to catch unsuspecting mosquitoes. It was hard to believe we'd only been in this world a single day. Frost Cave, Salt Lake City, Sabrina, the police—they all seemed like mystical echoes from a former life. I curled up beside my children. Even the impending question of what had become of Mathoni and Mathonihah was no longer enough to stave off sleep.

The last sounds I heard were the songs of jungle birds and the lazy slur of the river. These noises acted as natural somnolents. Despite the weight of stress on my mind over decisions still to be made, I don't remember ever drifting into slumber so easily and so soundly.

CHAPTER 18

"Drink this," he said.

I drank it because I was about to lose my mind. To drink, to eat—I had to do something that might jar me back to reality, awaken me from this horrible nightmare. But as it turned out, the honeysweet drink sent me into a dream of its own. I began to hear the fluttering of butterfly wings about my head, like the propeller of an airplane. The voices around me began to fade and amplify and echo, like traffic on a distant interstate.

I remember being laid upon a bed of soft white fur, and I remember being lifted into the air and carried through the clouds. I rolled in the fur, and then I dropped off to sleep—forever.

Several times in my dreams, I made a conscious effort to try and wake up. I wanted to go down and make breakfast in the kitchen, as I had done so many times before. But no matter how hard I tried, I couldn't open my eyes.

Trapped in the world of sleep.

When I finally woke up, the process was very slow. I had a pounding headache. My fingers clutched at the white fur beneath my hands. When I glimpsed the green, leathery beast glaring down at me from the rim above my head, I thought I was hallucinating again. It was four feet long with a mane of sharp spikes. I shrieked. The lizard leaped off the rim and scampered into the foliage.

The next face I saw belonged to Marcos.

"An iguana," he announced matter-of-factly, as if making introductions between myself and the reptile. Then he added with a careless brush of the hand, "Harmless."

"Iguana?" I mumbled dazedly. I pressed my fists into my forehead to try and stop the pain. "What did you make me drink?"

"It's called Balche. Fermented bark and honey. Balam concocted it. You needed it. You were as white as a ghost."

"Don't ever . . . don't ever make me drink it again," I said wearily.

"It helped you sleep," said Marcos.

"I don't like that kind of sleep. Water . . . is there water?"

Marcos handed me a bag made of animal skin. Water sloshed inside it. I drank greedily. Afterwards, I wiped my mouth and asked, "How long was I out?"

"Just since last night."

I sat up. The sun was setting. I'd been asleep for twenty-four hours. We were still surrounded by mountains, but they looked different. Huge trees rose out of the earth, gripping the huge stones on the hillsides like the tentacles of an octopus. The company of King Jacob had camped within a cluster of towering trees.

"Where are we?"

"Ammonihah."

"Huh?"

"The land the Nephites call Ammonihah." He pointed. "The capital city is just over those hills. But we won't be going there; we're going around it. In about ten days, we'll reach my father's city."

Nephites. Ammonihah. It took a moment for these words to sink in.

"Book of Mormon?" I asked groggily.

"That's one *history of the Nephites. A rather jaded history. But it* is *the only history that appears to have survived into your century. So I can understand why it has fooled so many people."*

I closed my eyes and let the facts sort themselves out. Marcos was saying we were back in the days of the Book of Mormon, and yet he didn't believe in the Book of Mormon. A contradiction? Was it possible to believe in the existence of Nephites and deny the truthfulness of the Book of Mormon? The pounding in my head was almost audible.

But despite this bizarre revelation about the place in which I'd awakened, something deep inside me registered this news with an incredible sense of calm. I no longer felt overwhelmed by dizziness or panic. Something remarkable had happened—something beyond my under-

standing. Yet my mind consumed and digested this information as easily as anything I'd ever learned. We'd gone back almost two thousand years. Back to the time of the Nephites.

The time of the Nephites.

I realized I was lying within a kind of portable litter, like an emperor or a queen. But clearly I was not considered royalty. There was a loose leather collar around my neck, constricted just enough to keep me from slipping it over my head. It was attached to a rope that led up to a metal ring hooked to a horizontal pole at the top of the canopy. I felt like a dog tied to a clothesline.

It struck me that Marcos wore different clothes, ancient things, like the rest of them—leather sandals, breechcloth, and a kind of mantle that wrapped around his shoulders and covered only half of his chest. His calves, arms, and stomach were painted red.

And then to my revulsion I realized that my own clothes were different! I was draped in a wrap-around skirt and pullover with red and brown bands and gold weavings. I smelled my wrist. Perfume! My entire body had been perfumed! My face flushed. I wanted to shrivel up and die. I looked at Marcos with loathing.

He realized my thoughts and his own face reddened. He vigorously shook his head. "Not me! Balam changed your clothes. I wasn't even there."

Balam! That disgusting little man with the holes in his face. I thought I'd vomit.

"It's all right," Marcos assured me. "Balam is a eunuch. He's been that way all of his adult life. It was done to keep him pure and undefiled. Now he can focus all his energies on serving the divinities of light and darkness."

A eunuch? To keep him pure and undefiled? I'd never heard such a warped concept.

"Why did you kidnap me?" I demanded. "Why did you bring me here?"

Marcos smiled wryly. "It's supposed to be a surprise."

"A surprise?"

"Well, I suppose I could give you a hint. My father wants to reunite you with someone you care about very much."

"Reunite? I don't understand. Everyone I know is back—"

"Most likely you haven't seen this person for a number of years."

I pondered this, then caught my breath. "Aunt Jennifer? You're going to reunite me with my Aunt Jenny? You know where she is?"

Marcos frowned. "Well, no. Actually, this person is called Garth Plimpton."

I lurched toward him. "Garth? You have my Uncle Garth?"

"Oops," said Marcos. "Now I've spoiled the surprise."

"You kidnapped my Uncle Garth, too? When? Where is Jenny?"

"Slow down. I don't know anything about your Aunt Jenny. Frankly, I've never met your Uncle Garth, either. I only know what they've told me."

I stuck out my chin defiantly. "I want to see your father. I insist that you let me speak with him."

Marcos laughed. "I don't think you understand. My father is a king. Nobody insists on speaking with him."

My heart plummeted. "You're right, I don't understand. I don't understand any of this. But I have to have some answers. Please help me, Marcos."

Marcos looked sincerely sympathetic. "I'll do what I can. It's my job to keep you happy. But I can't make any promises. I feel as much like a fish out of water as you do. I really haven't spent too much time in this world—not since I was a small boy. My father wanted it that way. My home is back in our century, not here among these hillbillies. Next time I get a chance, I'll ask him about your aunt."

"Can't you ask him now?"

Marcos raised his eyebrows as if I'd requested something unthinkable. "My father is in his tent with Balam. No one disturbs my father when he is in trance with Balam the Diviner. It would mean certain death. The incantation may last through the night. When they are finished, my father will see the invisible space. Past, present and future will become one. He will know the true course for our people, and he will have the protection and nourishment of the Divine Jaguar."

I nearly cracked a mocking smile. He considered his home back in our century, yet he still believed in this mystical hogwash?

His father's tent stood in the middle of the clearing. Blue smoke seeped out of a shaft in the roof, mingling with the bloodred sunset. Jacob's men were gathered in various clusters. They talked in low, reverent tones, mesmerized by the rising smoke. They looked expectant, as if something important was about to happen.

I tried to sound polite as I asked, "You believe in all that stuff?"

"Not belief," he replied. "Knowledge."

I quirked an eyebrow. It sounded almost like a testimony, but not of the gospel—a testimony of ancient voodoo. He must have perceived my skepticism, because in a patronizing tone he said, "You are so naive, child. The world is so naive. They know so little of the true power that governs this planet. They are weak. It's up to us to make them strong." And then his thought processes did a 180-degree flip-flop: "You're so beautiful, Melody."

"Excuse me?"

"I'm sorry. I was just looking at you, and . . ." He leaned in closer. "I want to teach you our ways, Melody. Please let me show you the limitless power we possess. We hold the knowledge of the earth. Our rites have been handed down from the very foundation of the world. They are holy and pure."

The most unsettling feeling came over me. I was frightened, and yet strangely curious.

Fortunately, I had the presence of mind to reply, "Maybe some other time."

Marcos looked disappointed. "Yes. Some other time. I'm sure you're very hungry." I nodded. Marcos departed to go and fetch me something to eat.

Like everyone else, I found myself entranced by the blue smoke. Unexpectedly, my eyes filled with tears. I felt so alone, so confused. I thought about my family. By now they must have thought I was dead. I might as well have been; I was certain I would never see them again. I thought of my father. Was he still rotting in that miserable jail? What a stupid question. He wouldn't even be born for another two thousand years!

I thought about what Quinn had said to me that night. I gathered from his words that these men were somehow responsible for my father's arrest. They had framed him. They were murderers. I couldn't help wondering again if this was all a nightmare. The tears rolled out of my eyes. Why was this happening to me? Why was any *of this happening? I curled up against the back rim of the carrier, a little girl lost in a cyclone.*

All at once, an excited murmur gripped Jacob's men. They pointed at the smoke, gasping. I squinted my eyes in amazement. Could it be real? The blue smoke was undulating back and forth, like a cobra in a snake charmer's basket. What could be causing it to do that? I felt no breeze.

Suddenly the smoke began changing shapes. It curled outward, then it wrapped around and formed a face. A hideous face with two upper and lower fangs: the face of the Divine Jaguar.

The men of Jacob fell forward on their faces as the image continued its eerie metamorphosis. I pressed myself harder into the back rim of the carrier and hid my eyes.

"It can't be real," I whispered to myself. "It's not real."

A thought slapped me in the face—PRAY!

Two seconds later, I was on my knees—but not to worship the image in the smoke like everyone else. I was reaching out to my Father in Heaven. "Protect me," I pleaded. "I can't get through this without Thee. I can't!"

I continued to pray for a long time, while the sounds of drums and rattles and high-pitched whistles reverberated through the camp. But despite the distractions, I maintained my concentration.

And soon, I no longer felt alone.

CHAPTER 19

"Awake! Arise! Everyone arise! The mob is coming! They are killing all Christians!"

The cries began as part of my dreams and blended into reality. It was Mathoni and Mathonihah. It was still very dark; I could scarcely see better with my eyes open than closed. What time was it? It couldn't have been later than five or six in the morning. The shouts soon mixed with other voices, equally panicked.

Steffanie's moan pierced the darkness. "What is it, Dad?"

I peered over the rim of Samuel's elevated hut, off into the direction of the jungled hills. Immediately I saw the cause for concern. About two miles distant, faint flickers of torchlight descended the hill that stood directly beyond the rise that sloped down to the river. The flickers appeared and disappeared in the congested foliage. I guessed that the mob would be upon us in twenty minutes, maybe less. The light of the stars was veiled by a layer of clouds. Except for the dimming coals of the central fire, the only other light was a glimmer of deep red against the eastern hills—the portent of a violent and desperate day for the people of Christ.

Shadows emerged from the tents. Others ran to and fro, gathering up supplies and children. Another shadow rushed into the hut. It was Chief Mathoni, now draped in a simple tunic. All the finery of his office had been discarded.

"Father!" Mathoni located Samuel in the darkness and roused him. "Awake! We have to leave this place! *All* of us!"

"Leave?" said the old prophet, disoriented.

Mathoni scooped his father into his arms and stood him on his feet. He pointed toward the distant torches. "It's a mob from the city of Laman, Father. They're coming to destroy this place."

"Is that you, Mathoni?" Samuel asked.

"Yes, Father. Mathonihah is also here. We are spreading the word. All Christians must flee for their lives. You must come with us."

"But I can't leave today, my son," said Samuel. "I have patients. Many patients."

Mathonihah, wielding a torch that he'd ignited in the coals of the fire, ascended the ramp. A welcome burst of light filled the hut. Mathonihah was followed by Shemnon, who had slept near the fire.

"Is he coming?" Mathonihah asked his brother.

"I can't make him understand!" replied Mathoni in exasperation.

"Then we'll carry him," said Mathonihah.

"It's useless. He would fight us every step."

"We'll bind him if we have to!"

"At his age it would kill him," said Mathoni.

"Brother," Mathonihah pleaded, "he will die for certain if he remains. Our father is the best known Christian in Melek. The mob will tear him apart! His healing arts will not save him today."

"It is good to rise at such an early hour," said Samuel obliviously. "I must make breakfast for my sons." He began calling for Menoah, his nursemaid, while Mathonihah tried again to explain the situation to his father.

Shemnon took Mathoni by the arm. "What is your destination?"

"Across the river, at least for now," said Mathoni. "My attendants are spreading the word to all the Christian settlements upriver that we will gather at the Hill Abithar. From there, I do not know."

Mathonihah's pestering to convince Samuel to leave had caused the prophet/healer to wrap his arms around a corner post. The stubborn old man wasn't going anywhere. His patients, he argued, would not be able to find him.

Mathonihah shrieked in frustration and turned back to his brother. "What are we to do?"

"We will inquire of the Lord," said Mathoni. "If it is God's will that our father remain in this place, then we will depart without him. He will be in the Lord's hands."

Harry piped in. "What are you saying? You can't just leave him here."

I put my arm around my boy's shoulder. "They may not have a choice, son."

"You'd just leave him to the mob? Samuel the Lamanite?" He repeated his name as if we had all forgotten who he was.

I was touched by Harry's concern. But I knew that Mathoni was only trying to set aside his feelings and learn the will of the Lord. Maybe God *would* protect Samuel. Maybe he would tell the mob something that would inspire them to abandon their evil designs. Or perhaps, as a testimony against them at judgment day, Samuel the Lamanite was destined to become a martyr.

The tension was relieved when a wrinkled but firm hand rested on Harry's arm. Harry looked into the face of the prophet. Samuel the Lamanite was calmly smiling. His countenance had changed. The senility seemed to have vanished—gone like the snap of a hypnotist's fingers. Everyone in the hut sensed the change. His features seemed to emit a translucent glow. Even last night when I had watched him perform miracles as a healer, the change had not seemed nearly so dramatic.

"Your course is clear," he said, his voice even and strong. "You will journey to Bountiful." The pronouncement resonated though us all.

Mathonihah was reluctant about his next question. "Will you be coming with us, Father?"

"No," he said firmly.

Mathonihah started to protest. "But we can't leave you here. The people of Laman have sworn an oath. Any Christian they lay their hands on will be—"

Samuel interrupted. "All will be well, my son. All will be well." He turned to Mathoni. "You will lead them, my firstborn. They will follow you. Those who gather at the Hill Abithar will follow you to Bountiful."

Mathoni took both his father's hands in a last pleading effort. "They will not follow me, Father. They no longer trust me. I was chief to a wicked people. But they will follow you."

"They will do as you say," Samuel declared. "If I were to go with you, my son, you would be overtaken. All would be lost. Because I will stay, they will falter. No one will overtake you."

Mathoni nodded, his eyes to the ground. "I understand."

"Go and make the announcement," Samuel commanded.

Mathoni gazed into his father's eyes a moment longer, gaining strength from the power contained in them. Finally, the sons embraced their father. They did not expect to see their father again in this life. Shemnon and my children watched in plaintive silence.

Someone down at the tents shouted, "I hear them!"

The shrieks of the mob raged in the distance. They were closing in faster than I had expected. The urgency finally settled over Samuel's sons, and they descended the ramp in long strides. We followed on their heels—all except Harry. As I reached the bottom, I turned back to see him standing next to the prophet. Samuel spoke to him in low tones; I couldn't hear the words. Harry listened with solemn attentiveness. I'd never seen such a reverent expression on my boy's face. I considered going back to fetch him, but the urge was interrupted by Mathoni's announcement. Everyone ceased their preparations for departure to listen. Even those already boarding their canoes paused before shoving off to hear the words of Samuel's eldest son.

"The prophet has spoken," Mathoni declared. "The will of the Lord is made known. Today we will gather at the Hill Abithar. Tomorrow we will journey to Bountiful."

Many repeated the name of the place under their breaths. A few questions were asked. Some wondered about family and friends living upriver, but no one challenged the propriety of Samuel's words. To these people, Bountiful was as foreign to their daily experience as Moscow or Timbuktu. Yet a kind of elation settled over them—a resurgence of hope. They'd patiently borne the indignities of persecution for three long years, and now this new directive was as healing for them as any of Samuel's medicines. They embraced it joyfully. The gathering place had finally been named. It was to be Bountiful.

Harry joined us at the bottom of the ramp. He looked back one last time to see Samuel standing in the doorway. The venerable prophet watched the first canoes take to the waters. Heavy mist on the river made it impossible to see the opposite shore, but the dugouts slipped fearlessly into the murkiness. Because their prophet had spoken, no fog would hinder the people of Christ.

Mathoni organized the exodus as best he could in the few remaining minutes. When he'd finished, Shemnon approached and informed him that he would not be traveling to Bountiful with them at this time.

"I must go to Zarahemla," he said. "My wife is there. And my son."

"Yes," Mathoni agreed. "You must confer with Nephi. You must tell him what has happened here."

"I will," he promised.

Mathoni invited Shemnon to take his father's canoe. He and his brother would cross the river with one of the other families. Shemnon turned toward me and prepared to express his farewell. I stopped him.

"Wait," I said. "If you'll still have us, I'd like to go with you to Zarahemla."

Shemnon grinned. He knew the hazards of traveling alone, and the prospect of companionship made him deeply grateful. "Get your family into the canoe," he instructed. "We have no time to spare."

My decision to go to Zarahemla had fixed upon me in an instant. I recalled what Shemnon had said about people in Zarahemla knowing the location of Jacob's secret city. There had to be someone in that city who would tell me. Someone who would break the oath. But even if I couldn't find anyone, the Prophet Nephi was my key to learning what had happened to Garth. If I could learn where Garth had been sent to preach, it might lead me to his captors. Like Shemnon, I couldn't think about Bountiful right now. I only hoped the decision would not prove disasterous for my family.

In the last few moments before our canoes took to the water, Mathoni approached me and returned both of our backpacks. He'd left them near the fire when he first entered the encampment. "One of my attendants retrieved them in the confusion," he said.

What incredible luck! Everything was still intact—the flashlights, the canteens, the Indian blankets, Sabrina's Book of Mormon. The only item missing was Harry's pocketknife. I found it incomprehensible that Mathoni had thought of such a thing while evading a bloodthirsty mob. "You shouldn't have gone to the trouble," I said. "It wasn't worth risking your life."

"Consider it an apology for how I mistreated you in the marketplace."

"Mistreated me? You saved my life and the lives of my children. There is no conceivable reason for you to apologize."

"Then I return them in friendship," said Mathoni, smiling warmly. "And God willing, we shall both meet again—in Bountiful."

The canoe carrying my family and the one carrying Samuel's sons were the last to shove off. As Shemnon handed me the other oar, the torches were already visible through the trees. I hadn't paddled a canoe since I'd earned a merit badge for it in Boy Scouts, but the swish of an arrow over our heads helped me recall everything I needed to know.

As the mob emerged by the dozens from the surrounding woods, I raised my head to see if I could spot Samuel the Lamanite one last time in the pale light. I thought perhaps I could see his outline, still poised at the edge of the ramp, but the dark backdrop of the forested hill made it difficult to be certain. Mathoni and Mathonihah's canoe had already disappeared into the fog. The mob noticed that we were headed downriver instead of toward the opposite side, and they began to pursue us along the bank.

"Paddle!" Shemnon shouted.

We struggled to reach the point where the rivers converged. From there, the current would carry us out away from the bank. Another arrow bit the surface of the water just behind our tail. "Get down!" I barked at the children. They prostrated themselves on the floor.

We reached the convergence just as more men armed with bows emerged from the woods. Five or six of them gathered at the corner where the two rivers joined. They fired their bows, but we had paddled out far enough out now that the arrows torpedoed harmlessly under the surface of the water. Our canoe melted into the mist.

My daughter raised her head and looked back toward the elevated hut. We could barely see it now as the river curved around a wide bend. "What will they do to Samuel?" she asked.

"I'm not sure, honey," I said sorrowfully, although I feared I knew all too well.

We could still hear the cries of the mob, more savage than ever. No doubt they had found the aged prophet by now. All at once I saw a flame burst upwards in the midst of the fog. Then another flame, and another. The mob had set fire to the hut and all the tents. The flames climbed higher and higher. Even after our canoe had finished making its way around the bend, we could still see the glow above the trees. We stopped paddling and listened. The frenzied voices faded into the dawn. Steffanie broke down in tears.

"Like Abinadi of old," uttered Shemnon, recalling how another prophet had met a similar fate two hundred years before.

Samuel the Lamanite had foreseen it all so perfectly. He knew that by sacrificing himself, the mob's lust for blood would be satiated just long enough to allow the rest of us to escape. I marveled at his foresight and swallowed a painful lump in my throat.

Harry's emotions were not as easily discerned. His expression looked to be a mixture of shock, awe, and a glint of courage. He looked back at the fiery glow and said nothing, as if no one on earth might have convinced him that Samuel the Lamanite, the prophet of the sign, had just sealed his testimony with his life. Samuel couldn't die. He never would—not while a ten-year-old boy could keep him alive in his heart.

"What did he say to you, Harry?" I asked.

"Huh?"

"When you were alone with him in the hut, what did he say?"

"He said—" There was a crack in his voice, "he said to watch closely all that was about to happen. He said to learn what I could. It was all a shadow of things to come. Someday, before my life was over, I might see it all again."

He looked quizzical for an instant, then he threw off the expression and looked away. Harry was afraid to admit that he did not fully comprehend what Samuel had meant. I gazed back at the glow above the trees, wondering if I fully understood myself, and thinking that perhaps I understood better than I was ready to admit.

CHAPTER 20

The heavens were angry today. Clouds rolled across the sky like ocean waves, colliding with each other and breaking against the mountain tops. Yet stubbornly, the rain refused to fall. The turbulent sky seemed to confirm that Samuel the Lamanite had lost his life this day, yet the heavens were too bitter to shed any tears. I began to wonder if the three hours of destruction would commence at any moment. But because the storm procrastinated for so long, rumbling and threatening but never delivering, I dismissed the notion. Just the weather of the season.

Shemnon and I rowed in silence for much of the morning. My children planted themselves in the bottom of the dugout, emotionally and physically drained. Harry tried to sleep, but at every peal of thunder his eyes popped open and his body shuddered. Finally, Shemnon and I rested our oars and let the current carry us on its own. Steffanie climbed under my arm. She seemed to have forgiven me, at least a little, for having brought her to this terrible place. Either that, or her desperation for human tenderness had made her unparticular.

But even if Steffanie had begun to forgive me, I was far from forgiving myself. The thought kept tormenting me that when we were in Cody, Wyoming, I had been only a hundred short miles from my brother's residence in Billings, Montana. A four-hour detour—that's all it would have taken. The thought sickened me. What foolish notion had convinced me that my children would be better off in this place?

The river wound through narrow, moss-coated canyons, carrying our canoe north by northwest. The cliffs were alive with multiple species of birds, fluttering in and out of the crevices and crags. Shemnon told us we would have to abandon the canoe that evening; the current would soon become too difficult to navigate as it dropped into the valley and joined with the main branch of the River Sidon. By evening we would reach a settlement called Nahum Giff, and from there we would travel overland, due east, through a pass in the mountains. If there were no further delays, Shemnon expected to reach Zarahemla a day and a half later.

Around noon, after an enormous thunderclap, the rain finally commenced with a vengeance. Droplets boiled the surface of the river, and in a matter of minutes our canoe sloshed with several inches of rainwater. We sighted a shallow cavity along the cliff bank and paddled over to wait it out.

The cavity curled in about eight feet and ended. Inside, we found the cold remains of a campfire; river travelers had used this shelter before. My rain-soaked children dug into the backpacks to find dry clothing. Their spirits seemed to be lifting a little, and they joked about how they had needed a shower anyway. Steffanie showed us how ratty her hair had become. She raised her arms, curled her fingers into claws, and impersonated the Wicked Witch of the West: *"I'll get you, my pretty!"*

Shemnon had brought a sack of hard corn biscuits.

"Is that all we have to eat?" Harry inquired.

"Until the Lord blesses us with more," said Shemnon. "We should reach Nahum Giff before dark. There we will trade our canoe and buy food and supplies, with cacao beans to spare, I should think."

"Cacao beans?" repeated Harry.

"Money," I clarified. I remembered well all the bean-filled pouches that Nephites had carried at their waists when I was a boy.

"We will need anything extra to purchase clothing for the three of you," added Shemnon. "Otherwise, we'll have to convince everyone we meet that you are not sorcerers."

I had already taken a bite of biscuit when Shemnon announced that we would kneel and offer thanks. It occurred to me that I hadn't offered an official prayer to the Lord since . . . not since my escape from the Salt Lake County Jail. Had it really been that long? Because of my example (or lack of it), Harry and Steffanie hadn't prayed, either. Conspicuously, I stopped chewing and knelt down beside my son.

Shemnon's prayer lasted no less than fifteen minutes. Never in my life had I waited so long to eat a meal. He expressed gratitude for everything under the sun—our rescue in Laman, our narrow escape, our shelter from the storm. He thanked the Lord for the mission and example of Samuel the Lamanite, for the fact that our canoe did not leak, and for the life-giving rain.

What an ungrateful soul I was! It had been years since I'd felt truly grateful for anything—not since Renae's death. Shemnon, however, reminded me of how much I still possessed. I almost began to weep, but I decided it was best to be strong for the sake of my children. In the midst of Shemnon's prayer I began a prayer of my own, asking the Lord to forgive me and to strengthen me. My children fidgeted a lot, but when the prayer was over, I'm certain they were never so confident that the Lord had truly blessed something they were about to eat.

Harry and Steffanie ate their biscuits at the lip of the cavity. Fresh rainwater trickled down from above, merging into a single glistening cascade at the center of the overhang. They took turns standing open-mouthed beneath the stream.

Now and then I would catch myself watching Shemnon. I knew so little about him, yet I trusted him implicitly. Few people in my life had earned that status so quickly. He wasn't much of a conversationalist, and frankly, I couldn't discover an ounce of humor in the man. But this judgment may have been hasty and unfair, especially in light of all the dreary events we had encountered over the past two days. He seemed curiously shy, almost to the point that I wondered how he'd managed his calling as a missionary.

As yet, Shemnon hadn't graced us with a single question about our origin—not one inquiry about our unusual clothing, manners, or supplies. When he finally posed his first question, it was framed in a very roundabout way. I appreciated this approach, as I wasn't prepared to divulge everything at once.

"How long have you known Garplimpton, the pale prophet?" he inquired.

"Most of my life," I said. "His wife is my sister."

"I see," said Shemnon thoughtfully. "Perhaps by now he has returned to Zarahemla. You will see him again the day after tomorrow."

I shook my head. "I have reason to believe that Garth is in Jacobugath. He is also a prisoner of King Jacob."

Shemnon was flabbergasted. "Where did you hear this?"

"From Jacob himself, on the same day he kidnapped my daughter."

Shemnon furrowed his brow. "This is very odd. I have never heard of Jacob kidnapping anyone—leastwise a prophet or a missionary. He has only sought to murder such people. Why would he have taken Garplimpton captive?"

"That's the sixty-four-thousand-dollar question," I said.

"The what?"

"Umm, the question we'd all like to have answered. Somehow Jacob plans to use my daughter to force Garth to give up certain information. I couldn't tell you what that information is."

Shemnon thought about this. He shook his head again. "It's all very strange."

It occurred to me that Jacob might be as much of a mystery among these people as Garth or myself. "What is known about King Jacob of the Moon?" I asked.

"He may be the incarnation of the devil himself," said Shemnon. "I first knew of him in the days of Lachoneus the First. He is said to have fought beside the robbers during the Gadianton wars, a little more than twelve years ago. When the great general Gidgiddoni surrounded the robbers on the plains of Teancum, it was Jacob who betrayed the Gadianton leader, Zemnarihah, into Nephite hands. They hanged Zemnarihah upon a tree; but Jacob, because he professed a change of heart, was set free. In a few short years, he rose to become one of the three chief judges under Lachoneus the Younger.

"They made a former robber *a judge?*" I asked in amazement.

Shemnon looked downcast. "Evil does not enter a righteous heart uninvited. Many knew of Jacob's past, but he flattered all the right people. Wickedness always seeks its own."

It seemed incredible to me that a nation could turn away from righteousness so soon after fighting a war to preserve it.

"As a judge," Shemnon continued, "Jacob put many Christians to death."

"And the people just let him do this?"

"He did it secretly. It was unlawful to execute anyone without the governor's consent. When Lachoneus learned of Jacob's activities, he tried to have him removed. Shortly thereafter, Lachoneus himself was assassinated, and the government fell apart."

"Didn't anyone suspect Jacob?"

"Yes. Everyone suspected him. It was only a day later that he vied to make himself king. But he underestimated the number of his enemies. Even the most corrupt citizens of Zarahemla hated those who had conspired to destroy the government. Jacob and his followers fled the city by night. An army pursued, but he couldn't be overtaken."

"When we reach Zarahemla," I told Shemnon, "I need you to help me locate someone who knows how to reach Jacobugath, or who will at least introduce me to people who might help."

Shemnon frowned. "To even make such inquiries would stir up more ill feeling than you can imagine. To learn the answer would mean consorting with people in the darkest corners of the city."

"Is there anyone," I pleaded, *"anyone* who might have abandoned Jacob's band, perhaps even converted to Christ?"

"That is impossible," Shemnon snapped. "When a man . . . or a woman . . . utters the oaths of the Evil One, there is no escape. The chains are too strong. If escape is possible, it is only by the mercy and power of God. But this kind of mercy must be requested—and that is the one thing a member of a secret combination is taught never to do."

He spoke with a curious zeal, as if he knew this from personal experience. After a moment, the muscles in his face relaxed. He sighed. "I will help you, Jimhawkins. But do not be disappointed when we are halted at every turn. We should first seek counsel with the Prophet Nephi."

"Thank you," I said, still perplexed by the intensity of his emotions. I concluded that I was not the only one harboring secrets.

* * *

The rain stopped as suddenly as it had started. A ray of sunlight bore a chink in the clouds. We returned to our canoe, dumped out the rainwater, and set adrift again in the current. The bulk of the storm had fled south, leaving only swatches of gray clouds under an inviting blue sky. Harry and Steffanie watched an eagle descend upon the water, snatch up a fish in its talons, and fly away. By late afternoon, the steep canyon walls had given way to lush hillsides, some of which had been cleared and cultivated. Most of the landscape, however, remained rough and unpopulated.

That evening, we reached a community of huts that covered the bank on both sides of the river. According to Shemnon, the villages on the right and left shore were known as Nahum and Giff respectively. This place was a crossing station along the overland road to the city of Sidon in the west and Zarahemla in the east. The prosperity of the residents depended upon the number of travelers who requisitioned the local fleet of canoes and rafts to cross the river. Shemnon said it had been established by the stripling warriors of Helaman for the purpose of moving men and supplies in wartime.

I jumped into the soft mud along the bank and pulled our canoe out of the water. Shemnon immediately began haggling with the locals to see if anyone might be interested in purchasing a fine mahogany dugout. I noticed two other canoes under construction down the bank. Craftsmen tediously chipped away at wide tree trunks with stone axes and scrapers, leaving drifts of crimson wood shavings on either side of the operation. I figured anybody would have happily foregone such labor to buy a ready-made canoe. Within minutes, our dugout was surrounded by five or six prospects. Shemnon reached an agreeable price with the most determined of the lot. We received for our troubles a pouch of cacao beans and two feather quills filled with silver.

"Now we can dress you in the proper clothing," Shemnon told us.

I had already noted many locals gaping at us as if we were exotic animals and advising their children to keep away. It seemed to me that a change of clothing might fend off stares for a minute or so, but our pale features would soon draw them back. We simply did not *look* Nephite, and nothing we wore would change that. But perhaps we would no longer be labeled as sorcerers or Gadiantons.

For the convenience of travelers, a scant marketplace traded goods every day of the week, unlike other village markets that only opened one or two days out of seven. The selection was grim—strictly necessities associated with long-distance travel. We saw many animal hides in various stages of skinning and tanning. The smells of lime and turpentine mingled with the stench of decaying meat. Harry took special interest in a display of dead bats, hanging between two poles and strung out to their full wingspans. I couldn't guess what practical use anyone would have for these flying rodents; they reminded me of ingredients a witch might throw into a boiling kettle.

A shop featuring flint and bone tools also displayed two or three floormats stacked with clothing. Harry and I dredged up two cotton mantles, both brown with thin strips of red and black along the hem. We also purchased three pairs of coarse deer-leather sandals. The shoes were hard and flat, with a high guard at the heel. Tether strips wrapped them tightly in place over the ankle, leaving much of the foot exposed. The greasy-haired shopkeeper suggested a trade straight across—his clothing for ours. He even offered to throw in some turquoise neckbeads, but I politely declined. I especially wanted to retain our modern sneakers, worried that Nephite footwear would grind painful blisters into our feet.

As for women's clothing, the situation looked even grimmer. There wasn't much call for feminine apparel in these remote parts. Steffanie sorted through a few drab masculine outfits, then inquired of the shopkeeper if he stocked any of the colorful skirts she'd seen among the Lamanites. He shook his head. "Only what you see."

"Maybe I can be of assistance, young lady," announced a sonorous voice.

I'd seen the man who had spoken down by the river. He'd been standing with several other men, watching us intently. At the time, his interest hadn't seemed any more profound than anyone else's, but I noticed him because he wore a full beard. Beards seemed rather unique in this land. Facial hair on Nephites and Lamanites was generally thin and scraggly; most plucked their beards from the time they were very young. If the beard was stubborn, a mother might even go so far as to burn a child's face with a hot cloth. This man had inherited from his forebears whatever gene was responsible for thick and curled whiskers. Now that I thought about it, he'd never really left my peripheral vision. He'd followed us up from the river.

His clothing seemed as out of place as ours. The upper half of his one-piece mantle was leather with a violet-colored sash around the waist. The material bunched up in broad folds at his knees and again at his elbows in a style vaguely resembling eighteenth-century pantaloons, but without the stockings. Instead, he wore furry leg bands accented with beads. The bands dangled down from his knee and attached to his sandals, as if each leg were caught in some kind of furry net. A strange, mythical-looking bird had been tatooed on the backs of his hands. The men who stood behind him were also dressed and tattooed this way. The attire was obviously meant to identify him and his companions with some sort of occupation or organization.

With a smile on his lips that seemed vaguely predatory, he strolled up to my daughter. "In my train, I have garments and fashions from all over the world, some of which would look very fine on you." He raised a lock of Steffanie's hair. She pressed closer to me for protection.

"She is taken," Shemnon insisted curtly.

"Taken?" the man repeated. "By you, Nephite?"

Shemnon glanced at me. I didn't understand. *Taken?* It sounded as if Shemnon was telling him that my daughter was betrothed or married.

The man had caught Shemnon's glance in my direction. "Is she yours?" he inquired.

Shemnon sent me a discreet nod.

"Yes," I said. "She is mine."

"Your wife or your daughter?" The man grinned; the others laughed. The question was a subtle, double-edged insult. If she was my wife, it implied that I was too old and undeserving. If she was my daughter, to call her my wife made things equally awkward.

"Daughter," I replied uneasily.

Shemnon looked disappointed in my answer.

"And the boy?" the man asked. Harry moved behind me.

"My son," I said.

The bearded man looked pleased. "I am Kumarcaah of the Pochteca. I am a merchant of the exotic and the divine. My home is the volcano and my path is the stars. I see by your family's fair skin that you, too, are from a far distant land."

"They are Nephites," Shemnon declared.

Kumarcaah laughed. He didn't believe this for an instant.

"Come with me, friends," Kumarcaah invited. "Dine at my camp across the river. We will share good stories and the finest corn beer in all the lands. Bring your daughter and your son. Tonight you will be our honored guests."

"We must decline," said Shemnon.

Kumarcaah's patience with him was thinning. "I did not ask you, Nephite."

Shemnon had given me enough hints to indicate that this man had shady intentions, but as yet I was uncertain what those intentions might be. "No, thank you," I said. "Some other time."

Kumarcaah's eyes narrowed. He quickly recovered, however, and said, "I wish you would reconsider, friend. I could make you a very rich man."

"We are not interested."

The man turned up his hands. "Very well. Good evening to you, my friends."

He grinned one last time and rejoined his company. After exchanging a few words with them that I did not hear, the group began strolling toward the river, as if casually enjoying the sights and sounds of the village. A musical band was kicking up down at the water's edge, complete with whistles, flutes, and drums.

Shemnon hastily gathered up our clothes and piled them into my arms. He snatched up an extra mantle, estimated to be about Steffanie's size, and paid the shopkeeper. We left the marketplace at a brisk pace.

"What was that all about?" I asked.

"We have to leave this place—tonight," said Shemnon.

"But it's almost dark," Harry noted.

"We must get as far away from those men as possible."

"Who were they?" Steffanie asked.

"Pochteca," Shemnon declared. "Long-distance traders."

"What's wrong with them?" Harry wondered. "They were going to give us dinner. I'm *starving.*"

"You would not have enjoyed the conversation," Shemnon informed him.

"Why not?"

"It would have concerned you and your sister." Shemnon turned back to me. "We must change your clothes and purchase supplies as quickly as possible. The faster we are out of this village, the better. I almost wish you had said that Steffanie was your wife, though I doubt it would have made any difference. Those men are not accustomed to taking no for an answer. You are foreigners; that alone would justify their intentions. Because you are strangers, no one would interfere."

"Interfere with what?" I asked again. "What were their intentions?"

"The Pochteca trade in many things," said Shemnon. "But these days their most profitable commodity is not obsidian or salt or stingray spines. It is human beings. They want to sell your children as slaves."

CHAPTER 21

The audacity of the Pochteca was almost staggering. Who in their right minds would believe that a parent could willingly sell his children into slavery? As we filled our backpacks with various foodstuffs from the marketplace, Shemnon revealed that the men who had made the offer did not act without precedent. In the face of the economic chaos created by the dissolution of government, selling off a child or two was the best insurance against starvation for many of the poorer Nephites. It was also the surest means for many in the higher classes to hang on to their wealth.

"Trafficking in slaves, especially children, has become a common enterprise in our land," said Shemnon. "Your two children, because of their ages, their health, and their fair features, would be deemed particularly valuable. In the minds of men like Kumarcaah, it's an opportunity too good to pass up."

Slavery among the Nephites! When I was here as a boy, slavery had been squarely against the law. And here I was, willing to sacrifice everything I had to save my oldest daughter—a sacrifice I'd make for *any* of my children. The very idea that anyone could exchange their own flesh and blood for *money* enraged me.

"Who buys these children?" I demanded, imagining in my heart the slimiest of villains.

"There are always buyers," said Shemnon grimly. "The Pochteca will trade anywhere, even in the lands of their enemies if they can make a high enough profit. They will carry Nephite slaves far to the north and south. The children are never seen in their homeland again."

All at once, my anxiousness to get out of here exceeded that of Shemnon.

Our final purchases in the market were three sleeping mats and a pair of thin, itchy blankets. I envied my children, who would retain the soft Indian blankets. It was dark by the time we set out, making our way by moonlight toward a pass that ran between two ghostly peaks. I was determined not to break out the flashlights unless it became imperative. I still wasn't sure how Shemnon would react.

A mile was all we managed in the blackness. At one point, I heard something behind us—a scrape upon a rock. We held perfectly still and listened. No shapes appeared to be moving among the trees or brush. We continued on and heard nothing more. Without more evidence than a single sound, I was not ready to conclude that we were being followed; but I became extremely wary.

We located a clearing off to the side of the road and unrolled our sleeping mats. We could make out the faint flicker of several torchlights along the river. Shemnon had purchased a new flint, but we decided not to build a fire. Our dinner consisted of cold tomales and dry meat from an unspecified animal. The highlight of the meal was salted sunflower seeds, if such could be considered a highlight.

After eating, the children dozed off almost immediately. Shemnon remained alert. I decided to stay awake with him as long as I could, but I knew my stamina was no match for his.

We directed our eyes toward the village. Our hearing was dominated by crickets and the vague trickle of a small stream somewhere above. In the darkness, I did not have a clear perception of the lay of the land. On either side of us, the hills were smothered in dense thickets of shrub-like trees. To our left I perceived a ravine meandering into the valley by a southward course.

"Would they follow us in the dark?" I asked.

"Yes," said Shemnon. "If they know we're here, they'll be coming. If not tonight, at first light."

His certainty was disturbing. I wondered if we should have camped farther off the main road, down in the ravine.

Shemnon rejected this. "From here we can see their torches as they approach."

"What if they don't bring torches?"

"They're not so desperate yet to search in the dark. If they come, they will bring torches."

"We'll stay up in shifts."

Shemnon nodded and agreed to take the first watch.

I suddenly realized the enormity of this man's sacrifice for our welfare. Anyone else would have politely skipped out on us. If attacked by slave traders, I doubted very much if a Nephite would be allowed to live. Just being in our presence placed Shemnon at a substantial risk. "Tomorrow," I told him, "if you decide to go on alone, I'll understand. I assume the road is marked clearly enough. We should be able reach Zarahemla by ourselves."

Shemnon looked hurt. "To abandon strangers in a strange land is the act of a barbarian," he said.

"But you have a wife and child."

Shemnon gazed off toward the river for a long time. "I also have a promise. As I serve my fellowman, my family will be protected. I will return to them safely." He spoke solemnly, as if the promise had been issued under an inspired hand. This fact alone made it seem that we were eminently better off to keep him with us. We might prove beneficiaries of the promise by association.

"Without this promise," Shemnon continued, "I would not have come." He spoke somberly, as if he shuddered to think how close he had come to denying himself the blessings of God. "I lost one family. I couldn't bear to lose another."

"You were married before?" I asked.

Shemnon nodded. It took him great courage to tell me about it. Several times he faltered, and I thought he might break off the account. But he drudged on with his tale; recounting it seemed to be part of the process of healing.

His first wife was named Nemrah. She had been betrothed to him since infancy, as was the custom in the land of Bountiful. Shemnon smiled as he recalled her passion for life, then frowned as he remembered how this passion had made her infinitely impatient. She'd wanted so badly to know the deep mysteries of heaven and earth, but she rejected the gospel path to such knowledge. "She envied the ways of the Gadiantons," said Shemnon, "and spoke of such things as eagerly as the things of God. In reality, she saw very little difference between the two."

He explained that whenever a friend or kinsmen was ill, Nemrah would as soon prescribe the oracles of magic as call upon the powers of the priesthood. In her mind they were one and the same, and Shemnon's efforts to distinguish between the two fell on deaf ears. In the end, she did indeed come to see them as two different things, and the secret ways of the Gadiantons were declared to be far superior. The last thing Nemrah had said to him was, "I cannot devote my days to you and my nights to the Divine Jaguar!" That very day she joined herself permanently to the ranks of the Gadiantons.

"When she left," Shemnon concluded gravely, "she was carrying my child in her womb. I never saw the baby, nor did I ever see Nemrah again."

The story seemed to exhaust him. In certain ways he still blamed himself, particularly for the loss of his unborn child to the world of darkness. I no longer wondered where Shemnon had acquired his expertise on secret combinations. When he had said it was impossible to break the chains of the Evil One without requisitioning the mercy of God, he had spoken from experience. Leaving his second family while he preached in the land of Melek must have been very difficult, and his determination to reach his wife and child before traveling to Bountiful made more sense to me now.

I was about to express my deepest thanks to him for what he'd done for my family when I saw him lean forward with a start. Three torchlights had broken away from the village and were beginning a slow ascent up the trail.

"They know we're here," said Shemnon.

I wasn't about to doubt him, but to me it was only three faint sparks wandering away from the village. "How can you be certain?" I asked.

We watched for another minute. The torches were indeed climbing toward us.

"No one travels these roads at night," Shemnon insisted, "except villains like the Pochteca."

"What do we do?"

"We have to hide," said Shemnon.

"Where?"

He looked around. "We'll climb into the ravine and make our way down toward the river."

This seemed ridiculous. In the morning we'd end up back at the village, and have to face them all over again. "What if we climbed higher up the road?" I suggested.

"They have torches," he reminded me. "In the dark they would easily overtake us."

"We won't be in the dark," I said, reaching to unzip one of the backpacks.

Shemnon became uneasy. He'd already seen the contents of these backpacks on the temple steps in Laman. I don't think he believed we were actual Gadiantons, but our clothing and tools seemed to suggest some sort of association with them. Might we have stolen these things from King Jacob?

I pulled out one of the flashlights and switched on the beam. Shemnon gasped.

"Sorcery!" he cried, shielding his eyes.

"No, no," I said. "In my land, we use these to light our way in the dark. They are gifts from the Lord." I'd never really thought of flashlights as heavenly gifts, but it made perfect sense. After all, what *were* they if not the divine inspiration of some twentieth-century inventor?

"Have you ever heard the story of the Brother of Jared?" I asked Shemnon.

"Yes," he replied uncertainly. "Nephi has told us many of these stories."

"Do you remember when the finger of God touched the sixteen stones to light the way to the promised land?"

"Yes."

"These instruments work in sort of the same way." I tried to hand him the flashlight. "Take it. It's okay."

Steffanie roused. "What's happening?"

"We have to leave," I said.

"What time is it?" mumbled Harry.

I continued to coax Shemnon. "Just hold it in your hand."

"Will it burn?"

"Of course not."

Shemnon set his fingers against the plastic casing, retracting his hand twice before he believed me that the surface was cool. Then he gripped it firmly and shined it back at us. He shined it all around and up toward the sky, expecting, I suppose, to see the light beam bore a hole in the clouds and reflect off the surface of the moon.

"Only God could cause such a miracle," he decided. "Your people must be very righteous to have received such blessings."

"Well, I don't know about that."

Then I thought about it. Never had the miracles of God and the ingenuity of man seemed so perfectly meshed. It almost seemed unfair that the wonders of modern technology belonged to our generation alone. I concluded that the term "dispensation of the fulness of times" meant more than just spiritual knowledge.

We pointed out the approaching torches to Harry and Steffanie. Within minutes we were hiking up the trail again, penetrating deeper into the mountain pass. After an hour we reached an overlook. The lights of the village were almost too faint to distinguish now, and we could no longer see the tiny torchlights. Whoever had been coming up the trail must have discovered our empty camp, given up, and turned back.

* * *

The next morning Harry, Steffanie, and I changed into our Nephite apparel. The mantle that Shemnon had grabbed for Steff was yellow with decorated black bands at the borders. I told her she looked like a bumble bee. I don't think she appreciated my sense of humor.

Within a few hours of embarking that morning, my prophecy that Nephite sandals would wear blisters into our feet began to be fulfilled. The tethers also wore raw, red lines into our legs. How could the Nephites stand to wear such things? Their feet must have looked like massive callused lumps. Shemnon had spent a lifetime walking from place to place and I don't think I could have driven a nail into his foot with a hammer. Harry and Steff only agreed to wear the sandals with double pairs of socks. As a result, we stopped periodically to pick off hundreds of burrs.

We generally avoided all other travelers. Sometimes we would slip off the road and wait for them to pass; twice we took a roundabout trail to keep us at a safe distance.

I asked Shemnon why we were being so cautious. "You think we might run into more slave traders?"

"Not necessarily," he replied. He explained that avoiding strangers had become a necessary custom in the wilderness of Zarahemla. There were so many criminals and marauders in the mountains that strangers who drew near were usually judged to have wrongful intentions. It had been this way since the days of Gadianton, when the robbers had made the mountains their domain. Shemnon said a spirit of mutual trust and camaraderie had once thrived among travelers, but that era was long gone.

The rain fell again shortly after lunch and continued all afternoon. It finally broke as we reached the top of the pass, looking east into the crumpled green velvet hills of the Sidon Valley. Golden light from the setting sun painted fans between tiers of charcoal clouds. We decided to camp here tonight. Shemnon promised we would reach Zarahemla tomorrow afternoon. He prepared dinner while the children and I built a circle of rocks for a fire. As we worked, a tiny deer with limpid eyes came out of the bush and grazed not more than ten yards away. We kept perfectly still. It took a full minute before it spotted us. Then it stopped, pointed its feet like a ballerina, and skipped away.

Night descended. The cloudy sky was torn by patches of black infinity, alive with stars. Fireflies added to the innumerable pinpoints of light. Having overcome his initial shyness, Shemnon tossed out dozens of questions regarding our origin. I told him all I could without mentioning time travel. Yet I now wonder if he might have grasped such concepts as well as anyone with half an imagination.

As Steffanie chewed the crusty tortilla that Shemnon had made for us that evening, she hurt her tooth on a small rock that had been ground into the dough. Shemnon didn't understand why she was so distressed. In his day, this was a natural and expected hazard.

"What I wouldn't give right now for a meatball sandwich," Steffanie pined.

"How 'bout a T-bone steak at the Wagonmaster?" suggested Harry.

"Or a shrimp bowl at Mulboons." Steff licked her lips.

"I got it," said Harry. "All-You-Can-Eat at Chuck-A-Rama." Back at home, it had always been Up-Chuck-A-Rama, but at the moment the mere thought of it sent our salivary glands into overdrive.

Shemnon asked many questions to try and grasp the particulars of our society. By the end of the evening he knew all about rock concerts, four-wheeling, line-dancing, and water parks. He also could have listed each of my children's favorite TV programs and borne witness to their misery at having missed all the episodes that week. I considered trying to explain television, but I didn't want to short-circuit the poor guy's brain on the first night that he felt comfortable asking questions.

Before everyone had settled down to sleep, I arose to place one last chunk of wood on the fire and discovered Steffanie reading Sabrina's Book of Mormon by flashlight. When I leaned closer, she slid the book under her arm, as if I'd caught her doing something mischievous.

"What part were you reading?" I inquired politely.

"I don't know," she replied. "Just reading."

Under her hand I noticed the heading for 3 Nephi, Chapter 11. "I see. The part about Christ. My favorite. What did you think of it?"

She bristled slightly. "What am I supposed to think of it?"

I grinned. "Does this mean that you're starting to believe it?"

"Does it matter if I believe it or not?"

My grin sagged. "Well, of course it matters."

"If all of this is true, what does it change?"

I pulled in my chin. "It changes everything. It changes the way you look at every aspect of your life."

She shut the book. "I wish it *wasn't* true. I wish it was all just a fairy-tale. It was easier when I didn't believe there was a God. Now I have to wonder why He doesn't care."

"Doesn't *care?* The very fact that we even have a Book of Mormon shows us how much He cares."

"So he gave us a book. Big deal."

Once again, my middle daughter had raised the hair on the back of my neck. "Maybe you should read it before you say something as silly as that."

"It's not gonna help us get home. It's not gonna help us find Melody. It won't protect us from the people who want to hurt us. It won't take away the blisters on my feet. It has no practical use whatsoever!"

"It turns our minds to God," I said. "God is the one who helps us."

"When?"

"What do you mean, 'when'? All the time. Every day. How do you think we've come as far as we have?"

"Shemnon."

"Shemnon?"

"He's the one who took us to the camp of Samuel the Lamanite, isn't he? He's the one who saved us from the slave traders."

"Well, who do think brought Shemnon into our lives?"

"Luck."

"There's no such thing. There's nothing you can name that isn't touched by the hand of God."

"Give me a break, Dad. So that's why my sister was kidnapped, eh? The hand of God?"

"God can't control men, Steff. We have our agency"

"What about Mom? Why did she die? Was that the hand of God, too?"

I glared at the campfire. I knew the appropriate reply. I should have said something about God's eternal plan, or how the pains of life are but an instant, or how life's trials can be a testament of God's love. I might have given her much the same speech I'd given to Harry that night on the Wyoming highway. But for some reason, at that exact moment, I couldn't seem to grasp the concepts; they suddenly seemed so abstract and intangible. I was having a genuine stupor of thought. This disturbed me greatly. My daughter was struggling; she needed to be comforted. This was no time to flake out.

"It kills you, doesn't it?" she said finally.

"What?"

"Not having all the answers. It kills you."

"No, I can—I have—" It was no use. I leaned back and sighed. "How long have you known that I didn't have all the answers?"

She smiled tenderly. "It's a recent discovery."

She leaned over to kiss my cheek. Somehow the revelation that I was human did not appear to have crushed her last bud of faith, as I had always feared since the day I became a parent. Actually, it gave her a great deal of relief. From now on, I hoped she would feel confident enough to search out the truths of God for herself. No longer would she feel like I was always trying to take credit. The transition wouldn't be all that easy for me, however; I liked being in a position to steer and control and manipulate gospel explanations in just the right way. It would be hard to let go.

My daughter lay her head on my shoulder. We watched the fire together and let the flames draw us in. I'm not certain which one of us fell asleep first.

It began as a peaceful, dreamless night. I might have expected to awaken to the welcoming glow of a rising sun. Instead, I awakened in pitch blackness with the feel of cold obsidian against my throat.

"Try anything," said a familiar voice, "and I'll slit you from one end to the other like a snake."

CHAPTER 22

"Kill the Nephite!" shouted Kumarcaah.

"He's getting away!" cried one of his men.

I caught a glimpse of Shemnon's shadow fleeing into the woods and several more shadows pursuing, bows loaded, daggers drawn. A flurry of arrows zipped after the figure in the darkness. Tips shattered against boulders or imbedded in the trunks of trees, but none met their target. Shemnon had escaped.

Harry tried to slip into the woods on the other side of the road, but was caught and wrestled to the ground, kicking and screaming, by three men twice his size. He bloodied one of their noses with his elbow, but in the end, like Steffanie and myself, he was bound hand and foot and laid beside us in a row like the trophies of a game hunter.

"Should we kill the old man?" one of them inquired, referring, I believe, to me. "He's not worth his own weight in salt."

"Leave him for now," said Kumarcaah. "His back appears to be good. He has most of his teeth. He'll profit us a senine or two."

"He'd never survive the march north. If we can't sell him in Zarahemla, I say we give him to the reds."

"Agreed," said Kumarcaah.

Give me to the reds? It sounded as if they were planning to turn me over to the Communists. I had a feeling their definition was even more ominous. An image of blood sacrifice came to mind.

"Here! Look at these!" cried someone excitedly.

Daylight increased, but because of my position on the ground, I couldn't see what they were doing. I suspected they were rummaging through our backpacks.

Kumarcaah approached and stood over me. "How does this work?" he demanded. I lifted my head. He held one of our flashlights. "These are the lights that you use to travel at night. Yes?" He kicked me in the arm to encourage a reply.

"Yes," I confirmed. They must have seen the glow of our flashlights as we ascended the slope the night before last.

Kumarcaah had been fiddling with it as he spoke. Without needing my instruction, he pressed the correct button and the flashlight ignited. The other slave traders gathered around it in awe. Having traveled to distant lands in search of strange and exotic merchandise, the light beam did not appear to frighten them as much as it might frighten an uncosmopolitan peasant.

"It will earn us a fortune!" someone exclaimed.

"Yes, if we were to sell it," countered Kumarcaah. "These I will keep."

"Should we stoke the fire and brand the new slaves?" someone asked.

"There'll be plenty of time for that in Zarahemla."

They kept us face down on the ground for another half hour while the bulk of their supply train, which had camped somewhere nearby, arrived at our location. I could hear Steffanie beside me whispering an angry, reproachful prayer. She didn't understand how God could allow this to happen. She told God she *hated* Him. She told Him she wanted nothing to do with Him. Harry, on the other side of her, cringed at her tone. "Don't pray like that," he said. "It's not right."

"It's how I feel," she replied through hot tears.

"Dad," Harry pleaded, "don't let her pray like that."

"The Lord has been with us up to now," I reminded them, sounding as confident as I could with my face in the dirt. "We can't lose hope."

When the supply train arrived, the cords on our hands and feet were loosed. A stiff leather collar was strapped around each of our necks. They wrapped an extra apparatus around my hips that restricted the movement of my arms and kept my hands at my waist. It reminded me of the fetters worn by hard-core criminals as they were taken to and from the courtroom. For my children, the collar was presumed to be enough to discourage an escape attempt.

The Pochteca caravan consisted of no less than seventy people, all traveling on foot. Half of them were porters with heavy bales of merchandise on their backs. Most of them were slaves like us and wore similar collars. There were six other children besides Harry and Steffanie—all destined to be sold as slaves. The oldest was about fifteen. All of them looked filthy and miserable, forced to walk in concert like a chain gang with a connecting line attached to their collars. There was a similar line of eight adults—five women and three men, looking sickly and bent. These were the ones judged too weak to carry bales like the others.

Many of the other men in the train, including those who had attacked us in the dark, were soldiers. They marched at the front and rear of the column, wielding long spears and wearing wooden helmets crafted to look like some sort of mythical animal. I decided it was the head of an eagle. The wearer's face peeked out from inside the eagle's mouth, as if the bird were swallowing him. A similar symbol was also woven into the feathers on their shields, like a company logo.

The remainder of the men were elders and apprentices of the Pochteca. Kumarcaah, of course, was the chief elder of the group.

Because I was declared to be "unbroken," they connected my collar into the center of the chain of adult slaves, behind a woman with large boils on her legs. My children were tied at the front of a separate line. I guess because they looked healthier than the other children, the Pochteca presumed it would force the rest to march a little faster.

A taskmaster was assigned to keep us in line. He shouted in our faces, "Anyone caught speaking will lose their tongues!" He sliced a chunk out of the air with his blade to demonstrate. The injunction was directed primarily at me, as the others already knew this rule by heart and would never have dreamed to disobey. The children, as far as I could tell, were not issued such a harsh rule. Having no tongues might lessen their market value. Speechless adults, I supposed, could even be considered an asset—more work, less talk. For the children, disobedience meant several lashes with a switch.

It was an excruciating moment when my children were marched to the rear of the train where I could no longer see them. I desperately wanted to call out their names, but it would have been the last time I'd have ever spoken.

Where was Shemnon? He was our last ray of hope. Maybe, for the sake of his own neck, he'd finally decided it was best to abandon us. Without Shemnon, it seemed we had no allies left in this world. But what could one Nephite do against an armed caravan?

As we descended into the valley, I could see a distant ribbon of silver that was surely the River Sidon. We bypassed dozens of outlying hamlets and settlements. The corn in the fields stood twelve feet high, with morning glory and squash vines spiraling up the stems.

The population of this area had tripled since I was a child. As we passed through the countryside, the local peasants took great delight in gawking at the slaves. Some looked away in shame. I wondered if a few of them had actually sold children to trading companies like this.

About midday, the gleaming white walls of the Nephite capital appeared in the distance. The city was huge! When I was young, the walls encircling the city had not extended across the river; now they surrounded another full square mile on the opposite bank. The Sidon flowed right through the center of town. Years ago, the wall had been constructed chiefly of timber and earthworks; now the timber had been reinforced by plaster and stone. It stood twice as high, making it much easier to imagine Samuel the Lamanite poised upon the bulwarks declaring the word of God. The image gave me courage. If God could protect Samuel against the slings and arrows of his enemies, he could surely protect us.

The road into the city was heavy with travelers, most of whom moved to one side or the other, parted by the spears of our lead soldiers. While walking with Shemnon the day before, he had explained to me that the entire city had been sectioned off by the various tribes and kinships, each with their own separate laws of government. The heads of the various tribes had instituted general laws that would prevent them from trespassing against one another, but there was no agreement about whose responsibility it was to maintain and protect the city. I saw no soldiers or lookouts above the city gate. How long, I wondered, could this place hold out against a foreign invasion? If Jacob's army was even half as strong as he boasted, he'd conquer Zarahemla in a single day.

Garbage and filth seeped, protruded, decayed, and slithered almost everywhere I looked. And I had thought the city of Laman was bad! The stench in most neighborhoods was unbearable. Much of the sewer system with its gutters and drainage canals, constructed a generation earlier, had become clogged and damaged through neglect, and now refuse leaked into the streets. No one would fix any section which extended beyond the borders controlled by his individual tribe. Therefore, *none* of it got fixed.

Prostitutes and beggars lined the main street. Surprisingly, I saw very few children. Now and then I would catch a tiny head or hand disappearing around a corner or behind a ledge. Children were understandably terrified of the Pochteca.

I noted the same flat foreheads and squinting eyes on men and women under thirty. Had a strange, disfiguring disease afflicted the younger generation?

Despite the degradation, business was booming in the Zarahemla marketplace. Never in the history of the Nephites had they enjoyed such an abundance and variety of goods. I saw heaping piles of grain, beautifully crafted statues and pottery, stacks of lumber, corrals of live animals, mountains of tools and textiles, and a food selection that would have rivaled any Albertson's or Smith's.

Prices were high. Yesterday Shemnon had explained that for several years now, all prices had been fixed by corrupt market administrators who siphoned off a large chunk of the profits. Merchants paid levies to every tribe represented in Zarahemla. The poor were helpless against this kind of inflation; they had no recourse but beggary and crime. Many shopkeepers wore weapons and would not hesitate to cut the throat of anyone caught trying to steal. Roving "policemen," paid by the merchants, carried clubs to batter thieves to death on the spot.

We wouldn't be the only slaves for sale. All along the market streets I noted men, women, and children wearing collars attached to long poles. As we marched along the avenue, they watched us with glazed, listless expressions on their faces.

There was a wide, dusty space at the west end of the market where long-distance traders like the Pochteca gathered to sell wares to the local merchants. It was also a place where preferred customers could purchase certain items at wholesale. Many of the merchants left their canopies and blankets in the hands of underlings while they followed our train to get first dibs on the new commodities.

For the first time in nine hours, I got a close-up view of my children. They looked exhausted and sunburned, a layer of trail dust caking their skin. Nevertheless, their faces beamed when they saw me, and my heart came into my throat. All the slaves, except those who helped sort out the bales, were forced to sit in a cluster under the hot afternoon sun. My throat was parched; most of us hadn't partaken of water for several hours. My children and I continued to exchange nervous but encouraging glances. No one had announced whether the ban on speaking had been lifted, so we remained silent and waited in the heat for the next phase of our fate to reveal itself.

My eyes continually wandered about the plaza, looking for some sort of opportunity that might allow me to escape. In a sitting position, my hands were able to reach my neck. All I needed was to have our taskmaster distracted long enough to allow me to unstrap the collar—a process which might take as long as two or three minutes, since I wasn't exactly certain how the strap worked. Somewhere in this city lived an enclave of Christians. If I escaped, how could I find them? What would I do about my children? I realized I could never leave them, even if it meant my own freedom. And yet if I did nothing, our eventual separation was inevitable. We might never see each other again. I would find myself vainly searching for *three* children in this ancient and hostile world.

After an hour of contemplation, no solution, no plan came to mind. The heat had made me drowsy. I was practically the only slave still awake; even my children had succumbed to slumber, their arms over their heads to shield them from the sun. I began to feel lightheaded. My mind had begun drifting in and out of consciousness when I heard someone's voice utter the words, "How much for him?"

I raised my chin and let my eyes swim into focus. Before me stood a man in his early fifties. I vaguely perceived other men around him, but at the moment my attention rested only on him. His mantle was so blue that I became lost in the color. I concentrated on his face. His eyes were bright and full of light. The contours of his face were sharp and distinguished, as though chiseled by a sculptor's hands. I would have sworn I'd seen his face before.

"Jonas?" I whispered.

If he'd heard me utter the name of the mysterious figure who had helped me escape from the Salt Lake County Jail, he did not react. Then I realized there were obvious differences between the two faces. Jonas' hair had been platinum white; this man's hair was dark. There were subtle differences in his nose and forehead, as well. The eyes, however, looked the same. They might have easily been the exact same eyes.

At last I focused on another face. Shemnon! He was standing right behind the man in the blue mantle. How had I missed him? Also in the group stood Kumarcaah and two other elders of the Pochteca. I felt an urge to warn Shemnon—to tell him to run. But nobody seemed inclined to do him any harm. His escape in the wilderness was no longer of consequence to the Pochteca. This morning, Kumarcaah's motives for killing Shemnon had been to keep him from interfering, but such motives no longer applied. As far as the Pochteca were concerned, they'd captured us fair and square. Plainly, we were foreigners. A Nephite's accusation that we had been enslaved against our will made no difference here.

Kumarcaah pointed back at me. "You mean the pale one with the blue eyes?"

He knew perfectly well that I had been the object of inquiry; Shemnon's presence made this obvious. But this was business, and Kumarcaah played the game well.

"How much will it cost to set him free?" the blue-cloaked man repeated, steady indignation in his voice.

"He's a strong slave and in good health. I couldn't take less than ten senine of gold for him. Then, if you choose to free him, it is nothing to me." Apparently my value had inflated since that morning, when Kumarcaah had said I was only worth a senine or two.

There was no hesitation on the part of the blue-cloaked man. He called for one of his attendants to step forward. This man carried a wooden box. A customary blanket was laid out for him to sit upon while weighing out the proper weight of gold.

"This man had two children," said the man draped in blue. "Where are they?" Shemnon aided him by pointing toward Harry and Steffanie, still asleep in the midst of the other slaves.

Kumarcaah shook his head. "The boy and girl are not for sale." Apparently he'd decided he could make a lot more money selling them in a distant land.

Shemnon's eyes flashed rage. "You cannot separate a father from his children!"

The man in the blue mantle placed a silencing hand on Shemnon's shoulder. He continued his negotiations with Kumarcaah in the same tone of steady indignation. "Name your price, trader. What is your price to restore this family to the freedom you deprived them of only hours ago?"

Kumarcaah begrudged the inference. "I am a businessman," he said. "I have broken no statutes. Are these people members of your tribe? Are they claimed by any tribe in Zarahemla?"

"After today, they will be part of *my* tribe," the bluecloaked man said emphatically. "Is that understood?" I could only guess that he was making this point in case Kumarcaah had aspirations to round us up again at the first opportunity.

Kumarcaah studied the man's eyes, affirming to himself that these people would likely pay any price he might name. "Ten limnah—each," he declared.

"And for the others?"

The Pochteca chief raised his eyebrows. "You want to buy *all* the children?"

The man in the blue mantle produced another wooden box and dropped it on the blanket beside the first box. "Here is thirty limnah of gold and fifty onti of silver. You may have it all. Give me the children."

Kumarcaah scratched his beard, wondering, perhaps, if he might finagle a little more. For a moment, I thought he'd reject the offer—even raise the price on Harry and Steffanie on some technicality. But with a slight bow, he finally acquiesced. With a flit of his hand he directed one of his men to collect the merchandise, another to gather up the two boxes.

"You have negotiated a splendid bargain," said Kumarcaah. "Would you like me to have them branded before you take them? No extra charge."

He said this to be impudent. The man in the blue cloak did not reply. He stared hard into Kumarcaah's eyes, and I watched the slave merchant's pompous exterior crack a little. He even looked mildly frightened.

"Remove the collars," the blue-cloaked man demanded.

Kumarcaah nodded. The man in the blue mantle turned away and spoke something quietly to Shemnon.

My hands were freed and the collar was unstrapped. I massaged my neck; the sweat under the leather had made the skin raw and tender. Harry and Steffanie were released, along with the other six children. "You're free," someone said. The children rubbed their eyes in confusion, as if some of them had forgotten what that concept really meant.

Harry and Steffanie ran to me. I buried them in my embrace and kissed the crowns of their heads. Then I looked up and met the eyes of the man who had purchased our freedom. I perceived a deepening smile on his face, but before it could fully broaden, one of his men reminded him of urgent business elsewhere in the city. He and two of his entourage left the marketplace, while three other attendants remained with Shemnon to help care for the newly liberated children.

Shemnon approached me. "Who was he?" I asked, although I might have ventured a guess on my own.

"That was Nephi," Shemnon confirmed. "The prophet of the Church."

CHAPTER 23

We headed west—away from the marketplace, away from the slave traders, away from the filth and degradation which had overgrown this entire district of Zarahemla. I possessively held the hands of both my children. Some of the other slave merchants looked after us as we walked by, no doubt with the same greedy eye as Kumarcaah.

Shemnon told us how he had followed the Pochteca supply train all the way into the valley. "When I was certain they would reach Zarahemla before nightfall, I got ahead of them," he recounted. "I was fortunate to have found Nephi on the road leading from his estate. He came as soon as I explained the circumstances, postponing an important meeting with one of the tribal chiefs."

I was astonished at Nephi's financial sacrifice for the sake of strangers. "The prophet must be a wealthy man," I observed.

"Wealthy in the Spirit of the Lord," said Shemnon. "But as far as his worldly possessions, well . . . he was once one of the wealthiest men in Zarahemla. Most of his fortune is gone now; it was spent helping members of the Church. The majority of the Zarahemla Christians have lived inside the walls of his estate for the past six months."

"What for?"

"For protection. A few of them still maintain flocks and fields outside, but there has been much persecution. Now they are threatening to confiscate Nephi's land. This is the subject of his meeting today with the chief of the Mulekites."

"He postponed this meeting for us?" I marveled.

"I'm certain he would not have considered it an inconvenience.

Tonight we will rest at Nephi's estate. My wife and son are there; Nephi says they are doing well. There will be plenty of food and water. Your children must be terribly frightened after such an ordeal."

"Not me," said Harry defiantly. "It would take a lot more than some ugly goons wearing bird heads to frighten me."

"We're okay," added Steffanie, though the stress and fatigue in her voice told me otherwise.

My children had been through more trauma in the past week than most people experience in a lifetime. I yearned to give them a few days of peace. As for myself, I expected no such luxury. Secretly, I had hopes of leaving Harry and Steffanie here while I went off in search of my oldest daughter.

At last we passed before a building I recognized. I stood back from the courtyard gate to take it all in. Shemnon and my children stood with me while the others went on ahead.

"What is it?" asked Harry.

"It's the Holy Temple," I replied nostalgically. "I stood here in this exact spot when I was a child."

Like the walls of the city, the walls around the temple had also been heightened. But I could still see the top of the building, and I could see the puffs of sweet-smelling smoke floating upward from the altar of burnt offerings. A flood of memories washed over me. This is where I had once met the Prophet Helaman, Nephi's great-grandfather. It did my heart good to see at least one temple among the Nephites still in operation.

"After what I saw in Lamoni and Laman, I'd begun to think every temple in the land had been abandoned or destroyed," I said.

Shemnon shuffled his feet. He didn't wish to dampen my enthusiasm, but he explained sorrowfully that the believers in Christ had not been allowed inside these walls for two years. "Since we teach that the Law of Moses is to be fulfilled in Christ, the priests who reside here have decided we are not worthy to benefit from the ordinances performed herein. The first fruits of our fields and the firstlings of our flocks are no longer accepted. To them, we are no longer part of the covenant people."

"You mean this temple doesn't belong to the Church anymore?"

Shemnon shook his head. "Not to *our* church." He waxed philosophical: "When a people rejects the fulness of God, the last vestige of their faith can be seen in the habit and repetition of their traditions."

A short distance further down the highway stood an eight-foot stone barrier crawling with leafy vines. Behind the wall, rising two stories above the ground, leaned an old rickety platform. Some of the crossbeams were broken. At one time the tower might have supported the weight of a man, but a generation of wind and rain had rendered it unstable.

"This is it," said Shemnon. "The house of Nephi, the son of Nephi."

At those words, it struck me that a powerful sermon had once been delivered from this tower. At first I had wanted to credit the sermon to the man who had just emancipated us. But it wasn't Nephi, the current leader of the Church. It was his father of the same name.

From atop that platform, Nephi, the father of Nephi, had lamented the wickedness of his people, attracting a large multitude. He warned the people of impending destruction if they did not repent. Then he said something that sent a shock wave throughout the city. He announced that the chief judge of the land had just been murdered by the hand of his own brother. When his proclamations were verified, the people weren't quite sure what to think. Some said he was a prophet, others called him a demon, while still others felt he must be a god.

Nephi, the father of Nephi, was granted the power to seal on earth and in heaven. By that power he called forth a famine to stir up the people in remembrance of the Lord their God. Here was a man who was carried out of the midst of his persecutors by the Spirit, and by that same Spirit carried from congregation to congregation. But then, shortly after the sign of Christ's birth, he disappeared, never to seen or heard from again. He entrusted his son with leadership over the Church and stewardship over the sacred records. A lot of history had taken place on this spot. I had an odd premonition that the final chapter was about to be written.

Shemnon knocked on the gate. A face appeared overhead. "In whose name do you come?" asked the man dutifully.

"The Prince of Peace," Shemnon replied, and the gate was opened.

The place was almost magical, like the palace of a prince. The tower stood in the middle of an exquisite garden with fruit trees and flower beds. There were cement-enclosed pools and ditches fed by a spring. The house itself was built of stone and lime, with roof crests, tall chambers, and a great stone patio stretching before a front door framed by pillars. The roof was overlaid with neatly squared beams of dark wood, and the outside walls had been whitewashed and polished to glisten like silver.

Still, the property was not at the height of its elegance. Much of it had been converted into a refugee camp. The yard and much of the garden were covered with tents and awnings. There must have been a hundred and fifty families housed inside these walls. Along a strip on the eastern side of the property, a dozen children were engaged in what appeared to be a game of soccer. Their ball was a little smaller than a soccer ball, and it was black instead of white. But it had a surprisingly high bounce. It appeared to have been formed of pure rubber. A goal was scored by kicking the ball through a small wooden hoop elevated about five feet off the ground. It reminded me of a basketball hoop, except that it was turned on its side and had no net. I glanced at Steffanie, who excelled in both basketball and soccer, and wondered if she might find the game intriguing. Unfortunately, the events of the day had drained her. Nothing would have intrigued her at the moment but a hot bath and a soft bed.

The other children whom Nephi liberated had arrived just before us. They still looked disoriented and frightened as a group of mothers saw to their needs. Along the cement ditch, about twenty women washed clothes in the slow current. One of the women stopped scrubbing the moment we entered the gate. Her gaze locked on Shemnon. When recognition set in, she shrieked with excitement and hurdled the ditch. Shemnon captured his wife in both arms. Two seconds later, a boy of eight dislodged himself from the soccer game.

"Father!" He joined the embrace with his parents.

Just then, two men emerged from the house and cried Shemnon's name.

"Brother Timothy!" Shemnon shouted in return. "Brother Isaiah!"

In the blizzard of joyful reunion that ensued, my children and I were virtually forgotten for several minutes.

The first people to seek our acquaintance were the children. They gathered around Harry and Steffanie, fascinated by their blonde hair and pale skin. One girl touched Steffanie on the arm and said, "Their skin is like the pale prophet."

Steffanie caught her breath. "You know my Uncle Garth?"

To our astonishment, the girl replied, "Garplimpton? He is serving a mission with my father."

I grabbed the girl's shoulders. "Is your father here?"

My action had startled her. She shook her head.

I let go of her shoulders. "Where were they sent to preach?"

"The land of Gilgal," she replied.

"The pale prophet had a wife," I said. "Did he take her with him?" The girl looked away. She focused over my shoulder.

"No," said a voice behind me. "I don't think she went with him."

I turned abruptly. In the confusion I had not seen her approaching. I shouldn't have been surprised. It was just like her to sneak up from behind and milk the moment. When I saw her face, I was stupefied. I stood there, my jaw dangling. Finally, my lip started to quiver, as did my hands. I whispered her name.

"Jenny?"

Her coyness melted. She sent me a crooked smile—the one she always beamed when she was trying *not* to smile. When the tears finally swelled in her marine-blue eyes, it magnified the irises to twice their normal size.

"Hello, big brother," she said.

We clung tightly to one another, making no effort to silence our sobs. I touched her face and ran my fingers over her hair to assure myself that it was no illusion. She was real. She was here. Jenny's sobs became uncontrollable as she buried her face in my neck.

It took Harry and Steffanie a moment to register what was happening. After all, Jennifer looked so different. Not an ounce of makeup. I hadn't seen my sister without lipstick or eyeshadow in twenty years. Her long blonde hair was tied atop her head, Nephite fashion. She looked older.

"Aunt Jenny!" my children cried. They lunged toward her. She released me just in time to catch them.

I suddenly became aware of two small children, a boy and a girl, approximately four and two years old respectively, standing very near to my sister. They appeared to be *with* her. Both of them looked up at me, and then at Harry and Steffanie, with the most curious expressions—shy and wary, yet irresistibly fascinated. The children were not Nephite.

Jenny wiped her tears and knelt down beside them. She wound her arm around the little girl, glanced at the boy, then pointed up at me. "This is your Uncle Jim," she said. "And these are your cousins, Harrison and Steffanie." She stood again and introduced both of them to us. "This is Rebecca and Joshua—my children."

CHAPTER 24

Jennifer invited the three of us, along with her two toddlers, into the privacy of her tent. The children gorged themselves on baskets of cherries, plums, apples, and salted almonds. My emotions were saturated. My little niece, Rebecca, warmed up to me quickly. Once she had decided it was okay to sit in my lap, it was hard to get her off. Not that I minded. She was a gorgeous little girl. My nephew Joshua had flaming red hair, just like his father at that age. He took to Harry immediately, and insisted on giving him a tour of the compound. My sister tried to object, but Harry willingly gave in and allowed himself to be shown a secret spot in the garden where Joshua had once caught a salamander.

The flap on my sister's tent opened up toward the gardens and pools. It was a feast for the senses—tiny explosions of red, purple, and orange flowers, like little budding torch fires in the waning light of day. Several men were in the process of lighting actual torches along the perimeter wall for a baptismal ceremony to be performed that evening in the largest pool.

I couldn't get over the fact that my sister had managed to have children in ancient America when every avenue of modern science had failed to help them.

"How did it happen?" I asked.

"These are my two little miracles," Jenny replied. "There were no complications, except with Rebecca; she was born breech. But I had a blessing from Timothy, the prophet's brother, and my midwife did everything right."

"But the boy is four years old," I observed. "It doesn't make sense."

"What doesn't make sense?" asked Jenny. "After all, we've been here for five and a half years."

"Five and a half years!" I exclaimed.

I had to remind myself that time measured differently between our two worlds. Time in the Nephite perspective moved significantly faster, as if scurrying to catch up to the modern age. Still, I would never have guessed that the difference could add up to five and half years! Jenny herself was surprised that only two years and five months had elapsed since she and Garth had departed.

Something bizarre occurred to me. "How old are you, sis?"

Jenny bit her lip thoughtfully. "Garth figured it out once. The months are different here; they have twenty instead of twelve, and five extra days at year's end to make up the balance. Garth made up his own calendar based on the date when we left. According to that, I turned forty-one about seven months ago."

"You're kidding!" I shuddered at the ramifications.

Steffanie started laughing. "She's not your little sister anymore, Dad. She's older than you!"

"Wow," said Jenny. "That's really weird." My sister had always been the queen of understatement.

It suddenly occurred to me how many incredible events I had missed in my sister's life. "Why didn't you come back?" I asked mournfully. "We were expecting you on Christmas Eve. You said it would only be one year. Why did you stay so long?"

Jenny's shoulders fell. "I'm sorry. That's all we were planning to stay—one year. Then I got pregnant with Joshua. You know how difficult it was the last time. I couldn't risk going back through the tunnel in that condition, and I needed Garth to stay with me. Then, of course, I couldn't make the trip with an infant. A year later I was pregnant with Becky. Oh, Jim, I prayed every night that we could all go home. I wanted so much to raise my children in my own century. But before now, it's been impossible. And now, with all the unrest in Zarahemla . . . whenever we start to think about going home, it seems like everything is against us."

"We were starting to think we'd never see you again," Steffanie added. "Everybody was heartbroken, especially Melody."

"Where *is* Melody?" asked Jen. "Did she stay in Salt Lake?"

Steff and I glanced at one another. Who should tell her? The euphoria that had buoyed up our reunion abruptly vanished.

Jenny became concerned. "Is Melody all right?"

At that moment, something even more disturbing occurred to me. Jenny was totally unaware of Garth's circumstances. She had no idea that he had been captured; no idea that he had become a pawn in the hands of King Jacob. I didn't know where to begin.

"Melody is *not* all right, Jen," I began. "She was kidnapped. It happened four days ago. They brought her here. That's why we've come."

Jennifer was flabbergasted. "Who would kidnap Melody?"

"King Jacob of the Moon."

The blood drained from my sister's face. I unfolded every event of the previous week: the murder of Doug Bowman, my arrest, Jacob's visit to the Salt Lake County Jail. I told her that Jacob had once been called Boaz, one of the Gadiantons who had accompanied Mehrukenah in his search for the Sword of Coriantumr. Jenny knew all about Jacob's doings among the Nephites, but she was completely unaware of any connection between us. On that night so many years ago, when I had grappled with Boaz in my apartment, neither Garth nor Jenny had been present.

Jenny's face remained pale. "Why would Jacob kidnap Melody? What possible reason—?!"

I took my sister's hand. It was time to tell her about her husband. As I revealed everything Jacob had said about Garth, she seemed to age ten years before my eyes. She stood up from the floormat and walked toward the open flap of the tent with both hands clutched to her stomach.

And then she collapsed.

* * *

Everyone hovered around Jenny until she recovered. Her little boy, Joshua, climbed under her arm. I couldn't get him to move away. When she finally sat up, she asked for some water. As I helped her to drink it, she said, "I knew something was wrong. I've known for weeks, but I didn't understand. I didn't know what to do."

I helped prop up her head and urged her to take it easy. From the intensity of pain she seemed to feel when she collapsed, I wondered if there was something seriously wrong, perhaps some kind of digestive ailment, like an ulcer. Having not seen her husband for nearly nine months, it would have been understandable.

"The pain comes and goes," Jenny confessed. "They gave me some herbs—on that mat in the corner. They seem to help." The reddish leaves had been brewed into a tea that she kept sealed in a pottery flask. I retrieved it and helped her take four or five swallows. The more I contemplated my sister's health, the more concerned I became. She did not have the same constitution as the ancient Nephites.

"You need to be home," I told her. "You need to see a doctor."

"I won't leave without my husband," she said stubbornly.

I sighed. I might have expected such a reply. I cringed to think what might happen if her children lost both a father and a mother.

She grew impatient with my concern. "It's not that serious. I'm fine. I can travel."

"Travel? Do you expect to do some traveling?"

"Maybe. They say we might have to leave this place soon."

I recalled what Shemnon had said about the Mulekites threatening to confiscate Nephi's estate. "How soon will you know?"

"Today, we hope. That's where Nephi is now—pleading our cause at the palace. It used to be the governor's palace; now it belongs to the Mulekites. Everyone is anxious to hear what Nephi will say when he returns."

"Can they just steal someone's land whenever they feel like it?" Steffanie asked indignantly.

"This part of Zarahemla is controlled by the Mulekites," Jenny explained. "Nephi has paid them tribute for several years, but now they say he never legally owned the land in the first place. They say his father built it on the tithes and offerings of gullible Christians. It's not true. Nephi's father made clothing and textiles. But it doesn't matter; they do whatever they want. There's no law to protect the Christians."

"Where will everyone go?" Harry asked.

"The Mulekites have offered us some land just south of Zarahemla, near the river. Some of the men have seen it; they say it's good land, and there are several huts already built. Much of the ground has been burned off for raising crops. Nephi has always said we would leave Zarahemla one day. The time seems very close."

"Has anyone mentioned . . . Bountiful?" I wondered.

Jenny drew her eyebrows together. "Why?"

"I assume you know the scriptures," I said. "Bountiful is where the Savior will appear."

"It hasn't been mentioned," said Jenny.

I almost wondered if she'd forgotten. She seemed so caught up in the daily chore of survival that the bigger picture had escaped her. I could hardly fault her for it; even in our century it was so easy to lose perspective. Each day the sun rises and sets, the daily grind goes on. It's sometimes difficult to grasp the reality that one day, sooner than we expect, the final trump will sound, and heaven and earth will be rolled together like a scroll.

Outside in the garden pool, the baptism went on as scheduled. A young man with a flat forehead and squinted eyes received a remission of his sins. When he came out of the water, he shouted praises to God and embraced nearly everyone present with the exuberance of a child. Afterwards, he knelt on the ground and started sobbing. I sensed that the observers felt somewhat awkward at his gush of emotion. It did seem a bit overly theatrical. I scolded myself for thinking this; certainly to him it was a very sacred event.

About then, a commotion started at the front gate. Nephi and his attendants had returned from the palace. I left Jenny in the hands of my daughter while Harry and I went to see what he would say.

As the prophet made his way toward the raised patio before the door of his house, people grabbed at his cloak. "What is the outcome?" they asked anxiously. "What will become of us?"

Nephi ignored them as politely as he could. As he brushed past Harry and me, his eyes lingered a moment. Then he ascended the steps where he was met by his brother, Timothy. Timothy was younger and somewhat more stocky than Nephi, but his spiritual presence was no less compelling. Nephi whispered instructions into his ear. Then, to the people's profound disappointment, the prophet slipped inside his house.

Timothy faced the crowd. "Nephi will address everyone in the morning. Will all the elders of the Church come forward?"

I heard grumbling. Someone remarked, "Our fate hangs in the balance, and *he* will make us wait until morning."

"Why won't he talk to the people now?" Harry asked.

"I think he wants to consult with the other elders," I said.

Several men, including Shemnon, assembled on the patio and then followed Timothy through the door. I returned to my sister's tent to report the news. Steffanie had fallen asleep on a soft mattress of quilted cotton that Jenny had rolled out. My little niece and nephew were very near to dropping off, as well. Jenny leaned over them, softly singing "I Am a Child of God." Her eyes were moist. I put my arm around her shoulder. She stopped singing.

"Nephi will speak to us tomorrow," I told her.

She nodded. "Timothy once said that angels minister to the prophet daily. Sometimes I can feel their presence. It makes me feel better." She became quiet again. I could tell she was thinking of her husband.

"I have to tell you something, Jenny," I said. "I won't be in Zarahemla for long. I'll probably leave tomorrow—the next day at the latest."

She looked up to see if I was serious. "Where will you go?"

"To find Melody," I replied solemnly. "And to find Garth."

"Alone?"

I sighed deeply. "If I have to."

Jenny pinched off another tear. "I couldn't take it, Jim, if I were to lose my husband and my brother all at once."

"I'll be okay," I said. "You'll be praying for me."

"What about Steff and Harry?" she asked.

I looked at her pleadingly. "I have to leave them here, Jenny . . . if you'll have them."

"Of course," she sighed. "They'll be safe here. Garth always said if we remained close to the prophet, our family would be safe." She paused. "Jim, do you think he's alive?"

"Yes," I said, "I think they're *both* alive. I know it."

Jenny closed her eyes. Harry was already zonked beside his sister. I was in the process of rolling out my own quilted mattress when I heard Shemnon's voice outside the tent.

"Jim," he announced, "Nephi sent me. He wishes to speak with you at once."

CHAPTER 25

We found Nephi on the roof of his house. The other elders had been dismissed. Only the prophet and his brother were present, staring off thoughtfully at the luminous dust of the Milky Way. It was several seconds before they turned to acknowledge our presence. I couldn't help wondering if they had been conversing with heavenly messengers—a discussion which we had prematurely interrupted. It was probably my imagination.

Nephi turned to greet me. His eyes were bright, almost shining. "Jim Hawkins," he said. "I am Nephi, the son of Nephi. This is my brother, Timothy."

"It is good to meet you," said Timothy.

I was impressed that Nephi did not slur my name together, like the others. When I took the prophet's hand, I couldn't speak. I'd been concentrating so hard on how I might present myself to this great and noble spiritual giant that my tongue failed me at the critical moment. I could only grip his hand more firmly. Finally, I whispered, "Thank you." He knew I spoke of the moment he had saved my family from the Pochteca.

"I'm glad I still had the means to help," he said. "I wish I could do more for you, Jim."

Not since I'd emerged from the cave had a Nephite or Lamanite addressed me using only my first name. It must have been considered rude to use half a person's name, like calling Nephi "Neph" or Mormon "Morm." But how would Nephi have known that our custom was different? Even if Garth had taught him that the people in our land had two names, how would he have known where mine was divided? He might have just as easily called me "Jimha."

"Sit, my friend," said Nephi. "Rest yourself. You've had a very long and trying day. Shemnon tells me you have come a great distance on a very sad errand."

I sat slowly on the parapet, never taking my eyes off the prophet. "Then you know all about me?"

"Shemnon has told me that your daughter was taken captive by Jacob of the Moon. I am very sorry to hear this. Jacob is a ruthless man. Shemnon has also said that you are a friend to Garth Plimpton."

Nephi knew more than what Shemnon had told him; I felt this very strongly. But how much could he know?

Nephi continued. "Shemnon says that you also believe Garth Plimpton is Jacob's prisoner. This grieves me very much, not only because of my love for Garth, but because Garth was a companion to my son, Jonas."

Jonas. The name reverberated in my soul.

"Jonas is your son?"

"My youngest," said Nephi. "My oldest son, Nephi, returned from his mission to the land of Manti a week ago. Have you met Jonas before?"

I wasn't certain how to answer the prophet's question. To say that I had met him would have made no sense at all; the Jonas I knew existed twenty centuries in the future. And as far as I could tell, the mysterious white-haired policeman had been very close to Nephi's age. I might have been convinced that Jonas was the prophet's *brother,* but not his son. I decided it couldn't be the same Jonas.

"No," I replied. "I don't think so."

"Have you heard of him?" asked the prophet eagerly. "When Jacob spoke to you of Garth, did he mention my son?"

Again I answered, "No."

The prophet sighed. "I feel very strongly that he is still alive. But I don't know what has become of him. Jonas, too, may be a captive of King Jacob."

"Shemnon tells us you are seeking to know the location of the secret city, Jacobugath," said Timothy.

"Yes," I replied. "That's where Jacob is taking my daughter. I think it's where he's holding Garth."

"We may be able to help you," said Timothy reservedly. "There was a man baptized tonight. This man *may* know the answer to your question. His name is Lamachi."

"Yes," I said. "I saw him. He looked very happy about his baptism."

"Before tonight," said Timothy, "Lamachi belonged to the secret sect of Gadianton. He comes from a line of Gadiantons three generations long. He claims to be a descendant of Kishkuman himself. Three months ago, he sought to unite with our community. We have hidden him here ever since. It is certain that if he left the estate, he would be murdered."

"How do we know he is truly converted?" asked Shemnon skeptically.

"I have spoken with him at length," said Nephi. "I believe he is sincere, but his spirit is very fragile and immature."

"This is to be expected from someone who has witnessed the horrors that he has surely witnessed," added Timothy.

"I have blessed him on numerous occasions," said Nephi. "He suffers from terrible visions and nightmares. More than once he has awakened the entire compound with his screams."

"Will he tell me how to reach Jacobugath?" I asked.

"We hope so," replied Timothy. "He still feels bound by many of the dark oaths he has made. But the boy has come far; he may now be willing to reveal what we need to know."

"Don't trust him," said Shemnon sternly. "It is not beyond the conscience of a Gadianton to infiltrate the ranks of his enemies with the sole intent to destroy them. He should not have been allowed to enter our community so hastily."

Nephi spoke with mild reproach. "Brother Shemnon, any soul who comes to us with a broken heart and a contrite spirit, seeking a remission of sins in the name of Christ, shall have it granted."

Shemnon lowered his eyes. "Forgive me, Elder Nephi. I am . . . sometimes not very objective about such matters."

"There's something I still don't understand," I said. "Jacob kidnapped my daughter to coerce Garth into revealing some important information. What might Garth know that's so important?"

Nephi and Timothy looked at one another. I could see by their expressions that they thought they might know the answer.

Timothy explained. "Jonas and Garplimpton were sent to the Land of Gilgal to recover a branch of the Church that left Zarahemla three years ago, shortly after the governor's death. Among these were the city's wealthiest Christians. This was the time when tribal chiefs started to confiscate the property of Church members. These families were afraid their fortunes would be stolen."

"We tried to convince them to stay," said Nephi, "but I could not promise that their fortunes would be spared. What I *could* promise them, in the name of the Lord, was that if they remained, their temporal and eternal reward would be far greater. They flatly rejected the Lord's assurance."

"They took their fortunes with them," said Timothy. "Collectively, their treasures might be as great as the treasures of King Solomon. If Jacob knows that such a fortune exists, he would stop at nothing to obtain it for the purpose of building his kingdom."

So that's it, I thought. Jacob wanted to know where these wealthy Christians were hiding. With this money, he might finally obtain enough resources to launch his invasion of Zarahemla. Garth knew where these people were hidden. That's why Jacob needed Melody!

"I will introduce you to Lamachi tomorrow," said Timothy. "If he tells us what we want to know, we will organize a party of men to accompany you to Jacobugath. Strong and righteous men."

This was the most encouraging development yet. "I don't know what to say . . . except, thank you."

"If you can," said Nephi, "I would like you to find out what has happened to my son. I feel he is in great need of help."

"I'll do everything I can."

Nephi beamed with gratitude. "It saddens me that I cannot go with you. The Lord has commanded me to remain with my people. Tomorrow will be a trying day for them; for some, it will be the most trying day of their lives." He straightened himself. The meeting was at an end. "You must be very tired, Jim. Go and get some rest."

Again he looked at me in a strange, familiar way, as if I were an old family friend. *He knows who I am,* I thought again. *He knows all about me.*

"If it's possible," I said reticently, "I wonder, sir, if I could speak with you in private."

"The hour is very late," Timothy reminded his brother.

"It's all right," said Nephi. "I will speak with Jim privately."

Timothy hesitated; he was very protective of his older brother. But he and Shemnon did as directed and left me alone with the Lord's servant. Nephi sat beside me on the parapet.

I suddenly felt embarrassed to have taken the prophet's time. "I'm sorry," I said. "I shouldn't have bothered you."

"What troubles you, Jim?"

How could I tell him that I was feeling overwhelmed by my own secrets? If, by chance, Nephi knew who I was and where I was from, it would relieve me of a great burden.

"How is it," I asked, "that you know to call me by my first name?"

"It is the custom in your land, is it not?"

"Where did you learn our customs? From Garth Plimpton?"

"Garth taught me a great deal about your land," he replied, "and about your day."

"Then you know everything," I said softly. "You know that my home is in the future."

"I know only what Garth has told me," he replied. "I confess that your presence here is a mystery to me."

"Did Garth also tell you my name?"

"Actually, I first heard the name Jim Hawkins when I was a child. It came from the lips of my grandmother."

I felt a rush of adrenaline. Suddenly I knew who his grandmother was. I whispered her name. "Menochin."

It had been eighteen years since Muleki, the son of Teancum, had reported to me that Menochin had married Helaman, the son of Helaman. Until this moment, I hadn't made the connection.

"Then you remember her?"

"I could never forget her," I replied.

"She loved my grandfather very much," said Nephi. "But she always spoke very kindly of you—the pale-faced boy she had known a short while in her youth. She always kept a jade and silver necklace. She said you gave it to her. That necklace now belongs to my granddaughter, who bears her name."

The jade and silver necklace! It had all come full circle. So I *had* left my mark in the world of the Nephites—a legacy kept by the very first girl I had ever had a crush on.

"You must think I'm some kind of ghost," I said, "appearing and disappearing once every century."

Nephi laughed. I thought back and wondered if I had ever heard a prophet laugh. It was a wonderful sound. "I hadn't thought of it quite like that," he said. "I only know that your presence, as well as the presence of Garth and your sister, Jennifer, has proven a marvelous blessing for my people."

"For us as well," I said. "Some of the happiest memories of my life are here, in this land. I think about those days a lot. They seem so uncomplicated. My sense of purpose was so clear." I realized I was rambling. "I suppose everyone has a time in their life like that."

"You don't believe your purpose is as clear as it once was?" Nephi asked.

"It is, but—" I stopped myself. I didn't want to burden the prophet with my problems. Surely he didn't want to hear my endless pinings over the loss of my wife or the shattering of my life. He had plenty of his own problems. "It just seems more difficult than before."

"I think if you contemplate those memories from your childhood," said Nephi, "you'll realize that they are happy because of what you accomplished, what you overcame. They were probably no less difficult."

I considered this. He was right, of course.

"Push forward, Jim. I'm sure you have many happy memories yet to be born. Lasting happiness is the offspring of endurance."

"Then I should be a happy man one day very soon." The prophet did not crack a smile, and I immediately regretted my flippancy.

Nephi rested his hands on my shoulders. He looked at me squarely with his omniscient gaze. "Never forget, Jim. All of this—" his eyes quickly scanned earth and sky, "is but a moment. Then comes the glory. It beckons us like the first rays of the sun. And all we must do is endure to the very end. Afterwards, our sorrows will melt away so freely we'll wonder how we ever lost faith, even for an instant. It's all true, Jim. Our Savior will make it true. It won't be very long now."

These were the words I wished I'd spoken to my daughter the night before. Their impact on me was no less profound. For the last time on this long and furious day, I let my emotions drain. The prophet embraced me, and I drank in his spiritual power. In that moment, the eternities seemed to crystallize into one bright whole. My sorrows disappeared. They weren't just forgotten or set aside; they really vanished. In spite of all the uncertainly and turbulence, I felt true joy. The joy of endurance and hope.

The joy of my Savior.

CHAPTER 26

The first people had started to gather in front of Nephi's house shortly after sunrise. The front gates to the estate were frequently opened and closed to allow the entrance of Christians who had braved living outside the compound. By mid-morning, the crowd had swelled to over six hundred people, all anxious to learn their fate from the prophet of God. There was an unnatural agitation in the air, even before the prophet's appearance. Many people were trying to outguess each other as to what he would say. Several heated arguments had broken out.

Jenny and I and our children were seated upon the stone embankment that divided the courtyard from the garden. Around 9:00 a.m., Nephi and his brother emerged through the reed curtain hanging down over the doorway. The prophet looked cheerful, almost elated. As he took his position in the center of the patio, the chatter hushed. He surveyed the crowd a moment longer. Then he grinned widely. "Brothers and sisters," he began, "the news is glorious!"

"Then we are to stay?" inquired a man in front.

"No, Benjamin," Nephi replied. "We are to leave. Within the week."

There was murmuring. This was glorious news? Could it be glorious that Nephi was willing to abandon the estate that had been in his family for three generations?

Another man inquired, "Is this the decision of the Mulekite chief?"

"No, Brother Heshlom," said Nephi. "The decision of the chief was to let us stay until after the first harvest. The decision to leave belongs to the Lord."

More murmuring. This time it ended abruptly as Nephi raised his hand.

"When I was summoned to the palace yesterday morning," he said, "I already knew the demands they would place upon us. I was prepared to go and fight for my land. I was prepared to defend my rights under tribal law and, if necessary, pay a double tribute. But the Spirit whispered that my cause was vain. When we arrived, they brought up many false charges against us—against *all* Christians. They had many witnesses who testified how we had stolen their money by deceit and fraud. Some of these witnesses, as far as I recall, were never members of our Church! I felt impressed that if I resisted the Mulekite chief, every Christian in Zarahemla would pay the consequences. So I pleaded for time, and my request was granted."

"Then why are we to leave so soon?" asked Heshlom.

"We are not prepared," said another. "Our flocks . . . our fields"

"Let the prophet speak!" Timothy admonished.

"Rejoice, brothers and sisters!" Nephi shouted over the murmuring. "The long-awaited day of Lord is soon at hand! Even now, our Savior Jesus Christ prepares to make his triumphal return to Jerusalem in the land of our forefathers. We, too, must prepare for a great pilgrimage. It is not the word and will of God for us to remain in the land of Zarahemla. Our destination is north, to the land of Bountiful!"

My sister looked at me and nodded. So I'd been right.

The murmur now rose to a tumult. "Bountiful?" Heshlom protested. "Our home is here! Why would the Lord ask us to leave the sacred land of our ancestors?"

"Let the prophet finish!" Timothy pleaded. The disrespectful outbursts from the crowd distressed him greatly. Nephi, however, remained remarkably unruffled.

"Thus saith the Lord," Nephi proclaimed, "in Bountiful awaits a blessing for this people more glorious than they could possibly imagine! Prepare yourselves to receive the blessing of the Lord!"

A little old man cried out above the clamoring. "What is the significance? We have always been taught that the Messiah would appear at his temple here in Zarahemla!"

Timothy shook his head. "This is not the word of the Lord, Brother

Malchiah. It is only a tradition—a tradition that we have been taught since our childhoods."

"It was taught by your father!" Heshlom accused.

Timothy stood firm. "I never heard my father speak of this as anything other than a tradition."

"Then you were not listening to your own father!" cried Malchiah. "I heard him speak it with my own ears—as a revelation!"

Timothy looked astonished. He turned to the prophet. Nephi stood in silence, his arms folded, his brow furrowed. He had spoken the word of the Lord. He would leave it to his brother to address specific concerns.

Heshlom spoke up to support Malchiah. "And as your father spoke this revelation, he enjoined the words of Father Nephi of old." Heshlom quoted a scripture—one he had apparently memorized for the occasion. "'*Behold, I saw multitudes who had not fallen because of the great and terrible judgments of the Lord. And I saw the heavens open, and the Lamb of God descending out of heaven; and he came and showed himself unto them*'—Are not these multitudes the seed of Lehi? Where else could our Savior show himself to the seed of Lehi if not in Zarahemla? In Bountiful, they are the seed of Mulek and Jared!"

"Brethren, your memory fails you," said Timothy. "Most of you were children when my father last preached among you. Nephi has spoken the word and will of God."

Next, Shemnon ascended the porch. "Disciples of Christ, let us be unified. I now know with a surety why the Lord has allowed me to return so I could be here on this fateful day. I can confirm what Nephi has spoken. The Christians of Melek have received the same instructions of the Lord. They are even now gathering to Bountiful."

"The devil will ensnare all those who deny the ancient word of God!" Heshlom contended. "Should it surprise us that the Christians of Melek have been thus deceived? Read the scriptures! Only in *them* do ye have eternal life!"

Tempers continued to percolate. My children became frightened, and Becky and Joshua clung to my sister's skirt.

Nephi raised his arms again. This time the clamor did not die so easily. When it finally hushed, the prophet declared, "What I have received, all may receive whose hearts are prepared. Brethren and sisters, retire to your tents. Pray fervently to know the truth. In three days, we shall leave this land."

"What about our animals?" asked a woman. "Our property?"

Timothy responded, "We will take only enough provisions to survive the journey."

Heshlom had heard enough. He leaped up to the porch and stood in front of Shemnon and Timothy. "Fellow Christians, listen to reason. The Lord, through the generosity of the Mulekites, has provided us with a strip of fine land, ample grazing for our animals, and corn. Many of us have already been driven from our homes. Should we now, after suffering so much for the testimony of Christ, deny the gifts of God?"

Why didn't anybody shut this guy up? The prophet remained unmoved. In perfect tolerance, he waited for his opponent to finish speaking. Had I been in Nephi's position, I'd have likely konked the guy over the head, rolled him off to the side, and got back to business.

"I echo Nephi's challenge!" Heshlom proclaimed. "Retire to your tents. Seek the word of the Spirit. I testify that the confirmation you will receive will command you to remain *here*—in Zarahemla. I have already taken this challenge. I *knew* the words that would be spoken here before they were spoken. And I was told those words would be a lie!"

"I need no confirmation!" proclaimed an old woman in back. "The Spirit has already borne witness to me that Nephi is a prophet of God!"

"He healed my son!" cried a father. "My boy was deaf. Now he hears! I need no further sign!"

"Then you will follow a man blindly to your destruction!" cried Heshlom. "We have all witnessed miracles—and not just by Nephi. We cannot forget that the Lord, by this man's father—a far greater prophet than has ever been known among the Nephites—declared that when the Messiah shall come, he shall come to his temple in Zarahemla! And who will be surprised when Nephi the Seer, who disappeared from among us thirty-three years ago, returns on that day to stand with our Savior? Remember, Nephi's son would have no authority whatsoever if not for his father. I say we remain here until after the harvest, and then we accept the land bestowed upon us by the mercy of God."

Nearly a hundred people sent up a cheer in support of Heshlom. The others looked dazed and bewildered, mostly at the foolishness of their comrades. A fight broke out at the back of the yard; Shemnon rushed over to stop it. Nephi raised his voice to make one final appeal.

"People of Christ, let us not fight among ourselves! We do not seek to destroy the agency of our friends. We are all free to choose. I testify to the depths of my soul that all those who remain in Zarahemla are doomed to suffer its fate. But we will compel no one. Three days hence, we shall depart in peace."

"If you are to depart," said Heshlom, "then why wait three whole days? Let it be *tomorrow!* Or give me some reason why I should, in good conscience, allow you to poison any more minds than you have already poisoned. Depart, if you will—but do it *tomorrow!*"

Nephi and Heshlom exchanged a willful stare. How long, I wondered, had Heshlom been sowing seeds of prejudice and distrust? For how many weeks had he been gathering sympathizers? I wondered how Nephi might respond. Would he condemn his opponent? Would he order Heshlom and his followers off the property? Would he reject the demands of an apostate? Instead, Nephi's face fell into repose. He seemed to be looking past the crowd. It was only a moment before he focused on the people and said calmly, "We will depart tomorrow morning. This is the Lord's will."

Heshlom let out a spluttering laugh. "Another revelation, Nephi?"

Nephi ignored him and spoke to the gathering at large. "May the grace of our Lord Jesus Christ rest upon your hearts, as you seek the voice of the Spirit." He turned to enter solemnly into his house.

The spirit of contention did not lift in any degree. The crowd continued to waver on the cusp of an all-out riot as the supporters of Heshlom and the younger supporters of Nephi stood with their fists clenched, awaiting the slightest cue.

At that instant, a woman at the back of the crowd broke into song. She sang alone, oblivious to everyone around her. At first her voice seemed discordant and out of place. The woman was old; most people probably thought she was senile. But she persisted, and without warning, a wave of calmness began to penetrate the hearts of those directly around her. After a moment, her solitary voice was joined by others. Soon, the greater part of all the men and women present in the square raised their voices in a hymn of praise and thanksgiving to the Lord. Only Heshlom and about sixty of his more adamant followers remained unmoved and mocking.

"Do not be deceived by your emotions!" he cried. "Trust in the sacred word of God as revealed by the prophets of old!"

He continued this tirade, but shortly I could no longer hear what he was saying. The voices of the people had drowned him out. Before the hymn had concluded, he threw up his hands and departed.

I would have liked to join in the hymn, but I didn't know the words. Jenny knew them, however, and she sang as loudly as the rest. I drew my children close and listened. The lyrics had come from a biblical psalm:

Oh give thanks unto the Lord,
For he is good, his mercy endureth forever.
Let the redeemed of the Lord say so;
Whom he had redeemed from the hand of the enemy;
And gathered them out from the land,
From the east and from the west,
From the north and from the south.
They wandered in the wilderness in a solitary way;
They found no city to dwell in.
Hungry and thirsty, their soul fainted in them.
Then they cried unto the Lord in their trouble,
And he delivered them out of their distresses.
And he led them forth by the right way,
That they might go to a city of habitation;
That they might go to a city of habitation.

I noticed Nephi in the doorway. Like many others, his cheeks were wet with tears.

CHAPTER 27

In the course of a few short hours, the encampment of Nephi's estate was turned upside down as men and women began packing all the necessary food and provisions to make the journey to Bountiful. Heshlom's followers remained in the compound for a short while, trying to convince others to abandon this absurd expedition. A few converts were won, but the vast majority remained faithful to Nephi.

After the apostates had left, a rumor spread almost immediately that Heshlom would seek out the leaders of the various tribes in Zarahemla and warn them that the Christian community was preparing to make a sudden mass exodus. By so doing, Heshlom would fuel the same feelings of resentment and fear that had been incited when the followers of Jacob made their escape. Would the Christians, like the dissenters of King Jacob, flee to the north and build up an army that would one day return and reclaim the capital? It did not matter that the entire Christian population in Zarahemla and the region round about numbered less than fifteen hundred, or that the dissenters of Jacob had numbered four times that many. Fanatics were fanatics! The paranoia dredged up by the report would be the same, and the tribes of Zarahemla would scrape together an army to stop them.

Nephi hoped that because of political rifts between the tribes, it would take days, maybe weeks, before they would reach a consensus that might motivate them to assemble troops. But he couldn't take any chances; a single tribe acting independently from the others could still cause him considerable trouble.

Throughout the morning and into the afternoon Nephi circulated among the people, lending a hand whenever possible. He counseled them to take enough food to last seven days. Many complained that it would take at least two weeks to reach Bountiful, especially with women and small children, but the prophet promised that if they were obedient, the Lord would provide for them in the wilderness. Others approached the prophet to express concerns that they were too sick or elderly to make the journey.

"In the name of the Lord," the prophet said to the weak and infirm, "I promise that if you will join us, you will complete the journey to Bountiful and live to receive your blessing."

I was in the process of helping my sister pack food into bundles when Zedekiah, another of Nephi's elders, came to collect me. I was escorted to a softly lit inner chamber of Nephi's house with colorful mats and handsome vases, all of which Nephi would leave behind forever in the course of few hours. Here in this chamber I finally met Lamachi, the converted Gadianton. He was about eighteen years old and a very nervous fellow. When he spoke, his words came out rapidly, like the chatter of a chipmunk. But I felt his heart was basically sincere.

Earlier I had learned why his forehead was flat and his eyes squinted. When Lamachi was an infant, his parents had created the deformity by binding his head between two wooden boards. The squinting of the eyes was accomplished by hanging a little rubber ball between the newborn's eyebrows. Jenny explained that the practice was started by the Zoramites who lived east of Zarahemla, but over the years it had become fashionable for the general populace. Most considered high foreheads and squinting eyes the height of beauty. Nephi, however, considered it the height of vanity, and instructed members of the Church to avoid the practice.

Besides Timothy, the prophet's brother, three other men were also gathered in the chamber. Timothy introduced them to me one at a time. The first was Jonathan. Standing nearly six feet, two inches tall, he was a veritable giant in this day and time—a freak of nature. But his enormous stature contrasted with a round, boyish face. The next was Naaman, a gruff-looking man with graying hair despite the fact that he was in his mid-thirties. Timothy said he was an excellent tracker. The third was Gidgiddonihah—a name I wasn't certain I could pronounce in one breath. He had a shrewd face covered with a sparse beard, like the hair on a coconut. Timothy said he was the best living warrior in Zarahemla and the nephew of Gidgiddoni, the great Nephite general. These men, including Zedekiah, were the ones who had accepted the call to accompany me on my quest.

Our first order of business was to ask Lamachi about the location of the secret city. Timothy set the scene by describing the plight of my daughter, Garplimpton, and the prophet's son, Jonas. At last he put the question to Lamachi directly. "We must know, Lamachi, how to reach the city of Jacobugath. I assume that you know the route?"

"Of course," said Lamachi. "We all know it. All initiates are required to memorize a map so that one day we might journey to Jacobugath and receive our highest endowments at the hands of King Jacob and the Divine Jaguar."

I cringed at Satan's corrupt imitation of sacred things.

"Will you tell us where it is?" asked Timothy.

Lamachi shook his head briskly. "Oh, no. I cannot tell you that. I made an oath—a blood oath. If I were to tell, I would give myself over to the evil spirits. They would possess me. They would destroy me."

Timothy struggled to maintain his patience. "Lamachi, listen to me. Do you believe that the power of God is more powerful than the oaths of the Gadiantons?"

The boy's face became strained. I thought he might start weeping. "Yes," he squeaked. "Yes, I believe it. I know it is true. But—but—"

"Then you must tell us. It's the only way we might help our fellow disciples. The only way we might save their lives."

He arose and began pacing. "I can't tell it! Please don't make me break my oath, Brother Timothy! Please!"

Timothy hung his head. Everyone in the room became discouraged. None of us wanted to see the boy tormented beyond his own spiritual strength. I was beginning to think this interview was pointless. But then Lamachi turned to us abruptly, his expression illuminated.

"But I can take you there! Yes! There is no provision in the oath which states that I cannot take you there personally. But—" and he thought about his next provision very seriously, "—when we arrive, I cannot tell you that we have arrived. When we reach a particular city, you must ask someone else and he will *tell* you, 'yes, yes, yes, this is Jacobugath.' Then I will not have broken any oaths."

I watched several men raise a dubious eyebrow. Bizarre instructions, I thought. But I wondered if we had any choice but to agree to these conditions. Frankly, his loopholes struck me as rather tenuous; but if they helped him to feel secure, they were reasonable enough.

Lamachi suddenly grew very excited. "So can I go with you? I'll cause you no trouble, I promise. It's all for the glory of God, am I right? I would give my life for the Lord. It's the least I can do. The very, very, very least. Oh, please take me along."

Every man present looked uneasily at Lamachi. Timothy perceived the apprehension in the room and asked him to wait outside. After he was gone, Gidgiddonihah was the first to speak. "The boy's not right in the head. To take him along might cause our expedition far more harm than good."

"What choice do we have?" said Zedekiah. "If we sought to locate Jacobugath by ourselves, we might become lost in the wilderness forever."

"I have heard," said Naaman carefully, "that it is the objective of all Gadiantons to lead anyone who asks about Jacobugath into the wilderness so that they might be destroyed."

"I have also heard this," said Jonathan.

Everyone looked at me for my opinion. "I'm not sure I feel qualified to judge," I said. "Without the four of you, my chances would be far less than if we went with him or without him. All I know is, we have to reach Jacobugath as quickly as possible. Jacob is already four days ahead of us. Once he learns Garplimpton's secrets, he'll have no further use for either him or my daughter. Or Jonas, if he is there as well."

"That settles it," said Zedekiah, "We take the boy with us. It's the fastest way. Are we agreed?"

Gidgiddonihah sighed. "Agreed."

"Agreed," groaned Jonathan.

"I'll agree," said Naaman, "but I won't be responsible for him."

"I'll be responsible," I said.

"Then we'll depart in the morning with Nephi and the others," said Zedekiah. "We'll separate from the group when we reach the borders of the wilderness."

Timothy rose to adjourn the meeting. "God be with you all," he said.

CHAPTER 28

As the setting sun began to stripe the sky with purple and red, the first angry voices began to chant outside the walls of the compound.

"Dissenters!" they shouted.

"Traitors!"

"Death to Nephi the traitor!"

The campaign of Heshlom and his followers had proven far more successful than anyone might have imagined. Within a few short hours, the news of the Christian exodus had swept the marketplace and every corner of the city. As feared, the departure was immediately equated with the flight of King Jacob and his followers. Many even raised the unthinkable accusation that Nephi intended to join with the Gadiantons at Jacobugath.

Word reached Nephi that the militias of the various tribes were organizing a resistance at the city gates. Contingencies of the tribe of Benjamin were gathering at the north gate, Josephites and Zeniffites at the east, Mulekites at the west, and Zoramites, Jershonites, and Samites at the south. Their instructions were to cut down any known Christians who tried to leave the city. By the time darkness fell over Zarahemla, the mob of citizens outside the walls of Nephi's estate had expanded to nearly a thousand, all determined to wait out the night, mocking and abusing whoever might emerge with supplies and provisions on their backs.

I compared this mob to the one we had encountered in Melek. In Laman they were at least inflamed by a misguided sense of justice; but in Zarahemla there was no such sense. They were just plain vicious. I was beginning to understand why the Saints of the 1800s were terrified at the mere mention of the word "mob."

Jenny's children were playing near the walls as rocks were hurled into the compound. Steffanie plucked up the children just as a large chunk bounced very close to Rebecca.

"The situation is extremely dangerous," I overheard Timothy report to Nephi that evening. "If we try to exit by any gate, there will be bloodshed."

"Take courage, my brother," the prophet reassured him. "If the wind of faith is at our backs, no army on earth can prevail against us."

Despite this assurance, we did not grow complacent. Word quickly spread throughout the compound that we wouldn't wait until morning. It was thought that by daylight the resistance would become much more organized. There might even be a breach of the estate as the tribes made an effort to seize the prophet.

Most of us had done everything we could to prepare for the journey. My son, Harry, had even agreed to serve as a porter, although his pack was substantially lighter than most. My own load, at least until we were safely outside the city, would consist of my four-year-old nephew, Joshua. Steffanie would be responsible for Becky, while Jennifer carried a bale of food and supplies almost as heavy as her son. The plan, as laid out by Shemnon, was to reach some waterfalls known as the Falls of Gideon by daybreak. These falls, I was told, emptied into the Sidon River about four miles south of Zarahemla. But I still wondered how we were going to avoid an armed conflict at one of the city gates.

Around midnight, the Church elders fanned out through the compound to communicate our plan of escape. Shemnon briefed my family and about fifty others. "On the north," he explained, "where the river runs under the city wall, a bar of sand has built up against the west bank. By this means we shall exit the city. The way is very thin, but the prophet feels if we move quickly and efficiently, we will bypass the army at the north gate."

"Where is the north gate in relation to the river tunnel?" I asked.

"On the opposite bank," said Shemnon. "The nearest crossing is the Bridge of Pahoran in the center in the city. If the Benjaminites spot us, they will be helpless to stop us, except by firing arrows across the water in darkness. We are hoping the Benjaminites have not gathered as large a resistance as has been intimated."

"What about the people outside the estate?" asked someone else. "They are certain to follow us." The chants of the mob had doubled in momentum during the last hour.

"We have a prophet's assurance that if we are filled with faith, all will go well," said Shemnon. "No torches, except a single flame carried by Timothy, will be ignited until we are beyond the city walls. We are instructed to assemble in the courtyard. As soon as everyone is gathered, the gates to the estate will be opened. The prophet and his brother will lead us through the city."

Ten minutes later, the entire community of Christians stood ready to depart. A few stones continued to fly intermittently over the wall; I saw one person hit, but no serious injuries were sustained. In the dark it was difficult to see falling rocks. Our family stood up against the inside wall for protection.

Nephi and Timothy made their way through to the front gate and prepared to lead the procession out into the street. Timothy ignited his torch from one burning on the perimeter wall. Before opening the gate, the prophet faced the assemblage.

"Do not be afraid, little flock!" his voice trumpeted. "This night we shall march with the power of God! Shall we commence our journey, brothers and sisters? Shall we embark for the land of Bountiful?" A magnificent cheer shook the courtyard. Even the voices outside the gate fell silent at the sudden cry of jubilation.

Nephi's omniscient eyes scanned the faithful flock. I thought to myself that he also scanned the house, gardens, and dilapidated tower of the estate he was about to abandon. All his life, this place had been home. This was where he'd first learned the lessons of Christ from a loving father. It was where his children had been born; where some years ago the wife of his youth had passed away. Here was where he'd nurtured the faith to one day lead his people to a land where they might worship at the feet of the Holy Messiah.

Without another moment's hesitation, Nephi hoisted the cumbersome wooden latch. The gate fell open, revealing the dimly lit city street, rustling with hundreds of hostile citizens. The mob maintained an uneasy silence, but hatred smoldered in their eyes. Nephi was the first to emerge, with Timothy close at his side. The rest of us began to file in behind the two brothers. Every male and a great number of females were weighted down with heavy burdens. Mothers wore papooses strapped to their backs and chests, sometimes with an infant on either side.

My family was among the first wave of fifty who marched at the prophet's heel. Nephi led us eastward, in the direction of the marketplace. The mob followed. At first the jeering was light, directed mostly at Nephi and his brother. But about the time we passed beneath the temple gate, their behavior grew more unpredictable. I watched several move in nose-to-nose with certain people and spit forcefully into their faces. No one retaliated. We kept our eyes forward, trusting in Nephi's promise.

As we passed through the marketplace, I lowered Joshua from my shoulders and held him on my hip, fearing his elevation would make him a ready target for garbage or debris. An assailant sprang from the sidelines and pushed over a man wearing a heavy bale. His fall had a domino effect, and two other men toppled onto the cobbled street. The crowd was highly entertained by this. Our group wasted no time helping each other to their feet. We were fast approaching the river, where we would veer north until we reached the river's tunnel. But the mob was determined that they would not let us escape so easily.

At the eastern end of the market, Nephi and the rest of the column were forced to a halt. Blocking the roadway stood a cluster of several hundred people. These citizens were not content to shout insults and toss garbage. Molded into many fists were sizable stones. I felt my heartbeat quicken. I could see tension in my children's faces. Many of the families behind us couldn't see what was happening. They called forward to ask why we had stopped.

Timothy straightened his shoulders and took three steps toward the human barricade. "Let us pass!" he insisted. "We are not dissenters; neither are we traitors! We are leaving this city because it is the will of God!"

"Liar!" echoed several voices.

"Stone him!" shouted another. "Stone all of them!"

Timothy lifted his torch high overhead and roared, "Dare you defy the will of our Lord and Savior Jesus Christ?"

My memory of what happened next is something of a blur. Someone hurled a stone at Timothy. This act triggered a hailstorm of stones, like a volley of cannonfire from the enemy line. I couldn't tell whether the stones were tossed randomly into our ranks or whether they were aimed exclusively at Timothy, but the pandemonium they created among the disciples was the same. Bales were abandoned and the people dispersed, trampling each other and anyone else in their path. The human whirlpool carried Jenny in one direction, while Harry and Steffanie were carried in another. Little Becky was still in Steffanie's arms, and Jennifer cried out to her. I was knocked to the ground, where I draped myself over Joshua to protect him. For an instant, all I could see were legs and feet rushing every which way as the Christians sought cover among the stalls and canopies of the marketplace. I looked around to see who else might have fallen. Several others were groping on the ground like myself, but only one body seemed entirely devoid of life or movement.

Timothy lay in a heap, surrounded by a scattering of stones. The extinguished torch lay at his side. The mob was not satisfied that this man who had spoken to them so rudely was actually dead. One after another, individuals came forward and pummeled Timothy's body with more stones. When the last man had hurled a rock at his skull, the murderers raised up a frenetic cheer. Let this be a lesson, they seemed to saying, to any man who dares tell us we are defying God!

He was dead! What had become of Nephi? From my poor angle of vision, the prophet did not appear to be among the men and women struggling to stand. What had become of Nephi's promise? Hadn't he told us that tonight we walked with the power of God? Was it because we were lacking in faith? Were we unworthy of the Lord's protection?

Little Joshua stirred beneath me, and I rolled off the top of him. His eyes were wide with fright, but he seemed to be uninjured. I looked for my family. They were nowhere to be seen. I turned my eyes back toward the place where Timothy had fallen, and my focus settled on the prophet's blue mantle. He knelt over Timothy's shattered body, the tears on his cheeks glistening in the torchlight. The crowd did not relent; they continued to taunt him as he mourned silently over his brother.

"Go back, traitor!" they shouted. "Go home, or you'll get the same!"

Timothy's skull had been crushed. Nevertheless, Nephi lifted his brother's head gently from the ground and settled it on his lap, stroking his hair. He spoke tenderly into Timothy's ear. "Your time is not yet, younger brother," he said. "I need you too much."

A man leaned toward Nephi, waving his hands wildly. "Get out of here! Take the corpse with you!"

Nephi did not seem to hear him. Every pulse of energy in his soul seemed concentrated upon the body of his murdered brother.

Nephi rose to his feet. The crowd was unmoved by the tears on his cheeks. "What is the will of God now?" sneered a man.

Nephi's eyes focused on this man. So consuming was the indignation of his gaze that the man, as well as the mob, backed away several paces. As Nephi raised his arms above his head, the whole earth seemed to rise with them—drawn, hoisted, exalted toward heaven by invisible cords attached to his fingertips.

"Brother Timothy!" Nephi thundered. "By the power of Jesus Christ, arise and stand forth!"

The street fell gravely silent. The only sound was the flap of a few canopies in a light breeze. A voice somewhere burst out laughing, but no one joined the lone expression of mirth. Even that voice choked into silence as the hand of the prophet's brother twitched.

Timothy's eyelids fluttered opened. The sight of it wrenched a terrified gasp from the mob. They pressed back farther than before. There was a placid, mildly surprised look on Timothy's face as he reached out his hand toward Nephi. His older brother took the hand, but he did not help him to stand. As Timothy rose by his own strength, I could perceive no signs of disfigurement in his body. Every wound, every injury, every bruise had healed before our eyes. Nephi and his brother embraced.

The mob remained in a grip of terror, too stunned by what they had witnessed to make any move whatsoever. While they contemplated the power and judgment of God, Nephi presented Timothy to the scattered Christians. They began to emerge from behind the canopies and stalls, their expressions quiescent with wonder.

Their utterances began as whispers, but steadily swelled in passion and volume. "He lives. Timothy lives! Timothy is brought back from the dead!"

Within moments, the street was again teeming with hundreds of exultant disciples, praising God, their tear-stained faces shining in the torchlight. Had Jenny seen it? Had my children seen it? Where *were* they? I wanted to rejoice with them, shout Hosanna, and shower them in cascades of love and affection. I looked around. None of them were visible. But I wasn't worried. They had to be somewhere in this sea of enchanted faces.

Timothy leaned over and retrieved his torch from the place where it had fallen. He stepped up to one of the men who had pelted him with a stone. The man's eyes blinked rapidly, as if blinded by a light. He seemed certain that Timothy would strike him. Instead, Timothy leaned the tip of his torch toward the assailant's torch and lit it.

This time, as Nephi signaled the procession to move forward, the mob parted and allowed us to pass through unhindered. Incredibly, it didn't take more than a minute before their ire was re-inflamed.

"A Gadianton trick!" someone spat. "Nephi has a devil!"

But though some had started to doubt the miracle's authenticity, no one dared abuse us with more than a few flaccid taunts and jibes. "Get out, traitors!" became the new watchcry. "Leave our city! Leave here and never return!

When we reached the shores of the river Sidon, we turned north, keeping close to the stone embankment at the water's edge. As Joshua still clung to my neck, I continually scanned the flow of faces for Jenny and my children. None of them appeared, but considering the density of the dimly lit masses, I wasn't surprised.

A quarter mile later, we reached the tunnel where the river escaped beneath the city wall. As promised, a bank of sand five feet wide had built up against the left shoreline. In an era of lesser anarchy, the Nephites would have removed the sand bar to discourage anyone from using it as a passage into the city, but in the midst of so many self-serving tribes, no one had been willing to take the responsibility.

Walking four and five abreast, the people passed beneath the city wall. From where we were positioned, I could clearly see the city's northern gate across the river. As far as I could tell, there were only fifteen or twenty Benjaminite soldiers guarding the way. They noticed us almost immediately and assembled on the east bank. I heard the twang of several bowstrings, but to everyone's astonishment, not a single projectile struck a notable target. In fact, I never saw an arrow land in any location. I never even heard a splash in the water as an arrow fell short. It seemed as if the missiles simply sailed into the night and disappeared.

Timothy planted himself at the mouth of the tunnel, directing the people through four at a time. Every man, woman, and child paused to look into his eyes—to witness up close and personal his marvelous restoration to life. Some touched his face and arms to see for themselves that no bruise or injury remained. Timothy did not discourage this familiarity. He welcomed it in all humility.

I did not enter the tunnel when my turn came. I was determined to wait for Jenny and the children. Hundreds of bale-laden people filed past little Joshua and me. None of my family were among them. I was growing deeply concerned. I called out their names: "Jennifer! Steffanie! Harry!"

At last came a familiar reply. "Jim!" My distraught sister tore away from the line. She buried her son's face in kisses. "I couldn't find you!" Then her eyes cut left and right. "Where's my Becky?"

A chill gripped me. "She's not with you?"

Jenny's eyes flashed a mother's panic. "Where is she? Where's my baby?"

"Where are Harry and Steffanie?"

"I don't know! I couldn't reach them! I lost sight of them!"

The last of the Christians filed into the tunnel. Shemnon had positioned himself at the rear of the column to keep the line moving. When I saw him, I grasped his shoulders. "Have you seen my son and daughter?"

"Or my little girl?" Jenny added desperately.

"No," said Shemnon. "How long have they been missing?"

"I haven't seen them since everyone scattered."

"Come on," said Shemnon. "We'll go back to the market."

I handed Joshua to his disconcerted mother. Shemnon and I flew back down the banks of the river. We again found ourselves in the midst of the murderous masses, but the mob's fever had lost considerable potency and most of the crowd had ebbed away. The few who remained took no notice as we bolted through the market streets, switchbacking between the stalls and canopies, calling the names of Harry and Steffanie.

"What could have happened to them?" I panted.

"Would they go back to the estate?" Shemnon asked. "Might they have left something behind?"

"I can't imagine—"

At that instant we heard a faint cry; a little girl's cry, frightened and lost. We made our way to the next avenue of stalls, straining our ears, waiting for the sound to repeat itself. Finally we heard it again, closer now. Shemnon approached a dilapidated seller's booth. There, behind a fold of canvas, we found little two-year-old Becky, her eyes red from sobbing. I gathered her up in my arms and pressed her face against my cheek.

"Shhh, it's all right, now," I said. "It's all right."

"Where's my mommy?" she demanded.

"Your mommy is fine. Becky, where is Steffanie? Where is Harry?"

"I don't know," she peeped.

"Why did they leave you here?"

"I don't know," she repeated. "A man took them."

"A man? What man? *Who* took them?"

"I don't know," said little Becky, and she started crying again.

"Please try to remember," I pleaded with the two-year-old. "Please tell me, what did this man look like, Becky? Do you remember what he looked like?"

"Big man," she replied. "His face was all hairy."

My brain processed this information in less than a second. I thrust Becky into Shemnon's arms and took off down one of the darkened streets.

"Jimhawkins!" Shemnon called out to me. "Where are you going?"

There was no time to explain. My mind repeated a desperate

prayer: *Father, help me, Father, help me!* With the fury of a lion, I charged to the western end of the marketplace—the open square where the Pochteca had set up their camp. I knew my children would be there. I knew Kumarcaah had snatched them again, hoping he could double his profits. No doubt he'd have taken little Becky, too, if she hadn't been so young and delicate—so unlikely to survive long-distance travel.

At no other time in my life had I ever felt such an all-consuming, all-pervasive rage. There was nothing rational, nothing calculated in my behavior. I was operating on pure instinct now—the instinct of a father. The instinct of a man driven to wit's end.

As I entered the square, I spotted my children immediately. As I suspected, new collars had been strapped around their necks. Two Pochteca elders were attaching them at the tail of a string of slaves. I saw Kumarcaah, the bearded pirate, reveling over his recaptured prey. The caravan was making ready to leave, despite the lateness of the hour, anxious to get out of Zarahemla with their booty intact. But they'd moved too slowly.

I faltered only once in my step—to yank a wooden pole that supported an awning out of its dirt foundation. The awning collapsed and alerted them to my presence. When Kumarcaah spotted me, he signaled one of his warriors to attack. The warrior filled his hands with a jagged stone blade and charged, a shriek leeching out of his throat. I brought the pole behind my head like a baseball bat and swung. The shaft connected stiffly with his protruding Adam's apple, transforming his shriek into a clipped grunt. He sprawled backward, folding like a lawn chair.

Another man came at me. My swing struck the bridge of his nose. The knife flipped out of his hand, twirling like a pinwheel until it stuck in the earth. I snatched up the weapon and squeezed it in my fist. There was only one man now between myself and Kumarcaah. He armed himself with an ax and might have thrown it between my eyes if I hadn't thrust the pole's blunt tip into his stomach, doubling him over and forcing an explosive exhalation from his lungs. Kumarcaah tried to get away, but I used the pole to trip up his ankles. When he stopped rolling and opened his eyes, he found my face breathing down on him and the knife blade quivering against his throat. I recalled with satisfaction that not two days ago, he had held me in this same position. The way he looked back at me now, there must have been flames shooting out of my eyes.

"Let them go," I seethed. "I'll give you to the count of three. One! . . ."

Other warriors and elders of the Pochteca were gathered around us, but none of them dared move in while I tightened the blade against their leader's neck.

"Two! . . ."

"Release them!" Kumarcaah commanded. "Both of them! *Now!*"

I would have done it. My anger was so intense, I would have killed him in cold blood. Something inside me had wanted to do it badly. But as soon as he cried the command and my children were set free, the emotion slipped into oblivion. I was grateful not to have colored my hands in blood. My children were as wide-eyed with surprise as everyone else—especially Harry, who up until now had never seen me do anything more outrageous than jaywalking in front of the Valley Fair Mall.

"Head toward the river," I instructed Harry and Steffanie. "Find Shemnon and Rebecca. Run!"

As soon as my children had disappeared between the booths and stalls, the warriors and elders of the Pochteca began edging toward me. I grabbed Kumarcaah by the scruff of his baggy cloak and hoisted him to his feet, never removing the blade from his pulsing jugular.

"Don't try anything," I warned the others.

I backed away slowly, using Kumarcaah's body as a shield in case someone had armed himself with a bow. In such a position, Kumarcaah had the audacity to level a threat.

"If we ever cross paths again," he sneered, "I pledge to feed your flesh to the vultures."

"Glad to know it." I pulled the blade away from his throat and smashed the stone handle down sharply on the back of his head. Kumarcaah crumbled. As the elders and warriors surged forward to aid their leader, I fled into the night.

CHAPTER 29

The next morning I watched the sunrise creep upward from behind the Falls of Gideon. My children slept on either side of me, their heads nestled against my shoulders. Frankly, I was starting to lose a little circulation in my arms, but I bore the discomfort. I clasped them tightly, my two gems, my pair of pearls. My heart ached as I considered that I was leaving them this morning, as soon as we had eaten breakfast and I had received a blessing under the hands of the Prophet Nephi. I would go to search for my one remaining jewel. I had no idea when I might see Harry, Steffanie, or Jennifer again.

"Dad, I want to go with you," Harry had insisted the night before. "If you leave me, I'll just follow you."

"No you won't," I said sternly. "You'll take care of your sister and your Aunt Jenny and your little cousins. They have a long journey ahead, and they need a man."

Steffanie overheard. Usually she would have laid into me for expressing such chauvinist drivel, but today she ignored it, even reinforced it.

"We need you, Harry," she said. "Dad will be fine, as long as we're praying for him." She caught my raised eyebrow and smiled back. It appeared as if a fragile but certain seed of faith was growing in the heart of my youngest daughter.

The morning was glorious and blissful, full of promise. The therapeutic roar of the falls had rejuvenated my senses. Small frogs mewed like kittens in the reeds along the banks of the River Sidon. I watched a basilisk lizard leave a score on the marshy water off to our right with its swift-moving legs. The ripples gradually softened and absorbed, as if by the passage of an age. There were rain clouds threatening over the western mountains, determined to drench the land of Zarahemla with more life-giving moisture. All of these miracles suddenly seemed no less glorious than the one that had raised Timothy from the dead.

The camp of Christian refugees had only been sleeping for two or three hours. Nephi had informed us that as soon as the sun had risen, the camp would prepare to march again. Just below the Falls of Gideon, the waters of the Sidon were wide and shallow; Nephi was determined to cross at this point. From there, the Christian disciples would follow much the same trail that I had once followed with Hagoth and the army of Teancum when we had marched toward the Land of Jershon. Bountiful was only a few days further north. Nephi wanted to reach the wilderness by nightfall and discourage the pursuit of a vengeful army from Zarahemla.

In that few moments before anyone had sounded a morning reveille, I contemplated the quest that lay ahead. The courage that had consumed me the night before had not entirely subsided. Never before this moment had I felt so hopeful, so confident, that Melody was alive and well, and that one day soon I would prevail and reunite my family. I thought perhaps I could feel her spirit, living and breathing somewhere in this ancient world. If I concentrated, I wondered if I could actually hear the pulse of her thoughts, and I wondered if I could transmit some glimmer of fatherly love and assurance across the expanse. Had my oldest daughter abandoned all hope of rescue? All hope of ever seeing any of us again?

Almost.

I'd nearly decided there was nothing left for me. I felt so far from home, so far from everything that I had once known, that I might have easily forgotten my previous life. Simply passed it off as some bizarre dream or fantasy. This *was reality. This had* always *been reality. I had always been a nobody in a primitive world, a slave to demonic savages.*

I might have lost my mind entirely. I might have gone catatonic, refused to eat, buried my face in a corner and waited to die. But it was during those terrible days and weeks that I learned how to hear the Spirit. I wish

I could explain it. I wish I could describe the feeling so clearly and flawlessly that everyone who's ever been sad or scared could recognize it instantly and accept its comfort. Maybe the Holy Ghost was meant *to defy perfect description through language. That way we have to figure it out for ourselves, by learning what it really means to listen.*

Nephi laid his hands upon each of us who had committed ourselves to the expedition. He blessed us with endurance beyond our natural capacities. We were warned to avoid the advice of solitary strangers, and told that only through following the voice of the Spirit could we possibly succeed in our task. In addition to this, I received a personal promise. Nephi said if I "repulsed the arm of flesh," I would see my loved ones again on the rolling plains of Bountiful. Such a pointed condition worried me a little, but I couldn't think about it now.

It was less than an hour after sunrise when I embraced my sister and each of my children in our final good-byes. Jenny and Steffanie were weeping; Harry tried to look brave. My own tears were mingled with rain as the first heavy droplets fell out of the sky. I used this to my advantage. I hoped I left them with a lingering image of a father with his chin held high, a pinnacle of stamina and confidence, even if inside it was all butter and butterflies.

"I'll see you in a few weeks," I staunchly assured them. "Melody and Garth will be with me. I promise."

I caught a strange glint in Harry's eye, as if he still harbored the thought that he might try to follow me. I warned him again to remain with his sister and his aunt. If only I had been blessed with children who were a little less self-willed.

With you as our father, how could we have turned out any other way?

And so with my family, Shemnon, Timothy, and the Prophet Nephi looking on through the threads of rain, the six of us—including myself, Zedekiah the Elder, Gidgiddonihah the warrior, Jonathan the giant, Naaman the tracker, and Lamachi the freshly converted Gadianton—we started down a narrow, cobbled trail that writhed its way into the jungle foliage. We had no idea how many days it would take us to reach the dark city of Jacobugath. Lamachi wouldn't tell us. He also wouldn't tell us the secret passwords needed to get beyond the checkpoints where Jacob's assassins were rumored to be lying in wait. A long and treacherous journey lay ahead—a journey that thus far, no one had been known to survive.

But the most ominous question of all related to none of this. It related to time itself. How much remained before the just wrath of God turned this land inside out with fire and destruction? Every rumble of thunder and jolt of lightning overhead drew this question back to the forefront of my mind.

Our adventure in the land and time of the Feathered Serpent had only begun.

PHOTO BY "PICTURE THIS...by Sara Staker"

About the Author

For over ten years, Chris Heimerdinger has brought adventure and fantasy to LDS readers. At first his intention was to make this a sideline and continue his ambition to become a film director or write books for the national market. Each time he would finish an LDS novel, he would sit down to write something for the national market, but the inevitable result was a "stupor of creativity." He says that only by turning his attention back to an LDS-oriented project would the ideas start to flow again and the writer's block disappear. Thus he concluded that writing for the Latter-day Saint market was where he belonged, at least for the present.

"Artists should be driven and motivated by the things they care about the most," Chris explains. "If I didn't write stories on gospel themes and subjects, it would, in essence, be a denial of who I am."

Readers will also enjoy Chris' other books published in the *Tennis Shoes Adventure Series,* which include *Tennis Shoes Among the Nephites; Gadiantons and the Silver Sword; The Feathered Serpent, Parts One and Two; The Sacred Quest* (formerly *Tennis Shoes and the Seven Churches); The Lost Scrolls;* and *The Golden Crown.* His other books published by Covenant include *Daniel and Nephi; Eddie Fantastic;* and *A Return to Christmas* (currently published by Random House/Ballantine for a national readership).

Chris resides in Riverton, Utah, with his wife, Beth, and their three children, Steven Teancum, Christopher Ammon, and Alyssa Sariah. Check out Chris' web site and become a registered guest at **www.cheimerdinger.com.**

TENNIS SHOES
ADVENTURE SERIES

THE FEATHERED

SERPENT

PART 2

PROLOGUE

Recently I started collecting portraits of the Savior. Everybody has one or two. I have hundreds.

And yet none of them quite strikes me the way it should. I think of all the many artists throughout the ages, poised at canvas or clay, their eyes moist with tears, their hearts burning with prayer, seeking just the right line, just the right curve, and in the end having to submit to the limits of their medium. Two, or even three dimensions are simply not enough.

In spite of this, I find myself gathering up every painting, print, and statuette I can lay my hands on, from medieval wall paintings where his image was crowned by a glowing halo, to portraits by modern artists who invariably depict a being with long hair, beard, flowing white robe, warm eyes, and a smile subtle and penetrating, like the Mona Lisa.

My father is very patient with my obsession. He understands it, and even encourages it. From time to time he'll bring home to me yet another portrait by yet another master artist to add to my collection. Because even if a single painting doesn't quite capture the image, the whole of them together, nourished by the love of so many artists, comes very close.

But more importantly, each picture serves to remind me that there were once people who lived on this earth—people who once stood before his face, or brushed his shoulder, or took currency from his hand—who hardly noticed him at all. They saw only a man—just another among hundreds, among thousands. And then there were others who saw in his eyes something so familiar, so overwhelming, that it took no persuasion at all for them to kneel and call him Master.

For the first sixteen years of my life, I think I'd have been part of the first category. I'm sure I'd have looked right past him. It's not that I didn't believe in him. But in my mind I'd decided I already knew what he looked like. I'd squarely defined him according to my own desires and opinions. I left him no opportunity to define himself according to his Holy Spirit.

I'm not really certain how I let this happen. I suppose I wasn't quite satisfied by the place I seemed to have been assigned in his kingdom. The prospect of being only a wife and a mother, the eternal nurturer who stood at the sidelines, always subordinate to the leadership of men, didn't appeal to me very much. Especially when I considered that most men did a pretty poor job at the helm. But whenever I expressed such feelings, I was always informed that my views were at variance with the way of heaven and the will of the Master. So, to an extent, I created my own Master, in my own image—a person whose views of the universe were in harmony with my own.

Don't get me wrong. I'm not saying I was some sort of ultra-feminist. I just preferred to believe that my Savior wanted for me exactly the things that I wanted for myself. Whatever made me happy, made him happy. It never occurred to me that I might have turned the whole thing exactly backwards—that I might, in all humility, approach the Master, and rather than telling him who he was or who I wanted him to be, that I might ask him instead. That I might inquire to know his heart, and then to know who he wanted me to be. Although at that time I doubt I would have been prepared for the answer.

But one look into the Master's eyes, one touch from the flesh of his hand, one breath of his presence, and all the towers of opinion we've built through years of study and labor come crumbling down. Suddenly we find ourselves willing to say, "This time, Master, I'll build whatever you want me to build."

So this is my objective. Now and for the rest of mortality. I'll strive for it until that day when I can look into his eyes and breathe in his presence again and forever.

All my portraits help me to remember this goal. Because each image of the Master, no matter how unequal or imperfect the artist's stroke, takes me back to that one moment, as long ago as eternity and as recent as a single heartbeat, when I—Melody Hawkins—had the honor, the privilege, and the glory to bathe his feet with my tears.